CISCO

Course Booklet

CCNA Cybersecurity Operations

Cisco Press

800 East 96th Street
Indianapolis, Indiana 46240 USA

Cisco | Networking Academy
Mind Wide Open

CCNA Cybersecurity Operations Course Booklet

Copyright © 2018 Cisco Systems, Inc.

Published by:
Cisco Press
800 East 96th Street
Indianapolis, IN 46240 USA

Printed in the United States of America

First Printing March 2018

Library of Congress Control Number: 2018931073

ISBN-13: 978-1-58713-437-1

ISBN-10: 1-58713-437-3

Editor-in-Chief
Mark Taub

Alliances Manager, Cisco Press
Arezou Gol

Executive Editor
Mary Beth Ray

Managing Editor
Sandra Schroeder

Senior Project Editor
Tonya Simpson

Editorial Assistant
Vanessa Evans

Cover Designer
Chuti Prasertsith

Composition
codemantra

Indexer
Erika Millen

Warning and Disclaimer

CISCO

Trademark Acknowledgments

All terms mentioned in this book that are known to be trademarks or service marks have been appropriately capitalized. Cisco Press or Cisco Systems, Inc., cannot attest to the accuracy of this information. Use of a term in this book should not be regarded as affecting the validity of any trademark or service mark.

Special Sales

For information about buying this title in bulk quantities, or for special sales opportunities (which may include electronic versions; custom cover designs; and content particular to your business, training goals, marketing focus, or branding interests), please contact our corporate sales department at corpsales@pearsoned.com or (800) 382-3419.

For government sales inquiries, please contact governmentsales@pearsoned.com.

For questions about sales outside the U.S., please contact intlcs@pearson.com.

Feedback Information

At Cisco Press, our goal is to create in-depth technical books of the highest quality and value. Each book is crafted with care and precision, undergoing rigorous development that involves the unique expertise of members from the professional technical community.

Readers' feedback is a natural continuation of this process. If you have any comments regarding how we could improve the quality of this book, or otherwise alter it to better suit your needs, you can contact us through email at feedback@ciscopress.com. Please make sure to include the book title and ISBN in your message.

We greatly appreciate your assistance.

Americas Headquarters	Asia Pacific Headquarters	Europe Headquarters
Cisco Systems, Inc.	Cisco Systems (USA) Pte. Ltd.	Cisco Systems International BV Amsterdam,
San Jose, CA	Singapore	The Netherlands

Cisco has more than 200 offices worldwide. Addresses, phone numbers, and fax numbers are listed on the Cisco Website at **www.cisco.com/go/offices**.

Cisco and the Cisco logo are trademarks or registered trademarks of Cisco and/or its affiliates in the U.S. and other countries. To view a list of Cisco trademarks, go to this URL: www.cisco.com/go/trademarks. Third party trademarks mentioned are the property of their respective owners. The use of the word partner does not imply a partnership relationship between Cisco and any other company. (1110R)

Contents at a Glance

Contents

Command Syntax Conventions

The conventions used to present command syntax in this book are the same conventions used in the IOS Command Reference. The Command Reference describes these conventions as follows:

- **Boldface** indicates commands and keywords that are entered literally as shown. In actual configuration examples and output (not general command syntax), boldface indicates commands that are manually input by the user (such as a **show** command).

- *Italic* indicates arguments for which you supply actual values.

- Vertical bars (|) separate alternative, mutually exclusive elements.

- Square brackets ([ ]) indicate an optional element.

- Braces ({ }) indicate a required choice.

- Braces within brackets ([{ }]) indicate a required choice within an optional element.

About This Course Booklet

Your Cisco Networking Academy Course Booklet is designed as a study resource you can easily read, highlight, and review on the go, wherever the Internet is not available or practical:

- The text is extracted directly, word for word, from the online course so you can highlight important points and take notes in the "Your Chapter Notes" section.

- Headings with the exact page correlations provide a quick reference to the online course for your classroom discussions and exam preparation.

- An icon system directs you to the online curriculum to take full advantage of the images embedded within the Networking Academy online course interface and reminds you to do the labs, interactive activities, packet tracer activities, watch videos, and take the chapter quizzes.

Refer to **Online Course** for Illustration   Refer to **Lab Activity** for this chapter   Go to the online course to take the quiz and exam.   Refer to **Interactive Graphic** in online course   Refer to **Packet Tracer Activity** for this chapter   Refer to **Video** in online course

The Course Booklet is a basic, economical paper-based resource to help you succeed with the Cisco Networking Academy online course.

Course Introduction

0.0 Welcome to CCNA: Cybersecurity Operations

0.0.1 Message to the Student

Refer to
Online Course
for Illustration

0.0.1.1 Welcome

Today's organizations are challenged with rapidly detecting cybersecurity breaches and effectively responding to security incidents. Teams of people in Security Operations Centers (SOCs) keep a vigilant eye on security systems, protecting their organizations by detecting and responding to cybersecurity threats. CCNA Cybersecurity Operations v1.0 (CyberOps) prepares candidates to begin a career working with associate-level cybersecurity analysts within SOCs.

The Student Support page includes a link to the NetAcad Facebook page and our LinkedIn page. It also contains Additional Resources and Activities for each chapter.

Refer to
Online Course
for Illustration

0.0.1.2 A Global Community

When you participate in the Networking Academy, you are joining a global community linked by common goals and technologies. Schools, colleges, universities, and other entities in over 160 countries participate in the program.

Look for the Cisco Networking Academy official site on Facebook© and LinkedIn©. The Facebook site is where you can meet and engage with other Networking Academy students from around the world. The Cisco Networking Academy LinkedIn site connects you with job postings, and you can see how others are effectively communicating their skills.

Refer to
Online Course
for Illustration

0.0.1.3 More than Just Information

The netacad.com learning environment is an important part of the overall course experience for students and instructors in the Networking Academy. These online course materials include course text and related interactive media, paper-based labs, and many different types of quizzes. All of these materials provide important feedback to help you assess your progress throughout the course.

The material in this course encompasses a broad range of technologies that facilitate how people work, live, play, and learn by communicating with voice, video, and other data. Networking and the internet affect people differently in different parts of the world. Although we have worked with instructors from around the world to create these materials, it is important that you work with your instructor and fellow students to make the material in this course applicable to your local situation.

Refer to
Interactive Graphic
in online course

0.0.1.4   How We Teach

E-doing is a design philosophy that applies the principle that people learn best by doing. The curriculum includes embedded, highly interactive e-doing activities to help stimulate learning, increase knowledge retention, and make the whole learning experience much richer – and that makes understanding the content much easier.

Interactive Activities

Interactive activities are embedded within the chapters as checks for understanding. Some of these use "drag and drop" to complete the activity (Figure 1). Others use a "checkbox" method to complete them (Figure 2). You can check your score immediately. You can also reset and do the activity as many times as you like.

Labs

Labs are activities that are designed to be performed on physical equipment (Figure 3). Some labs are written as class or small group activities that may or may not involve equipment. It is very important to learn and practice physical skills by using the labs in this course in preparation for a career in IT. Working on physical equipment not only develops skills, but also reinforces knowledge and builds confidence. This is very important as you move into the IT field.

Packet Tracer

In the Networking chapters, you will configure a simple network using Packet Tracer, the Networking Academy network simulation tool (Figure 4). Click here to download the latest version of Packet Tracer. Packet Tracer may look complicated at first glance, but is easy to work with, and there are many tutorials to help you learn how to use it. Packet Tracer is a very robust tool that you will use regularly as you participate in more advanced networking courses.

Assessments

Each chapter in this course has an online quiz. These are scored automatically, showing you the areas where you excel, as well as any areas where you may want to do some additional study or practice. There is also an online, end-of-course final exam.

Refer to
Online Course
for Illustration

0.0.1.5   Ethical Hacking Statement

Ethical Hacking Statement

The Cisco Networking Academy Program is focused on creating the global problem solvers needed to build, scale, secure, and defend the networks that are used in our businesses and daily lives. The need for well-trained cybersecurity specialists continues to grow at an exponential rate. Training to become a cybersecurity specialist requires in depth understanding and exposure to how cyber attacks occur, as well as how they are detected and prevented. These skills will naturally also include learning the techniques that threat actors use to circumvent data, privacy, and computer and network security.

In this course, learners will use tools and techniques in a "sandboxed", virtual machine environment that allows them to create, implement, monitor, and detect various types of cyber attacks. The hands-on training is performed in this environment so that students can gain the necessary skills and knowledge needed to thwart these and future cyber attacks. Security holes and vulnerabilities that are created in this course should only be used in an ethical manner and only in this "sandboxed" virtual environment. Experimentation with these tools, techniques, and resources outside of the provided sandboxed virtual environment is at the discretion of the instructor and local institution. If the learner has any doubt about which computer systems and networks are part of the sandboxed virtual environment, they should contact their instructor prior to any experimentation.

Unauthorized access to data, computer, and network systems is a crime in many jurisdictions and often is accompanied by severe consequences, regardless of the perpetrator's motivations. It is the learner's responsibility, as the user of this material, to be cognizant of and compliant with computer use laws.

0.0.1.6   Course Overview

CCNA Cybersecurity Operations 1.0 covers knowledge and skills needed to successfully handle the tasks, duties, and responsibilities of an associate-level Security Analyst working in a Security Operations Center (SOC).

Upon completion of the CCNA Cybersecurity Operations 1.0 course, students will be able to perform the following tasks:

- Explain the role of the Cybersecurity Operations Analyst in the enterprise.
- Explain the Windows Operating System features and characteristics needed to support cybersecurity analyses.
- Explain the features and characteristics of the Linux Operating System.
- Analyze the operation of network protocols and services.
- Explain the operation of the network infrastructure.
- Classify the various types of network attacks.
- Use network monitoring tools to identify attacks against network protocols and services.
- Use various methods to prevent malicious access to computer networks, hosts, and data.
- Explain the impacts of cryptography on network security monitoring.
- Explain how to investigate endpoint vulnerabilities and attacks.
- Identify network security alerts.
- Analyze network intrusion data to verify potential exploits.
- Apply incident response models to manage network security incidents.

Cybersecurity and the Security Operations Center

1.0 Introduction

1.0.1 Welcome

Refer to
Online Course
for Illustration

1.0.1.1 Chapter 1: Cybersecurity and the Security Operations Center

In this chapter, you will learn about the who, what, and why of cyberattacks. Different people commit cybercrime for different reasons. Security Operations Centers work to combat cybercrime. People prepare for work in a Security Operations Center (SOC) by earning certifications, seeking formal education, and by using employment services to gain internship experience and jobs.

Refer to
Lab Activity
for this chapter

1.0.1.2 Activity - Top Hacker Shows Us How It is Done

In this class activity, you will view a TED Talk video that discusses various security vulnerabilities. You will also research one of the vulnerabilities mentioned in the video.

1.1 The Danger

1.1.1 War Stories

Refer to
Online Course
for Illustration

1.1.1.1 Hijacked People

Sarah stopped by her favorite coffee shop to grab her afternoon drink. She placed her order, paid the clerk, and waited while the baristas worked furiously to fulfill the backup of orders. Sarah pulled out her phone, opened the wireless client, and connected to what she assumed was the coffee shop's free wireless network.

However, sitting in a corner of the store, a hacker had just set up an open "rogue" wireless hotspot posing as the coffee shop's wireless network. When Sarah logged onto her bank's website, the hacker hijacked her session, and gained access to her bank accounts.

Click here for a quick look at a video posted in 2008 demonstrating how one wireless network was vulnerable to hacking. In this course, you will learn about security technologies that easily prevent this type of attack.

Refer to
Online Course
for Illustration

1.1.1.2 Ransomed Companies

Rashid, an employee in the finance department of a major, publicly-held corporation, receives an email from his CEO with an attached PDF. The PDF is about the company's third quarter earnings. Rashid does not remember his department creating the PDF. His curiosity is peaked, so he opens the attachment.

The same scenario plays out across the organization as dozens of other employees are successfully enticed to click the attachment. When the PDF opens, ransomware is installed on the employees' computers and begins the process of gathering and encrypting corporate data. The goal of the attackers is financial gain, because they hold the company's data for ransom until they are paid.

Click here to see a dramatization of how this ransomware attack could happen.

Refer to
Online Course
for Illustration

1.1.1.3   Targeted Nations

Some of today's malware is so sophisticated and expensive to create that security experts believe only a nation state or group of nations could possibly have the influence and funding to create it. Such malware can be targeted to attack a nation's vulnerable infrastructure, such as the water system or power grid.

This was the purpose of the Stuxnet worm, which infected USB drives. These drives were carried by five Iranian component vendors, with the intention of infiltrating nuclear facilities supported by the vendors. Stuxnet was designed to infiltrate Windows operating systems and then target Step 7 software. Step 7 was developed by Siemens for their programmable logic controllers (PLCs). Stuxnet was looking for a specific model of the Siemens PLCs that controls the centrifuges in nuclear facilities. The worm was transmitted from the infected USB drives into the PLCs and eventually damaged many of these centrifuges.

Zero Days, a film released in 2016, attempts to document the development and deployment of the Stuxnet targeted malware attack.

Note   Search for the Zero Days film if the link does not work for your country of residence.

Refer to
Lab Activity
for this chapter

1.1.1.4   Lab - Installing the CyberOps Workstation Virtual Machine

In this lab, you will install VirtualBox on your personal computer. You will then download and install the CyberOps Workstation Virtual Machine (VM).

Refer to
Lab Activity
for this chapter

1.1.1.5   Lab - Cybersecurity Case Studies

In this lab, you will analyze the given cases and answer questions about them.

1.1.2   Threat Actors

Refer to
Online Course
for Illustration

1.1.2.1   Amateurs

Threat actors include, but are not limited to, amateurs, hacktivists, organized crime groups, state sponsored, and terrorist groups. Threat actors are individuals or a group of individuals who perform cyberattacks against another individual or organization. Cyberattacks are intentional, malicious acts meant to negatively impact another individual or organization.

Amateurs, also known as script kiddies, have little or no skill. They often use existing tools or instructions found on the Internet to launch attacks. Some are just curious, while others try to demonstrate their skills by causing harm. Even though they are using basic tools, the results can still be devastating.

Refer to
Online Course
for Illustration

1.1.2.2   Hacktivists

Hacktivists are hackers who protest against a variety of political and social ideas. Hacktivists publicly protest against organizations or governments by posting articles and videos, leaking sensitive information, and disrupting web services with illegitimate traffic in distributed denial of service (DDoS) attacks.

Refer to
Online Course
for Illustration

1.1.2.3   Financial Gain

Much of the hacking activity that consistently threatens our security is motivated by financial gain. These cybercriminals want to gain access to our bank accounts, personal data, and anything else they can leverage to generate cash flow.

Refer to
Online Course
for Illustration

1.1.2.4   Trade Secrets and Global Politics

The past several years have seen many stories about nation states hacking other countries, or otherwise interfering with internal politics. Nation states are also interested in using cyberspace for industrial espionage. The theft of intellectual property can give a country a significant advantage in international trade.

Defending against the fallout from state-sponsored cyberespionage and cyberwarfare will continue to be a priority for cybersecurity professionals.

Refer to
Online Course
for Illustration

1.1.2.5   How Secure is the Internet of Things?

The Internet of Things (IoT) is all around us and quickly expanding. We are just beginning to reap the benefits of the IoT. New ways to use connected things are being developed daily. The IoT helps individuals connect things to improve their quality of life. For example, many people are now using connected wearable devices to track their fitness activities. How many devices do you currently own that connect to your home network or the Internet?

How secure are these devices? For example, who wrote the firmware? Did the programmer pay attention to security flaws? Is your connected home thermostat vulnerable to attacks? What about your DVR? If security vulnerabilities are found, can firmware in the device be patched to eliminate the vulnerability? Many devices on the Internet are not updated with the latest firmware. Some older devices were not even developed to be updated with patches. These two situations create opportunity for threat actors and security risks for the owners of these devices.

In October 2016, a DDoS attack against the domain name provider Dyn took down many popular websites. The attack came from a large number of webcams, DVRs, routers, and other IoT devices that had been compromised by malicious software. These devices formed a "botnet" that was controlled by hackers. This botnet was used to create an enormous DDoS attack that disabled essential Internet services. Dyn has posted a blog here to explain the attack and their reaction to it.

Avi Rubin, professor of Computer Science at Johns Hopkins University, highlights the dangers of not securing all our connected devices. Click here to view his TED talk.

Refer to
Lab Activity
for this chapter

1.1.2.6   Lab - Learning the Details of Attacks

In this lab, you will research and analyze IoT application vulnerabilities.

1.1.3   Threat Impact

Refer to
Online Course
for Illustration

1.1.3.1   PII and PHI

The economic impact of cyberattacks is difficult to ascertain with precision; however, according to an article in Forbes, it is estimated that businesses lose $400 billion annually to cyberattacks.

Personally identifiable information (PII) is any information that can be used to positively identify an individual. Examples of PII include:

- Name

- Social security number

- Birthdate

- Credit card numbers

- Bank account numbers

- Government issued ID

- Address information (street, email, phone numbers)

One of the more lucrative goals of cybercriminals is obtaining lists of PII that can then be sold on the dark web. The dark web can only be accessed with special software and is used by cybercriminals to shield their activities. Stolen PII can be used to create fake accounts, such as credit cards and short-term loans.

A subset of PII is protected health information (PHI). The medical community creates and maintains electronic medical records (EMRs) that contain PHI. In the U.S., handling of PHI is regulated by the Health Insurance Portability and Accountability Act (HIPAA). The equivalent regulation in the European Union is called Data Protection.

Most hacks on companies and organizations reported in the news involved stolen PII or PHI. In only three months in 2016, the following attacks occurred:

- In March 2016, a data breach at a health care provider exposed the personal information of 2.2 million patients.

- In April 2016, a laptop and portable drives were stolen from a government agency that included personal information for as many as 5 million people.

- In May 2016, a data breach at a payroll company exposed the payroll, tax, and benefits information of over 600,000 companies.

Refer to
Online Course
for Illustration

1.1.3.2   Lost Competitive Advantage

Companies are increasingly worried about corporate espionage in cyberspace. An additional major concern is the loss of trust that comes when a company is unable to protect its customers' personal data. The loss of competitive advantage may come from this loss of trust rather than another company or country stealing trade secrets.

Refer to
Online Course
for Illustration

1.1.3.3   Politics and National Security

It is not just businesses that get hacked. In February 2016, a hacker published the personal information of 20,000 U.S. Federal Bureau of Investigation (FBI) employees and 9,000 U.S.

Department of Homeland Security (DHS) employees. The hacker was apparently politically motivated.

The Stuxnet worm was specifically designed to impede Iran's progress in enriching uranium that could be used in a nuclear weapon. Stuxnet is a prime example of a network attack motivated by national security concerns. Cyberwarfare is a serious possibility. State-supported hacker warriors can cause disruption and destruction of vital services and resources within an enemy nation. The Internet has become essential as a medium for commercial and financial activities. Disruption of these activities can devastate a nation's economy. Controllers, similar to those attacked by Stuxnet, also are used to control the flow of water at dams and the switching of electricity on the power grid. Attacks on such controllers can have dire consequences.

Refer to **Lab Activity** for this chapter

1.1.3.4   Lab - Visualizing the Black Hats

In this lab, you will research and analyze cybersecurity incidents to create scenarios how organizations can prevent or mitigate an attack.

1.2   Fighters in the War Against Cybercrime

1.2.1   The Modern Security Operations Center

Refer to **Online Course** for Illustration

1.2.1.1   Elements of a SOC

Defending against today's threats requires a formalized, structured, and disciplined approach which is executed by professionals at Security Operations Centers. SOCs provide a broad range of services, from monitoring and management, to comprehensive threat solutions and hosted security that can be customized to meet customer needs. SOCs can be wholly in-house, owned and operated by a business, or elements of a SOC can be contracted out to security vendors, such as Cisco's Managed Security Services.

The major elements of a SOC, shown in the figure, are people, processes, and technology.

Refer to **Online Course** for Illustration

1.2.1.2   People in the SOC

The SANS Institute (www.sans.org) classifies the roles people play in a SOC into four job titles:

- **Tier 1 Alert Analyst** - These professionals monitor incoming alerts, verify that a true incident has occurred, and forward tickets to Tier 2, if necessary.

- **Tier 2 Incident Responder** - These professionals are responsible for deep investigation of incidents and advise remediation or action to be taken.

- **Tier 3 Subject Matter Expert (SME)/Hunter** - These professionals have expert-level skill in network, endpoint, threat intelligence, and malware reverse engineering. They are experts at tracing the processes of the malware to determine its impact and how it can be removed. They are also deeply involved in hunting for potential threats and implementing threat detection tools.

- **SOC Manager** - This professional manages all the resources of the SOC and serves as the point of contact for the larger organization or customer.

This course offers preparation for a certification suitable for the position of Tier 1 Alert Analyst, also known as Cybersecurity Analyst.

The figure from the SANS institute graphically represents how these roles interact with each other.

Refer to **Online Course** for Illustration

1.2.1.3 Process in the SOC

The day of a Tier 1 Analyst begins with monitoring security alert queues. A ticketing system is frequently used to allow analysts to select alerts from a queue to investigate. Because the software that generates alerts can trigger false alarms, one job of the Tier 1 Analyst might be to verify that an alert represents a true security incident. When verification is established, the incident can be forwarded to investigators or other security personnel to be acted upon, or resolved as a false alarm.

Refer to **Online Course** for Illustration

1.2.1.4 Technologies in the SOC

As shown in the figure, a SOC needs a security information and event management system (SIEM), or its equivalent. This system combines data from multiple technologies. SIEM systems are used for collecting and filtering data, detecting and classifying threats, analyzing and investigating threats, and managing resources to implement preventive measures and address future threats. SOC technologies include one or more of the following:

- Event collection, correlation, and analysis
- Security monitoring
- Security control
- Log management
- Vulnerability assessment
- Vulnerability tracking
- Threat intelligence

Refer to **Online Course** for Illustration

1.2.1.5 Enterprise and Managed Security

For medium and large networks, the organization will benefit from implementing an enterprise-level SOC. The SOC can be a complete in-house solution. However, many larger organizations will outsource at least part of the SOC operations to a security solutions provider.

Cisco has a team of experts who help ensure timely and accurate incident resolution. Cisco offers a wide range of incident response, preparedness, and management capabilities:

- Cisco Smart Net Total Care Service for Rapid Problem Resolution
- Cisco Product Security Incident Response Team (PSIRT)
- Cisco Computer Security Incident Response Team (CSIRT)
- Cisco Managed Services
- Cisco Tactical Operations (TacOps)
- Cisco's Safety and Physical Security Program

Refer to
Online Course
for Illustration

1.2.1.6   Security vs. Availability

Most enterprise networks must be up and running at all times. Security personnel understand that for the organization to accomplish its priorities, network availability must be preserved.

Each business or industry has a limited tolerance for network downtime. That tolerance is usually based upon a comparison of the cost of the downtime in relation to the cost of ensuring against downtime. For example, in a small retail business with only one location, it may be tolerable to have a router as a single point of failure. However, if a large portion of that business's sales are from online shoppers, then the owner may decide to provide a level of redundancy to ensure that a connection is always available.

Preferred uptime is often measured in the number of down minutes in a year, as shown in the figure. For example, a "five nines" uptime means that the network is up 99.999% of the time or down for no more than 5 minutes a year. "Four nines" would be a downtime of 53 minutes a year.

However, security cannot be so strong that it interferes with the needs of employees or business functions. It is always a tradeoff between strong security and permitting efficient business functioning.

Refer to
Interactive Graphic
in online course

1.2.1.7   Activity - Identify the SOC Terminology

1.2.2   Becoming a Defender

Refer to
Online Course
for Illustration

1.2.2.1   Certifications

A variety of cybersecurity certifications that are relevant to careers in SOCs are available from several different organizations.

Cisco CCNA Cyber Ops

The CCNA Cyber Ops certification provides a valuable first step in acquiring the knowledge and skills needed to work with a SOC team. It can be a valuable part of a career in the exciting and growing field of cybersecurity operations.

CompTIA Cybersecurity Analyst Certification

The CompTIA Cybersecurity Analyst (CSA+) certification is a vendor-neutral IT professional certification. It validates knowledge and skills required to configure and use threat detection tools, perform data analysis, interpret the results to identify vulnerabilities, threats and risks to an organization. The end goal is the ability to secure and protect applications and systems within an organization.

(ISC)^2 Information Security Certifications

(ISC)^2 is an international non-profit organization that offers the highly-acclaimed CISSP certification. They offer a range of other certifications for various specialties in cybersecurity.

Global Information Assurance Certification (GIAC)

GIAC, which was founded in 1999, is one of the oldest security certification organizations. It offers a wide range of certifications in seven categories.

Other Security-Related Certifications

Search for "cybersecurity certifications" to find information about other vendor and vendor-neutral certifications.

Refer to
Online Course
for Illustration

1.2.2.2   Further Education

Degrees

Anyone considering a career in the cybersecurity field, should seriously consider pursuing a technical degree or bachelor's degree in computer science, electrical engineering, information technology, or information security. Many educational institutions offer security-related specialized tracks and certifications.

Python Programming

Computer programming is an essential skill for anyone who wishes to pursue a career in cybersecurity. If you have never learned how to program, then Python might be the first language to learn. Python is an open-source, object-oriented language that is routinely used by cybersecurity analysts. It is also a popular programming language for Linux-based systems and software-defined networking (SDN).

Refer to
Online Course
for Illustration

1.2.2.3   Sources of Career Information

A variety of websites and mobile applications advertise information technology jobs. Each site targets a variety of job applicants and provides different tools for candidates to research their ideal job position. Many sites are job site aggregators. Job site aggregators gather listings from other job boards and company career sites and display them in a single location.

Indeed.com

Advertised as the world's #1 job site, Indeed.com attracts over 180 million unique visitors every month from over 50 different countries. Indeed.com is truly a worldwide job site. It helps companies of all sizes hire the best talent and offers the best opportunity for job seekers.

CareerBuilder.com

CareerBuilder serves many large and prestigious companies. As a result, this site attracts specific candidates that typically have more education and higher credentials. The employers posting on CareerBuilder commonly get more candidates with college degrees, advanced credentials and industry certifications.

USAJobs.gov

The United States federal government posts any openings on USAJobs. Click here to learn more about the application process.

Salary Information

The website glassdoor.com provides salary information for different job types, companies, and locations. Search for "cyber security analyst" to see salaries and requirements for current job openings.

Refer to
Online Course
for Illustration

1.2.2.4   Getting Experience

Internships

Internships are an excellent method for gaining entry into the cybersecurity field. Sometimes, internships turn into an offer of full time employment. However, even a temporary internship allows you the opportunity to gain experience in the inner workings of a cybersecurity organization. The contacts you make during an internship can also prove to be a valuable resource as you continue your career. Click here to read an article by Forbes about the 10 best websites for internships.

Cisco Cybersecurity Scholarship

To help close the security skills gap, Cisco introduced the Global Cybersecurity Scholarship program in 2016. Cisco is motivated to increase the pool of talent with critical cybersecurity proficiency. Registration opens in spring and awards are announced in late fall. Click here to learn more about the scholarship.

Temporary Agencies

If you are having difficulty finding your first job, a temporary agency can be a great place to start. Most temporary agencies will help you polish your resume and make recommendations on additional skills you may need to obtain to make yourself more attractive to potential employers.

Many organizations use temporary agencies to fill job openings for the first 90 days. Then, if the employee is a good match, the organization may offer to buy the contract from the temporary agency, converting the employee to a full-time, permanent position.

Your First Job

If you have no experience in the cybersecurity field, then you will most likely look for a company that is willing to train you for a position similar to a Tier 1 Analyst. Working for a call center or support desk may be your first step into gaining the experience you need to move ahead in your career.

How long should you stay in your first job? Generally, you want to make it through a full review cycle before leaving a company. That is, you typically want to make it past 18 months. Potential employers will normally want to know if you met or exceeded expectations in your current or past jobs.

Refer to
Lab Activity
for this chapter

1.2.2.5   Lab - Becoming a Defender

In this lab, you will research and analyze what it takes to become a network defender.

1.3   Summary

1.3.1   Conclusion

Refer to
Online Course
for Illustration

1.3.1.1   Chapter 1: Cybersecurity and the Security Operations Center

In the beginning of the chapter you learned that people, companies, and even nations can all fall victim to cyberattacks. There are various types of attackers, including amateurs who attack for fun and prestige, hacktivists who hack to further a political cause, and professional hackers who attack for profit. In addition, nations may attack other nations to gain economic advantage through the theft of intellectual property, or to damage or destroy the assets of another country. The networks that are vulnerable to attack are not just business networks of PCs and servers, but also the thousands of devices on the Internet of Things.

Security Operations Centers (SOC) are responsible for preventing, detecting, and responding to cybercrime. SOCs consist of people following processes to use technologies to respond to threats. There are four main roles in the SOC. Tier 1 analysts verify security alerts using network data. Tier 2 responders investigate verified incidents and decide on how to act. Tier 3 SME/Hunters are experts and are able to investigate threats at the highest level. The fourth role is the SOC managers. They manage the resources of the center and communicate with customers. Customers can be internal or external. A SOC may be operated by a single company or may provide services to many companies. Finally, although network security is extremely important, it cannot interfere with the ability of the company and its employees to fulfill the mission of an organization.

In order to work in a SOC, you learned that you can study to earn certifications that are offered by a number of different organizations. In addition, you can pursue degrees in higher education that are relevant to cyber operations, and learn other skills such as programming in Python. Job leads can be found at a number of employment websites, and agencies can help you to find temporary jobs, internships, or permanent employment.

Go to the online course to take the quiz and exam.

Chapter 1 Quiz

This quiz is designed to provide an additional opportunity to practice the skills and knowledge presented in the chapter and to prepare for the chapter exam. You will be allowed multiple attempts and the grade does not appear in the gradebook.

Chapter 1 Exam

The chapter exam assesses your knowledge of the chapter content.

Your Chapter Notes

Windows Operating System

2.0 Introduction

2.0.1 Welcome

Refer to
Online Course
for Illustration

2.0.1.1 Chapter 2: Windows Operating System

From its humble beginnings over 30 years ago in 1985, the Windows operating system has seen many iterations; from Windows 1.0 to today's current desktop version, Windows 10, and server version, Windows Server 2016. Click here for a graphical view of timeline for Windows desktop and server versions.

This chapter covers some of the basic concepts of Windows, including how the operating system works and the tools used to secure Windows endpoints.

Refer to
Lab Activity
for this chapter

2.0.1.2 Class Activity - Identify Running Processes

In this lab, you will use TCP/UDP Endpoint Viewer, a tool in Sysinternals Suite, to identify any running processes on your computer.

2.1 Windows Overview

2.1.1 Windows History

Refer to
Online Course
for Illustration

2.1.1.1 Disk Operating System

The first computers did not have modern storage devices such as hard drives, optical drives, or flash storage. The first storage methods used punch cards, paper tape, magnetic tape, and even audio cassettes.

Floppy disk and hard disk storage requires software to read from, write to, and manage the data that they store. A Disk Operating System (DOS) is an operating system that the computer uses to enable these data storage devices to read and write files. The DOS provides a file system which organizes the files in a specific way on the disk. MS-DOS is a DOS created by Microsoft. MS-DOS used a command line as the interface for people to create programs and manipulate data files, as shown in the figure.

With MS-DOS, the computer had a basic working knowledge of how to access the disk drive, and load the operating system files directly from disk as part of the boot process. When it was loaded, MS-DOS could easily access DOS because it was built into the operating system.

Early versions of Windows consisted of a Graphical User Interface (GUI) that ran over MS-DOS with the first being Windows 1.0 in 1985. The disk operating system still controlled the computer and its hardware. A modern operating system like Windows 10 is not considered a disk operating system. It is built on Windows NT, which stands for "New Technologies". The operating system itself is in direct control of the computer and its hardware. NT is an OS with support for multiple user processes. This is much different than the single process, single user MS-DOS.

Today, anything that used to be accomplished through the command line interface of MS-DOS can be accomplished in the Windows GUI. You can still experience what it was like to use MS-DOS by opening a command window, but what you see is no longer MS-DOS, it is a function of Windows. To experience a little of what it was like to work in MS-DOS, open a command window by typing **cmd** in Windows Search and pressing **Enter**. These are some commands that you can use:

- **dir** - shows a listing of all the files in the current directory (folder)
- **cd** *directory* - changes the directory to the indicated directory
- **cd..** - changes the directory to the directory above the current directory
- **cd** - changes the directory to the root directory (often C:)
- **copy** - copies files to another location
- **del** - deletes one or more files
- **find** - searches for text in files
- **mkdir** - creates a new directory
- **ren** - renames a file
- **help** - displays all the commands that can be used, with a brief description
- **help** *command* - displays extensive help for the indicated command

Refer to
Online Course
for Illustration

2.1.1.2   Windows Versions

Since 1993, there have been more than 20 releases of Windows that are based on the NT operating system. Most of these versions were for use by the general public and businesses because of the file security offered by the file system that was used by the NT OS. Businesses also adopted NT OS-based Windows operating systems. This is because many editions were built specifically for workstation, professional, server, advanced server, and datacenter server, to name just a few of the many purpose-built versions.

Beginning with Windows XP, a 64-bit edition was available. The 64-bit operating system was an entirely new architecture. It had a 64-bit address space instead of a 32-bit address space. This is not simply twice the amount of space because these bits are binary numbers. While 32-bit Windows can address a little less than 4 GB of RAM, 64-bit Windows can theoretically address 16.8 million terabytes. When the OS and the hardware all support 64-bit operation, extremely large data sets can be used. These large data sets include very large databases, scientific computing, and manipulation of high definition digital video with special effects. In general, 64-bit computers and operating systems are backward-compatible with older, 32-bit programs, but 64-bit programs cannot be run on older, 32-bit hardware.

With each subsequent release of Windows, the operating system has become more refined by incorporating more features. Windows 7 was offered with six different editions,

Windows 8 with as many as five, and Windows 10 with eight different editions! Each edition not only offers different capabilities, but also different price points. Microsoft has said that Windows 10 is the last version of Windows, that Windows has become a service rather than just an OS. They say that rather than purchasing new operating systems, users will just update Windows 10 instead.

Refer to
Interactive Graphic
in online course

2.1.1.3   Windows GUI

Windows has a graphical user interface (GUI) for users to work with data files and software. The GUI has a main area that is known as the Desktop, shown in Figure 1. The Desktop can be customized with various colors and background images. Windows supports multiple users, so each user can customize the Desktop to their liking. The Desktop can store files, folders, shortcuts to locations and programs, and applications. The Desktop also has a recycle bin icon, where files are stored when the user deletes them. Files can be restored from the recycle bin or the recycle bin can be emptied of files, which truly deletes them.

At the bottom of the desktop is the Task Bar. The Task Bar has three areas that are used for different purposes. At the left is the Start menu. It is used to access all of the installed programs, configuration options, and the search feature. At the center of the Task Bar, users place quick launch icons that run specific programs or open specific folders when they are clicked. Finally, on the right of the Task Bar is the notification area. The notification area shows, at a glance, the functionality of many different programs and features. For example, a blinking envelope icon may indicate new email, or a network icon with a red "x" may indicate a problem with the network.

Often, right-clicking an icon will bring up additional functions that can be used. This list is known as a Context Menu, shown in Figure 2. There are Context Menus for the icons in the notification area, and also for quick launch icons, system configuration icons, and for files and folders. The Context Menu provides many of the most commonly used functions by just clicking. For example, the Context Menu for a file will contain such items as copy, delete, share, and print. To open folders and manipulate files, Windows uses the Windows File Explorer.

Windows File Explorer, also shown in Figure 2, is a tool used to navigate the entire file system of a computer, including multiple storage devices and network locations. Using the Windows File Explorer, you can easily create folders, copy files and folders, and move them around to different locations and devices. Basically, the tool has two main windows. The one on the left allows quick navigation to storage devices, parent folders, and child folders. The one on the right shows the content of the location that is selected in the left pane.

Refer to
Online Course
for Illustration

2.1.1.4   Operating System Vulnerabilities

Operating systems consist of millions of lines of code. Installed software can also contain millions of lines of code. With all this code comes vulnerabilities. A vulnerability is some flaw or weakness that can be exploited by an attacker to reduce the viability of a computer's information. To take advantage of an operating system vulnerability, the attacker must use a technique or a tool to exploit the vulnerability. The attacker can then use the vulnerability to get the computer to act in a fashion outside of its intended design. In general, the goal is to gain unauthorized control of the computer, change permissions, or manipulate data.

Even though the CLI has many commands and features, it cannot work together with the core of Windows or the GUI. Another environment, called the Windows PowerShell, can be used to create scripts to automate tasks that the regular CLI is unable to create. PowerShell also provides a CLI for initiating commands. PowerShell is an integrated program within Windows and can be opened by searching for powershell and clicking the program. Like the CLI, PowerShell can also be run with administrative privileges.

These are the types of commands that PowerShell can execute:

- **cmdlets** - These commands perform an action and return an output or object to the next command that will be executed.

- **PowerShell scripts** - These are files with a .ps1 extension that contain PowerShell commands that are executed.

- **PowerShell functions** - These are pieces of code that can be referenced in a script.

To see more information about Windows PowerShell and get started using it, type **help** in PowerShell, as shown in the figure. You will be provided with much more information and resources to start using PowerShell.

There are four levels of help in Windows PowerShell:

- **get-help** *PS command* - Displays basic help for a command

- **get-help** *PS command* [*-examples*] - Displays basic help for a command with examples

- **get-help** *PS command* [*-detailed*] - Displays detailed help for a command with examples

- **get-help** *PS command* [*-full*] - Displays all help information for a command with examples in greater depth

2.2.1.4   Windows Management Instrumentation

Refer to **Online Course** for Illustration

Windows Management Instrumentation (WMI) is used to manage remote computers. It can retrieve information about computer components, hardware and software statistics, and monitor the health of remote computers. You can open WMI control by searching for computer management, and then right-click the **WMI Control** entry under **Services and Applications**, and choosing **Properties**. The WMI Control Properties window is shown in the figure.

These are the four tabs in the WMI Control Properties window:

- **General** - Summary information about the local computer and WMI

- **Backup/Restore** - Allows manual backup of statistics gathered by WMI

- **Security** - Settings to configure who has access to different WMI statistics

- **Advanced** - Settings to configure the default namespace for WMI

Some attacks today use WMI to connect to remote systems, modify the registry, and run commands. WMI helps them to avoid detection because it is common traffic, most often trusted by the network security devices and the remote WMI commands do not usually leave evidence on the remote host. Because of this, WMI access should be strictly limited.

Refer to
Online Course
for Illustration

2.2.1.5　The net Command

Windows has many commands that can be entered at the command line. One important command is the **net** command, used in the administration and maintenance of the OS. The **net** command supports many other commands that follow the **net** command and can be combined with switches to focus on specific output.

To see a list of the many **net** commands, type **net help** at the command prompt. The figure shows the commands that the **net** command can use. To see verbose help about any of the net commands, type **net help** *command*.

These are some common net commands:

- **net accounts** - Sets password and logon requirements for users
- **net session** - Lists or disconnects sessions between a computer and other computers on the network
- **net share** - Creates, removes, or manages shared resources
- **net start** - Starts a network service or lists running network services
- **net stop** - Stops a network service
- **net use** - Connects, disconnects, and displays information about shared network resources
- **net view** - Shows a list of computers and network devices on the network

Refer to
Online Course
for Illustration

2.2.1.6　Task Manager and Resource Monitor

There are two very important and useful tools to help an administrator to understand the many different applications, services, and processes that are running on a Windows computer. These tools also provide insight into the performance of the computer, such as CPU, memory, and network usage. These tools are especially useful when investigating a problem where malware is suspected. When a component is not performing the way that it should be, these tools can be used to determine what the problem might be.

Task Manager

The Task Manager, shown in Figure 1, provides a lot of information about what is running, and general performance of the computer. There are seven tabs in the Task Manager:

- **Processes** - All of the programs and processes that are currently running are shown here. The CPU, memory, disk, and network utilization of each process is displayed in columns. You can examine the properties of any of these processes, or end a process that is not behaving properly or has stalled.

- **Performance** - A view of all the performance statistics provides a useful overview of the CPU, memory, disk, and network performance. Clicking each item in the left pane will show detailed statistics of that item in the right pane.

- **App history** - The use of resources by application over time provides insight into applications that are consuming more resources than they should be. Click **Options** and **Show history for all processes** to see the history of every process that has run since the computer was started.

- **Startup** - All of the applications and services that start when the computer is booted are shown in this tab. To disable a program from starting at startup, **right-click** the item and choose **Disable**.

- **Users** - All of the users that are logged on to the computer are shown in this tab. Also shown are all the resources that each user's applications and processes are using. From this tab, an administrator can disconnect a user from the computer.

- **Details** - Similar to the Processes tab, this tab provides additional management options for processes such as setting a priority to make the processor devote more or less time to a process. CPU affinity can also be set which determines which core or CPU a program will use. Also, a useful feature called Analyze wait chain shows any process for which another process is waiting. This feature helps to determine if a process is simply waiting, or is stalled.

- **Services** - All the services that are loaded are shown in this tab. The process ID (PID) and a short description are also shown along with the status of either Running or Stopped. At the bottom, there is a button to open the Services console which provides additional management of services.

Resource Monitor

When more detailed information about resource usage is needed, you can use the Resource Monitor, shown in Figure 2. When searching for the reason a computer may be acting erratically, the Resource Monitor can help to find the source of the problem. The Resource Monitor has five tabs:

- **Overview** - General usage for each resource is shown in this tab. If you select a single process, it will be filtered across all of the tabs to show only that process's statistics.

- **CPU** - The PID, number of threads, which CPU the process is using, and the average CPU usage of each process is shown in this tab. Additional information about any services that the process relies on, and the associated handles and modules can be seen by expanding the lower rows.

- **Memory** - All of the statistical information about how each process uses memory is shown in this tab. Also, an overview of usage of all the RAM is shown below the Processes row.

- **Disk** - All of the processes that are using a disk are shown in this tab, with read/write statistics and an overview of each storage device.

- **Network** - All of the processes that are using the network are shown in this tab, with read/write statistics. Most importantly, the current TCP connections are shown, along with all of the ports that are listening. This tab is very useful when trying to determine which applications and processes are communicating over the network. It makes it possible to tell if an unauthorized process is accessing the network, listening for a communication, and the address with which it is communicating.

Refer to
Interactive Graphic
in online course

2.2.1.7 Networking

One of the most important features of any operating system is the ability for the computer to connect to a network. Without this feature, there is no access to network resources or the Internet. To configure Windows networking properties and test networking settings, the Network and Sharing Center, shown in Figure 1, is used. The easiest way to run this tool is to search for it and click it.

The initial view shows an overview of the active network. This view shows whether there is Internet access and if the network is private, public, or guest. The type of network, either wired or wireless, is also shown. From this window, you can see the HomeGroup the computer belongs to, or create one if it is not already part of a HomeGroup. This tool can also be used to change adapter settings, change advance sharing settings, set up a new connection, or troubleshoot problems.

To configure a network adapter, choose **Change adapter settings** to show all of the network connections that are available. Right-click the adapter you wish to configure and choose **Properties**, as shown in Figure 2. In the **This connection uses the following items:** box, highlight **Internet Protocol Version 4 (TCP/IPv4)** or **Internet Protocol Version 6 (TCP/IPv6)** depending on which version you wish to use (Figure 3). Click **Properties** to configure the adapter.

In the **Properties** dialogue box, shown in Figure 4, you can choose to **Obtain an address automatically** if there is a DHCP server available on the network. If you wish to configure addressing manually, you can fill in the address, subnet, default gateway, and DNS servers to configure the adapter. Click **OK** to accept the changes.

You can also use the **netsh.exe** tool to configure networking parameters from a command prompt. This program can display and modify the network configuration. Type **netsh /?** at the command prompt to see a list of all the switches that can be used with this command.

After the network configuration is complete, there are some basic commands that can be used to test connectivity to the local network, and the Internet. The most basic test is performed with the **ping** command. To test the adapter itself, type **ping 127.0.0.1** at the command prompt, as shown in Figure 5. This will make sure that the adapter is able to send and receive data. It also confirms that the TCP/IP protocol suite is properly installed in the computer. The 127.0.0.1 address is known as the loopback address.

Next, ping any host on the network. If you do not know any IP addresses of other hosts on the network, you can ping the default gateway. To find the address of the default gateway, type **ipconfig** at the command prompt, as shown in Figure 6. This command will return basic network information including the IP address of the host, the subnet mask, and the default gateway. You can also ping hosts on other connected networks to make sure that you have connectivity to those networks. The **ipconfig** command has many switches that are helpful when troubleshooting network issues. Type **ipconfig /?** to see a list of all the switches that can be used with this command.

When the ping command is issued, it will send four ICMP echo request messages to the indicated IP address. If there is no reply, there may be a problem with the network configuration. It is also possible that the intended host blocks ICMP echo requests. In this case, try to ping a different host on the network. Most often, there are four replies to the requests, showing the size of each request, the time it took to travel, and the time to live (TTL). TTL is the number of hops a packet takes along the path to its destination.

Domain Name System (DNS) should also be tested because it is used very often to find the address of hosts by translating it from a name. Use the nslookup command to test DNS. Type **nslookup cisco.com** at the command prompt to find the address of the Cisco webserver. When the address is returned, you know that DNS is functioning correctly. You can also check to see what ports are open, where they are connected, and what their current status is. Type **netstat** at the command line to see details of active network connections, as shown in Figure 7. The **netstat** command will be examined further later in this chapter.

Refer to
Online Course
for Illustration

2.2.1.8   Accessing Network Resources

Like other operating systems, Windows uses networking for many different applications such as web, email, and file services. Originally developed by IBM, Microsoft aided in the development of the Server Message Block (SMB) protocol to share network resources. SMB is mostly used for accessing files on remote hosts. The Universal Naming Convention (UNC) format is used to connect to resources, for example:

\\servername\sharename\file

In the UNC, servername is the server that is hosting the resource. This can be a DNS name, a NetBIOS name, or simply an IP address. The sharename is the root of the folder in the file system on the remote host, while the file is the resource that the local host is trying to find. The file may be deeper within the file system and this hierarchy will need to be indicated.

When sharing resources on the network, the area of the file system that will be shared will need to be identified. Access control can be applied to the folders and files to restrict users and groups to specific functions such as read, write, or deny. There are also special shares that are automatically created by Windows. These shares are called administrative shares. An administrative share is identified by the dollar sign ($) that comes after the share name. Each disk volume has an administrative share, represented by the volume letter and the $ such as C$, D$, or E$. The Windows installation folder is shared as admin$, the printers folder is shared as print$, and there are other administrative shares that can be connected. Only users with administrative privileges can access these shares.

The easiest way to connect to a share is to type the UNC of the share into the Windows File Explorer, in the box at the top of the screen which shows the breadcrumb listing of the current file system location. When Windows tries to connect to the share, you will be asked to provide credentials for accessing the resource. Remember that because the resource is on a remote computer, the credentials need to be for the remote computer, not the local computer.

Besides accessing shares on remote hosts, you can also log in to a remote host and manipulate that computer as if it were local, to make configuration changes, install software, or troubleshoot an issue with the computer. In Windows, this function is known as the Remote Desktop Protocol (RDP). When investigating security incidents, a security analyst uses RDP often to access remote computers. To start RDP and connect to a remote computer, search for remote desktop and click the application. The Remote Desktop Connection window is shown in the figure.

Refer to
Online Course
for Illustration

2.2.1.9   Windows Server

Most Windows installations are performed as desktop installation on desktops and laptops. There is another edition of Windows that is mainly used in data centers called Windows Server. This is a family of Microsoft products that began with Windows Server 2003. Today, the latest release is Windows Server 2016. Windows Server hosts many different services and can fulfill different roles within a company.

Note   Although there is a Windows Server 2000, it is considered a client version of Windows NT 5.0. Windows Server 2003 is a server based on NT 5.2 and begins a new family of Windows Server versions.

These are some of the services that Windows Server hosts:

- **Network Services** - DNS, DHCP, Terminal services, Network Controller, and Hyper-V Network virtualization

- **File Services** - SMB, NFS, and DFS

- **Web Services** - FTP, HTTP, and HTTPS

- **Management** - Group policy and Active Directory domain services control

Refer to **Lab Activity** for this chapter

2.2.1.10   Lab - Create User Accounts

In this lab, you will create and modify user accounts in Windows.

Refer to **Lab Activity** for this chapter

2.2.1.11   Lab - Using Windows PowerShell

The objective of the lab is to explore some of the functions of PowerShell.

Refer to **Lab Activity** for this chapter

2.2.1.12   Lab - Windows Task Manager

In this lab, you will explore Task Manager and manage processes from within Task Manager.

Refer to **Lab Activity** for this chapter

2.2.1.13   Lab - Monitor and Manage System Resources in Windows

In this lab, you will use administrative tools to monitor and manage system resources.

2.2.2   Windows Security

Refer to **Online Course** for Illustration

2.2.2.1   The netstat Command

When malware is present in a computer, it will often open communication ports on the host to send and receive data. The **netstat** command can be used to look for inbound or outbound connections that are not authorized. When used on its own, the **netstat** command will display all of the active TCP connections that are available.

By examining these connections, it is possible to determine which of the programs are listening for connections that are not authorized. When a program is suspected of being malware, a little research can be performed to determine its legitimacy. From there, the process can be shut down with the Task Manager, and malware removal software can be used to clean the computer.

To make this process easier, you can link the connections to the running processes in the Task Manager. To do this, open a command prompt with administrative privileges and use the command **netstat -abno**, as shown in the figure.

By examining the active TCP connections, an analyst should be able to determine if there are any suspicious programs that are listening for incoming connections on the host. You can also trace that process to the Windows Task Manager and cancel the process. There may be more than one process listed with the same name. If this is the case, use the PID to find the correct process. Each process running on the computer has a unique PID. To display the PIDs for the processes in the Task Manager, open the Task Manager, right-click the table heading and select **PID**.

Refer to
Online Course
for Illustration

2.2.2.2   Event Viewer

Windows Event Viewer logs the history of application, security, and system events. These log files are a valuable troubleshooting tool because they provide information necessary to identify a problem. To open the Event Viewer, search for it and click the program icon.

Windows includes two categories of event logs: Windows Logs, and Application and Services Logs. Each of these categories has multiple log types. Events that are displayed in these logs have a level: information, warning, error, or critical. They also have the date and time that the event occurred, along with the source of the event and an ID which relates to that type of event.

It is also possible to create a custom view. This is useful when looking for certain types of events, finding events that happened during a certain time period, displaying events of a certain level, and many other criteria. There is a built-in custom view called Administrative Events that shows all critical, error, and warning events from all of the administrative logs. This is a good view to start with when trying to troubleshoot a problem.

Refer to
Online Course
for Illustration

2.2.2.3   Windows Update Management

No software is perfect, and the Windows operating system is no exception. Attackers are constantly coming up with new ways to compromise computers and exploit bad code. Some of these attacks come so quickly that there is no defense against them. These are called zero-day exploits. Microsoft and security software developers are always trying to stay ahead of the attackers, but they are not always successful. To ensure the highest level of protection against these attacks, always make sure Windows is up to date with the latest service packs and security patches.

Patches are code updates that manufacturers provide to prevent a newly discovered virus or worm from making a successful attack. From time to time, manufacturers combine patches and upgrades into a comprehensive update application called a service pack. Many devastating virus attacks could have been much less severe if more users had downloaded and installed the latest service pack.

Windows routinely checks the Windows Update website for high-priority updates that can help protect a computer from the latest security threats. These updates include security updates, critical updates, and service packs. Depending on the setting you choose, Windows automatically downloads and installs any high-priority updates that your computer needs or notifies you as these updates become available. To configure the settings for Windows update, search for Windows Update and click the application.

The Update status, shown in the figure, allows you to check for updates manually and see the update history of the computer. There are also settings for the hours where the computer will not automatically restart, for example during regular business hours. You can also choose when to restart the computer after an update, if necessary, with the Restart options. Advanced options are also available to choose how updates are installed and get updates for other Microsoft products.

Refer to
Online Course
for Illustration

2.2.2.4   Local Security Policy

A security policy is a set of objectives that ensures the security of a network, the data, and the computer systems in an organization. The security policy is a constantly evolving document based on changes in technology, business, and employee requirements.

In most networks that use Windows computers, Active Directory is configured with Domains on a Windows Server. Windows computers join the domain. The administrator configures a Domain Security Policy that applies to all computers that join the domain. Account policies are automatically set when a user logs in to a computer that is a member of a domain. Windows Local Security Policy, shown in the figure, can be used for stand-alone computers that are not part of an Active Directory domain. To open the Local Security Policy applet, search for Local Security Policy and click the program.

Password guidelines are an important component of a security policy. Any user that must log on to a computer or connect to a network resource should be required to have a password. Passwords help prevent theft of data and malicious acts. Passwords also help to confirm that the logging of events is valid by ensuring that the user is the person they say that they are. Password Policy is found under Account Policies, and defines the criteria for the passwords for all of the users on the local computer.

Use the Account Lockout Policy in Account Policies to prevent brute-force login attempts. You can set the policy to allow the user to enter a wrong username and/or password five times. After five attempts, the account is locked out for 30 minutes. After 30 minutes, the number of attempts is reset to zero and the user can attempt to login again.

It is important to make sure that computers are secure when users are away. A security policy should contain a rule about requiring a computer to lock when the screensaver starts. This will ensure that after a short time away from the computer, the screen saver will start and then the computer cannot be used until the user logs in.

If the Local Security Policy on every stand-alone computer is the same, then use the Export Policy feature. Save the policy with a name, such as workstation.inf. Copy the policy file to an external media or network drive to use on other stand-alone computers. This is particularly helpful if the administrator needs to configure extensive local policies for user rights and security options.

The Local Security Policy applet contains many other security settings that apply specifically to the local computer. You can configure User Rights, Firewall Rules, and even the ability to restrict the files that users or groups are allowed to run with the AppLocker.

2.2.2.5 Windows Defender

Refer to **Online Course** for Illustration

Malware includes viruses, worms, Trojan horses, keyloggers, spyware, and adware. These are designed to invade privacy, steal information, damage the computer, or corrupt data. It is important that you protect computers and mobile devices using reputable antimalware software. The following types of antimalware programs are available:

- **Antivirus protection** - This program continuously monitors for viruses. When a virus is detected, the user is warned, and the program attempts to quarantine or delete the virus.

- **Adware protection** - This program continuously looks for programs that display advertising on your computer.

- **Phishing protection** - This program blocks the IP addresses of known phishing websites and warns the user about suspicious sites.

- **Spyware protection** - This program scans for keyloggers and other spyware.

- **Trusted/untrusted sources** - This program warns you about unsafe programs about to be installed or unsafe websites before they are visited.

It may take several different programs and multiple scans to completely remove all malicious software. Run only one malware protection program at a time.

Several reputable security organizations such as McAfee, Symantec, and Kaspersky, offer all-inclusive malware protection for computers and mobile devices. Windows has built-in virus and spyware protection called Windows Defender, shown in the figure. Windows Defender is turned on by default providing real-time protection against infection.

To open Windows Defender, search for it and click the program. Although Windows Defender works in the background, you can perform manual scans of the computer and storage devices. You can also manually update the virus and spyware definitions in the **Update** tab. Also, to see all of the items that were found during previous scans, click the **History** tab.

Refer to
Online Course
for Illustration

2.2.2.6   Windows Firewall

A firewall selectively denies traffic to a computer or network segment. Firewalls generally work by opening and closing the ports used by various applications. By opening only the required ports on a firewall, you are implementing a restrictive security policy. Any packet not explicitly permitted is denied. In contrast, a permissive security policy permits access through all ports, except those explicitly denied. In the past, software and hardware were shipped with permissive settings. As users neglected to configure their equipment, the default permissive settings left many devices exposed to attackers. Most devices now ship with settings as restrictive as possible, while still allowing easy setup.

To allow program access through the Windows Firewall, search for Windows Firewall, click its name to run it, and click **Allow an app or feature through Windows Firewall**, as shown in Figure 1.

If you wish to use a different software firewall, you will need to disable Windows Firewall. To disable the Windows Firewall, click **Turn Windows Firewall on or off**.

Many additional settings can be found under **Advanced settings**, as shown in Figure 2. Here you can create inbound or outbound traffic rules based on different criteria. You can also import and export policies or monitor different aspects of the firewall.

Refer to
Interactive Graphic
in online course

2.2.2.7   Activity - Identify the Windows Command

Refer to
Interactive Graphic
in online course

2.2.2.8   Activity - Identify the Windows Tool

2.3   Summary

2.3.1   Conclusion

Refer to
Online Course
for Illustration

2.3.1.1   Chapter 2: Windows Operating System

In this chapter, you learned about the history and architecture of the Windows operating system. There have been over 40 versions of Windows desktop, Windows server, and Windows mobile operating systems.

HAL handles all the communication between the hardware and the kernel. The CPU can operate in two separate modes: kernel mode and user mode. Applications that are installed are run in user mode, and operating system code runs in kernel mode.

NTFS formats the disk into four important data structures:

- Partition Boot Sector
- Master File Table (MFT)
- System Files
- File Area

Applications are generally made up of many processes. A process is any program that is currently executing. Each running process is made up of at least one thread. A thread is a part of the process that can be executed. Some of the processes that Windows runs are services. These are programs that run in the background to support the operating system and applications.

Each process in a 32-bit Windows computer supports a virtual address space that enables addressing up to four gigabytes. Each process in a 64-bit Windows computer supports a virtual address space of up to eight terabytes.

Windows stores all of the information about hardware, applications, users, and system settings in a large database known as the registry. The registry is a hierarchical database where the highest level is known as a hive. These are the five hives of the Windows registry:

- HKEY_CURRENT_USER (HKCU)
- HKEY_USERS (HKU)
- HKEY_CLASSES_ROOT (HKCR)
- HKEY_LOCAL_MACHINE (HKLM)
- HKEY_CURRENT_CONFIG (HKCC)

In this chapter, you also learned how to configure, monitor, and keep Windows secure. To do this normally requires that you run programs as Administrator. As administrator, you can create users and groups, disable access to the administrator and guest accounts, and use a variety of administrator tools including:

- All commands available to CLI and PowerShell
- Remote computer management using WMI and Remote Desktop
- Task Manager and Resource Monitor
- Networking configuration

As administrator, you will also have the ability to use all the Windows security tools including:

- The **netstat** command to look for inbound and outbound connections that are not authorized

- Event Viewer for access to logs that document the history of application, security, and system events

- Windows Update configuration and scheduling

- Windows Local Security Policy to secure stand-alone computers that are not part of an Active Directory domain

- Windows Defender configuration for built-in virus and spyware protection

- Windows Firewall configuration to fine-tune the default settings

As a cybersecurity analyst, you need a basic understanding of how Windows operates and what tools are available to help keep Windows endpoints secure.

Go to the online course to take the quiz and exam.

Chapter 2 Quiz

This quiz is designed to provide an additional opportunity to practice the skills and knowledge presented in the chapter and to prepare for the chapter exam. You will be allowed multiple attempts and the grade does not appear in the gradebook.

Chapter 2 Exam

The chapter exam assesses your knowledge of the chapter content.

Your Chapter Notes

Linux Operating System

3.0 Introduction

3.0.1 Welcome

Refer to
Online Course
for Illustration

3.0.1.1 Chapter 3: Linux Operating System

Linus Torvalds released the first Linux kernel in 1991 under the open source model. Originally developed for the Intel x86 chip architecture, Linux has grown to incorporate many different hardware configurations. Click here for a graphic showing how Linux is part of many of the computing platforms in use today.

In this chapter, you learn how to perform basic Linux operations as well as administrative and security-related tasks.

3.1 Linux Overview

3.1.1 Linux Basics

Refer to
Online Course
for Illustration

3.1.1.1 What is Linux?

Linux is an operating system created in 1991. Linux is open source, fast, reliable, and small. It requires very little hardware resources to run, and is highly customizable. Unlike other operating systems such as Windows and OS X, Linux was created, and is currently maintained by, a community of programmers. Linux is part of several platforms and can be found on devices anywhere from "wristwatches to supercomputers".

Another important aspect of Linux is that it is designed to be connected to the network, which makes it much simpler to write and use network-based applications. Because Linux is open source, any person or company can get the kernel's source code, inspect it, modify it, and re-compile it at will. They are also allowed to redistribute the program with or without charges.

A Linux distribution is the term used to describe packages created by different organizations. Linux distributions (or distros) include the Linux kernel with customized tools and software packages. While some of these organizations may charge for their Linux distribution support (geared towards Linux-based businesses), the majority of them also offer their distribution for free without support. Debian, Red Hat, Ubuntu, CentOS, and SUSE are just a few examples of Linux distributions.

Refer to
Online Course
for Illustration

3.1.1.2 The Value of Linux

Linux is often the operating system of choice in the Security Operations Center (SOC). These are some of the reasons to choose Linux:

- **Linux is open source** - Any person can acquire Linux at no charge and modify it to fit specific needs. This flexibility allows analysts and administrators to tailor-build an operating system specifically for security analysis.

- **The Linux CLI is very powerful** - While a GUI makes many tasks easier to perform, it adds complexity and requires more computer resources to run. The Linux Command Line Interface (CLI) is extremely powerful and enables analysts to perform tasks not only directly on a terminal, but also remotely because the CLI requires very few resources.

- **The user has more control over the OS** - The administrator user in Linux, known as the root user, or superuser, has absolute power over the computer. Unlike other operating systems, the root user can modify any aspect of the computer with a few keystrokes. This ability is especially valuable when working with low level functions such as the network stack. It allows the root user to have precise control over the way network packets are handled by the operating system.

- **It allows for better network communication control** - Control is an inherent part of Linux. Because the OS can be tweaked and adjusted in practically every aspect, it is a great platform for creating network applications. This is the same reason why many great network-based software tools are available for Linux only.

Refer to
Online Course
for Illustration

3.1.1.3 Linux in the SOC

The flexibility provided by Linux is a great feature for the SOC. The entire operating system can be tailored to become the perfect security analysis platform. For example, administrators can add only the necessary packages to the OS, making it lean and efficient. Specific software tools can be installed and configured to work in conjunction, allowing administrators to build a customized computer that fits perfectly in the workflow of a SOC.

These are a few tools that are often found in a SOC:

- **Network packet capture software** - This software is used for network packet captures. This is a crucial tool for a SOC analyst as it makes it possible to observe and understand every detail of a network transaction. The figure shows a screenshot of Wireshark, a popular packet capture tool.

- **Malware analysis tools** - In the case of new malware detection, these tools allow analysts to safely run and observe malware execution without the risk of compromising the underlying system.

- **Intrusion detection systems (IDSs)** - These tools are used for real-time traffic monitoring and inspection. If any aspect of the currently flowing traffic matches any of the established rules, a pre-defined action is taken.

- **Firewalls** - This software is used to specify, based on pre-defined rules, whether traffic is allowed to enter or leave the network.

- **Log managers** - Log files are used to record events. Because a large network can generate a very large number of events log entries, log managers are employed to facilitate log monitoring.

- **Security information and event management (SIEM)** - SIEMs provide real-time analysis of alerts and log entries generated by network appliances such as IDSs and firewalls.

- **Ticketing systems** - Ticket assignment, editing, and recording is done through a ticket management system.

Refer to
Online Course
for Illustration

3.1.1.4   Linux Tools

In addition to SOC-specific tools, Linux computers used in the SOC often contain penetration testing tools. Also known as PenTesting, a penetration test is the process of looking for vulnerabilities in a network or computer by attacking it. Packet generators, port scanners, and proof-of-concept exploits are examples of PenTesting tools.

Kali Linux is a Linux distribution created to group many penetration tools. Kali contains a great selection of penetration testing tools. The figure shows a screenshot of Kali Linux. Notice all the major categories of penetration testing tools.

3.1.2   Working in the Linux Shell

Refer to
Online Course
for Illustration

3.1.2.1   The Linux Shell

In Linux, the user communicates with the OS by using the CLI or the GUI. Linux often boots into the GUI by default, hiding the CLI from the user. One way to access the CLI from the GUI is through a terminal emulator application. These applications provide user access to the CLI and are often named as some variation of the word "terminal". In Linux, popular terminal emulators are Terminator, eterm, xterm, konsole, and gnome-terminal.

Click here to experience the Linux CLI in your web browser. Type the **ls** command to list the current directory content. Keep the tab open if you would like to try out some of the other commands discussed in this chapter.

The figure shows gnome-terminal, a popular Linux terminal emulator.

Note   The terms shell, console, console window, CLI terminal, and terminal window are often used interchangeably.

Refer to
Interactive Graphic
in online course

3.1.2.2   Basic Commands

Linux commands are programs created to perform a specific task. Use the **man** command (short for manual) to obtain documentation about commands. As an example, **man ls** provides documentation about the **ls** command from the user manual.

Because commands are programs stored on the disk, when a user types a command, the shell must find it on the disk before it can be executed. The shell will look for user-typed commands in specific directories and attempt to execute them. The list of directories checked by the shell is called the path. The path contains many directories commonly used to store commands. If a command is not in the path, the user must specify its location or the shell will not be able to find it. Users can easily add directories to the path, if necessary.

To invoke a command via the shell, simply type its name. The shell will try to find it in the system path and execute it.

Figures 1 and 2 shows a list of some basic Linux commands and their functions.

Note   The text here assumes the user has the proper permissions to execute the command. File permissions in Linux is covered later in this chapter.

Refer to
Online Course
for Illustration

3.1.2.3   File and Directory Commands

Many command line tools are included in Linux by default. To adjust the command operation, users can pass parameters and switches along with the command. The figure shows a few of the most common commands related to files and directories.

Refer to
Online Course
for Illustration

3.1.2.4   Working with Text Files

Linux has many different text editors, with various features and functions. Some text editors include graphical interfaces while others are command-line only tools. Each text editor includes a feature set designed to support a specific type of task. Some text editors focus on the programmer and include features such as syntax highlighting, brackets, parenthesis, check, and other programming-focused features.

While graphical text editors are convenient and easy to use, command line-based text editors are very important for Linux users. The main benefit of command-line-based text editors is that they allow for text file editing from a remote computer.

Consider the following scenario: a user must perform administrative tasks on a Linux computer but is not sitting in front of that computer. Using SSH, the user starts a remote shell to the remote computer. Under the text-based remote shell, the graphical interface is not available, which makes it impossible to rely on tools such as graphical text editors. In this type of situation, text-based programs are crucial.

The figure shows nano, a popular command-line text editor. The administrator is editing firewall rules. Text editors are often used for system configuration and maintenance in Linux.

Due to the lack of graphical support, nano (or GNU nano) can only be controlled with the keyboard. For example, **CTRL+O** saves the current file; **CTRL+W** opens the search menu. GNU nano uses a two-line shortcut bar at the bottom of the screen, where commands for the current context are listed. Press **CTRL+G** for the help screen and a complete list of commands.

Refer to
Online Course
for Illustration

3.1.2.5   The Importance of Text Files in Linux

In Linux, everything is treated as a file, this includes the memory, the disks, the monitor, the files, and the directories. For example, from the operating system standpoint, showing information on the display means to write to the file that represents the display device. It should be no surprise that the computer itself is configured through files. Known as configuration files, they are usually text files used to store adjustments and settings for specific applications or services. Practically everything in Linux relies on configuration files to work. Some services have not one, but several configuration files.

Users with proper permission levels can use text editors to change the contents of configuration files. After the changes are made, the file is saved and can be used by the related service or application. Users are able to specify exactly how they want any given application or service to behave. When launched, services and applications check the contents of specific configuration files to adjust their behavior accordingly.

In the figure, the administrator opened the host configuration file in nano for editing. Only the superuser can change the host file.

Note The administrator used the command **sudo nano /etc/hosts** to open the file. The command **sudo** (short for "superuser do") invokes the superuser privilege to use the nano text editor to open the host file.

Refer to
Lab Activity
for this chapter

3.1.2.6 Lab - Working with Text Files in the CLI

In this lab, you will get familiar with Linux command-line text editors and configuration files.

Refer to
Lab Activity
for this chapter

3.1.2.7 Lab - Getting Familiar with the Linux Shell

In this lab, you will use the Linux command line to manage files and folders and perform some basic administrative tasks.

3.1.3 Linux Servers and Clients

Refer to
Online Course
for Illustration

3.1.3.1 An Introduction to Client-Server Communications

Servers are computers with software installed that enables them to provide services to clients. There are many types of services. Some provide resources such as files, email messages, or web pages to clients upon request. Other services run maintenance tasks such as log management, memory management, disk scanning, and more. Each service requires separate server software. For example, the server in the figure requires file server software to provide clients with the ability to retrieve and submit files.

Client-server communications is discussed in more detail later in the course.

Refer to
Online Course
for Illustration

3.1.3.2 Servers, Services, and Their Ports

For a computer to be the server for multiple services, ports are used. A port is a reserved network resource used by a service. A server is said to be "listening" on a port when it has associated itself to that port.

While the administrator can decide which port to use with any given service, many clients are configured to use a specific port by default. To make it easier for the client, it is common practice to leave the service running in its default port. The figure shows a few commonly used ports and their services. These are also called "well-known ports".

Ports and their uses in network communications is discussed in more detail later in the course.

Refer to
Online Course
for Illustration

3.1.3.3 Clients

Clients are programs or applications designed to communicate with a specific server. Also known as client applications, clients use a well-defined protocol to communicate with the server. Web browsers are web clients used to communicate with web servers via the Hyper Text Transfer Protocol (HTTP). The File Transfer Protocol (FTP) client is software used to communicate with an FTP server. The figure shows a client uploading files to a server.

Refer to
Lab Activity
for this chapter

3.1.3.4 Lab - Linux Servers

In this lab, you will use the Linux command line to identify servers running on a given computer.

Refer to **Video** in online course

3.3.2.7   Video Demonstration - Applications, Rootkits, and Piping Commands

Click Play to view a demonstration of installing and updating applications, checking for a rootkit, and using piping commands.

Click here to read the transcript of this video.

3.4   Summary

3.4.1   Conclusion

Refer to **Online Course** for Illustration

3.4.1.1   Chapter 3: Linux Operating System

In this chapter, you learned how the Linux operation system is used in a SOC environment including:

- Linux tools that are used for security monitoring and investigation
- How to use the Linux shell to work with directory and files and how to create, modify, copy, and move text files
- The difference between server and client applications

In this chapter, you also learned how to perform basic Linux administration tasks including:

- How to view service configuration files
- What features need to be hardened on Linux devices
- The types and location of services logs used for monitoring purposes

You also learned about the various Linux file system types including:

- ext2, ext3, and ext4
- NFS
- CDFS
- Swap Partition
- HFSf+
- Master Boot Record

You learned how roles and file permissions dictate what users or groups can access which files and whether those users or groups have read, write, or execute permissions. You also learned how the root user or owner of a file can change permissions. These files can have hard links or symbolic links. A hard link is another file that points to the same location as the original file. A symbolic link, sometimes called soft link, is similar to a hard link in that applying changes to the symbolic link will also change the original file.

Finally, in this chapter you learned how to perform basic security-related tasks on a Linux host including:

- Installing and running applications from the command line
- Keeping the system up to date with apt-get update and apt-get upgrade
- Viewing the current processes and forks running in memory
- Using **chkrootkit** to check the computer for known rootkits
- Using piping to chain commands together, feeding one command output into the input of another command

As a cybersecurity analyst, you need a basic understanding of the features and characteristics of the Linux operating system and how Linux is used in a SOC environment.

Go to the online course to take the quiz and exam.

Chapter 3 Quiz

This quiz is designed to provide an additional opportunity to practice the skills and knowledge presented in the chapter and to prepare for the chapter exam. You will be allowed multiple attempts and the grade does not appear in the gradebook.

Chapter 3 Exam

The chapter exam assesses your knowledge of the chapter content.

Your Chapter Notes

Network Protocols and Services

4.0 Introduction

4.0.1 Welcome

Refer to
Online Course
for Illustration

4.0.1.1 Chapter 4: Network Protocols and Services

Cybersecurity analysts work to identify and analyze the traces of network security incidents. These traces consist of records of network events. These events, recorded in log files from various devices, are primarily composed of details of network protocol operations. Addresses identify which hosts connected to each other, within an organization, or to distant hosts on the Internet. Addresses held in log files also identify which hosts connected with, or attempted to connect with, hosts within an organization. Other traces, in the form of protocol addresses, identify what the network connections attempted to do, and whether this behavior was normal, suspicious, or damaging. Finally, network traces are recorded for the applications that enable us to receive and use information from the network. From all of these traces, cybersecurity analysts detect threats to the security of organizations and their data.

Cybersecurity analysts must understand the network on which normal data travels so that they can detect the abnormal behavior that is created by hackers, malevolent software, and dishonest users of the network. Protocols are at the heart of network communications and network services support the tasks that we perform using the network. This chapter provides an overview of how networks normally behave through a discussion of the protocols in the TCP/IP suite of protocols, and associated services that enable us to accomplish tasks on computer networks.

4.1 Network Protocols

4.1.1 Network Communications Process

Refer to
Interactive Graphic
in online course

4.1.1.1 Views of the Network

Networks come in all sizes. They can range from simple networks consisting of two computers to networks connecting millions of devices. Click the plus signs (+) in the figure to read about networks of different sizes.

Home office networks and small office networks are often set up by individuals that work from a home or a remote office and need to connect to a corporate network or other centralized resources. Additionally, many self-employed entrepreneurs use home office and small office networks to advertise and sell products, order supplies and communicate with customers.

In businesses and large organizations, networks can be used on an even broader scale to provide consolidation, storage, and access to information on network servers. Networks also allow for rapid communication such as email, instant messaging, and collaboration among employees. In addition to internal benefits, many organizations use their networks to provide products and services to customers through their connection to the Internet.

The Internet is the largest network in existence. In fact, the term Internet means a 'network of networks'. The Internet is literally a collection of interconnected private and public networks.

Refer to
Interactive Graphic
in online course

4.1.1.2   Client-Server Communications

All computers that are connected to a network and that participate directly in network communication are classified as hosts. Hosts are also called end devices, endpoints, or nodes. Much of the interaction between end devices is client-server traffic. For example, when you access a web page on the Internet, your web browser (the client) is accessing a server. When you send an email message, your email client will connect to an email server.

Servers are simply computers with specialized software. This software enables servers to provide information to other end devices on the network. A server can be single-purpose, providing only one service, such as web pages. A server can be multipurpose, providing a variety of services such as web pages, email, and file transfers.

Client computers have software installed, such as web browsers, email, and file transfers. This software enables them to request and display the information obtained from the server. A single computer can also run multiple types of client software. For example, a user can check email and view a web page while listening to Internet radio. Click the plus signs (+) in the figure to read about different clients in a client-server networks.

Refer to
Online Course
for Illustration

4.1.1.3   A Typical Session: Student

A typical network user at school, at home, or in the office, will normally use some type of computing device to establish many connections with network servers. Those servers could be located in the same room or around the world. Let's look at a few typical network communication sessions.

Terry is a high school student whose school has recently started a "bring your own device" (BYOD) program. Students are encouraged to use their cell phones or other devices such as tablets or laptops to access learning resources. Terry has just been given an assignment in language arts class to research the effects of World War I on the literature and art of the time. She enters the search terms she has chosen into a search engine app that she has opened on her cell phone.

Terry has connected her phone to the school Wi-Fi network. Her search is submitted from her phone to the school network wirelessly. Before her search can be sent, the data must be addressed so that it can find its way back to Terry. Her search terms are then represented as a string of binary data that has been encoded into radio waves. Her search string is then converted to electrical signals that travel on the school's wired network until they reach the place at which the school's network connects to the Internet Service Provider's (ISP) network. A combination of technologies take Terry's search to the search engine website.

For example, Terry's data flows with the data of thousands of other users along a fiber-optic network that connects Terry's ISP with the several other ISPs, including the ISP that is used by the search engine company. Eventually, Terry's search string enters the search engine company's website and is processed by its powerful servers. The results are then encoded and addressed to Terry's school and her device.

All of these transitions and connections happen in a fraction of a second, and Terry has started on her path to learning about her subject.

Refer to
Online Course
for Illustration

4.1.1.4   A Typical Session: Gamer

Michelle loves computer games. She has a powerful gaming console that she uses to play games against other players, watch movies, and play music. Michelle connects her game console directly to her network with a copper network cable.

Michelle's network, like many home networks, connects to an ISP using a router and modem. These devices allow Michelle's home network to connect to a cable TV network that belongs to Michelle's ISP. The cable wires for Michelle's neighborhood all connect to a central point on a telephone pole and then connect to a fiber-optic network. This fiber-optic network connects many neighborhoods that are served by Michelle's ISP.

All those fiber-optic cables connect to telecommunications services that provide access to the high-capacity connections. These connections allow thousands of users in homes, government offices, and businesses to connect Internet destinations around the world.

Michelle has connected her game console to a company that hosts a very popular online game. Michelle is registered with the company, and its servers keep track of Michelle's scores, experiences, and game assets. Michelle's actions in her game become data that is sent to the gamer network. Michelle's moves are broken up to groups of binary data that each consist of a string of zeros and ones. Information that identifies Michelle, the game she is playing, and Michelle's network location are added to the game data. The pieces of data that represent Michelle's game play are sent at high speed to the game provider's network. The results are returned to Michelle in the form of graphics and sounds.

All of this happens so quickly that Michelle can compete with hundreds of other gamers in real-time.

Refer to
Online Course
for Illustration

4.1.1.5   A Typical Session: Surgeon

Dr. Ismael Awad is an oncologist who performs surgery on cancer patients. He frequently needs to consult with radiologists and other specialists on patient cases. The hospital that Dr. Awad works for subscribes to a special service called a cloud. The cloud allows medical data, including patient x-rays and MRIs to be stored in a central location that is accessed over the Internet. In this way, the hospital does not need to manage paper patient records and X-ray films.

When a patient has an X-ray taken, the image is digitized as computer data. The X-ray is then prepared by hospital computers to be sent to the medical cloud service. Because security is very important when working with medical data, the hospital uses network services that encrypt the image data and patient information. This encrypted data cannot be intercepted and read as it travels across the Internet to the cloud service provider's data centers. The data is addressed so that it can be routed to the cloud provider's data center to reach the correct services that provide storage and retrieval of high-resolution digital images.

Dr. Awad and the patient's care team can connect to this special service, meet with other doctors in audio conferences and discuss patient records to decide on the best treatment unique to identify a specific host within a network. For example, if you looked at the IPv4 addresses for various devices in your home network, you will most likely see the same network portion. Figure 2 shows the IPv4 configuration for a Windows computer. Figure 3 shows the IPv4 address for an iPhone. Figure 4 shows the IPv4 configuration for an Xbox One gaming console. Notice that all three devices share the same network address portion, 192.168.10 and that each device has a unique host portion, .10, .7, and .12, respectively.

But how do hosts know which portion of the 32-bits identifies the network and which identifies the host? That is the job of the subnet mask.

Refer to
Interactive Graphic
in online course

4.2.3.3   IPv4 Subnet Mask and Network Address

The subnet mask is logically ANDed with the host address to determine the network address. Logical AND is the comparison of two bits that produce the results shown in Figure 1. Note how only a 1 AND 1 produces a 1.

To identify the network address of an IPv4 host, the IPv4 address is logically ANDed, bit by bit, with the subnet mask. ANDing between the address and the subnet mask yields the network address.

To illustrate how AND is used to discover a network address, consider a host with IPv4 address 192.168.10.10 and subnet mask of 255.255.255.0. Figure 2 displays the host IPv4 address and converted binary address. The host subnet mask binary address is added in Figure 3.

The yellow highlighted sections in Figure 4 identify the AND bits that produced a binary 1 in the AND Results row. All other bit comparisons produced binary 0s. Notice how the last octet no longer has any binary 1 bits.

Finally, Figure 5 displays the resulting network address 192.168.10.0 255.255.255.0. Therefore, host 192.168.10.10 is on network 192.168.10.0 255.255.255.0.

Refer to
Interactive Graphic
in online course

4.2.3.4   Subnetting Broadcast Domains

The 192.168.10.0/24 network can support 254 hosts. Larger networks, such as 172.16.0.0/16, can support many more host addresses (over 65,000). However, this can potentially create a larger broadcast domain. A problem with a large broadcast domain is that these hosts can generate excessive broadcasts and negatively affect the network. In Figure 1, LAN 1 connects 400 users that could each generate broadcast traffic. That much broadcast traffic can slow down network operations. It can also slow device operations because each device must accept and process each broadcast packet.

The solution is to reduce the size of the network to create smaller broadcast domains in a process called subnetting. These smaller network spaces are called subnets.

In Figure 2 for example, the 400 users in LAN 1 with network address 172.16.0.0 /16 have been divided into two subnets of 200 users each; 172.16.0.0 /24 and 172.16.1.0 /24. Broadcasts are only propagated within the smaller broadcast domains. Therefore a broadcast in LAN 1 would not propagate to LAN 2.

Notice how the prefix length has changed from a /16 to a /24. This is the basis of subnetting; using host bits to create additional subnets.

Note   The terms subnet and network are often used interchangeably. Most networks are a subnet of some larger address block.

Subnetting reduces overall network traffic and improves network performance. It also enables an administrator to implement security policies such as which subnets are allowed or not allowed to communicate together.

There are various ways of using subnets to help manage network devices. Network administrators can group devices and services into subnets that may be determined by a variety of factors:

- Location, such as floors in a building (Figure 3)
- Organizational unit (Figure 4)
- Device type (Figure 5)
- Any other division that makes sense for the network

A cybersecurity analyst does not need to know how to subnet. However, it is important to know the meaning of the subnet mask and that hosts with addresses on different subnets come from different places in a network.

Refer to **Video** in online course

4.2.3.5 Video Demonstration - Network, Host, and Broadcast Addresses

Click Play to view a demonstration of how the network, host, and broadcast addresses are determined for a given IPv4 address and subnet mask.

Click here to read the transcript of this video.

4.2.4 Types of IPv4 Addresses

Refer to **Interactive Graphic** in online course

4.2.4.1 IPv4 Address Classes and Default Subnet Masks

There are various types and classes of IPv4 addresses. While address classes are becoming less important in networking, they are still used and referred to commonly in network documentation.

Address Classes

In 1981, IPv4 addresses were assigned using classful addressing as defined in RFC 790. Customers were allocated a network address based on one of three classes, A, B, or C. The RFC divided the unicast ranges into specific classes:

- **Class A** (0.0.0.0/8 to 127.0.0.0/8) - Designed to support extremely large networks with more than 16 million host addresses. It used a fixed /8 prefix with the first octet to indicate the network address and the remaining three octets for host addresses.

- **Class B** (128.0.0.0 /16 – 191.255.0.0 /16) - Designed to support the needs of moderate to large size networks with up to approximately 65,000 host addresses. It used a fixed /16 prefix with the two high-order octets to indicate the network address and the remaining two octets for host addresses.

- **Class C** (192.0.0.0 /24 – 223.255.255.0 /24) - Designed to support small networks with a maximum of 254 hosts. It used a fixed /24 prefix with the first three octets to indicate the network and the remaining octet for the host addresses.

Note There is also a Class D multicast block consisting of 224.0.0.0 to 239.0.0.0 and a Class E experimental address block consisting of 240.0.0.0 – 255.0.0.0.

As shown in the figure, the classful system allocated 50% of the available IPv4 addresses to 128 Class A networks, 25% of the addresses to Class B and then Class C shared the remaining 25% with Class D and E. Although appropriate at the time, as the Internet grew it was obvious that this method was wasting addresses and depleting the number of available IPv4 network addresses.

Classful addressing was abandoned in the late 1990s for the newer and current classless addressing system. However, as we will see later in this section, classless addressing was only a temporary solution to the depletion of IPv4 addresses.

Refer to
Online Course
for Illustration

4.2.4.2   Reserved Private Addresses

Public IPv4 addresses are addresses which are globally routed between ISP routers. However, not all available IPv4 addresses can be used on the Internet. There are blocks of addresses called private addresses that are used by most organizations to assign IPv4 addresses to internal hosts.

In the mid-1990s, private IPv4 addresses were introduced because of the depletion of IPv4 address space. Private IPv4 addresses are not unique and can be used by any internal network.

These are the private address blocks:

- 10.0.0.0 /8 or 10.0.0.0 to 10.255.255.255

- 172.16.0.0 /12 or 172.16.0.0 to 172.31.255.255

- 192.168.0.0 /16 or 192.168.0.0 to 192.168.255.255

It is important to know that addresses within these address blocks are not allowed on the Internet and must be filtered (discarded) by Internet routers. For example, as shown in the figure, users in networks 1, 2, or 3 are sending packets to remote destinations. The ISP routers would see that the source IPv4 addresses in the packets are from private addresses and would, therefore, discard the packets.

Most organizations use private IPv4 addresses for their internal hosts. However, these RFC 1918 addresses are not routable on the Internet and must be translated to a public IPv4 addresses. Network Address Translation (NAT) is used to translate between private IPv4 and public IPv4 addresses. This is usually done on the router that connects the internal network to the ISP's network.

Home routers provide the same capability. For instance, most home routers assign IPv4 addresses to their wired and wireless hosts from the private address of 192.168.1.0 /24. The home router interface that connects to the Internet service provider (ISP) network is often assigned a public IPv4 address to use on the Internet.

4.2.5   The Default Gateway

Refer to
Online Course
for Illustration

4.2.5.1   Host Forwarding Decision

A host can send a packet to three types of destinations:

- **Itself** - A host can ping itself by sending a packet to a special IPv4 address of 127.0.0.1, which is referred to as the loopback interface. Pinging the loopback interface tests the TCP/IP protocol stack on the host.

- **Local host** - This is a host on the same local network as the sending host (from PC1 to PC2 in the figure). The hosts share the same network address.

- **Remote host** - This is a host on a remote network. The hosts do not share the same network address. Notice that R1, a router, is in between PC1 and the remote host. R1 is the default gateway for PC1 and PC2. R1's job is to route any traffic destined for remote networks.

As we have seen, the subnet mask is used to determine to which network an IPv4 host address belongs. Whether a packet is destined for a local host or a remote host is determined by the I P address and subnet mask combination of the source device compared to the IP address and subnet mask combination of the destination device. In the figure, PC 1 knows it is on the 192 . 168 . 10 . 0 / 24 network. Therefore it knows that PC 2 is also on the same network and that the server, Remote Host, is not on the same network. When a source device sends a packet to a remote host, then the help of routers and routing is needed. Routing is the process of identifying the best path to a destination. The router connected to the local network segment is referred to as the default gateway.

Refer to **Online Course** for Illustration

4.2.5.2   Default Gateway

As shown in the figure, three dotted decimal IPv4 addresses must be configured when assigning an IPv4 configuration to host:

- **IPv4 address** - Unique IPv4 address of the host

- **Subnet mask** - Used to identify the network/host portion of the IPv4 address

- **Default gateway** - Identifies the local gateway (i.e. local router interface IPv4 address) to reach remote networks

The default gateway is the network device that can route traffic to other networks. It is the router that can route traffic out of the local network.

If you use the analogy that a network is like a room, then the default gateway is like a doorway. If you want to get to another room or network you need to find the doorway.

Alternatively, a PC or computer that does not know the IP address of the default gateway is like a person, in a room, that does not know where the doorway is. They can talk to other people in the room or network, but if they do not know the default gateway address, or there is no default gateway, then there is no way out.

Refer to **Interactive Graphic** in online course

4.2.5.3   Using the Default Gateway

A host's routing table will typically include a default gateway. The host receives the IPv4 address of the default gateway either dynamically from Dynamic Host Configuration Protocol (DHCP) or configured manually. In Figure 1, PC1 and PC2 are configured with the default gateway's IPv4 address of 192.168.10.1. Having a default gateway configured creates a default route in the routing table of the PC. A default route is the route or pathway your computer will take when it tries to contact a remote network.

The default route is derived from the default gateway configuration and is placed in the host computer's routing table. Both PC1 and PC2 will have a default route for sending all traffic destined to remote networks to R1.

You can view the routing table for a Windows host using either the **netstat -r** or **route print** command, as shown in Figure 2.

4.2.6 IPv6

Refer to
Online Course
for Illustration

4.2.6.1 Need for IPv6

The depletion of IPv4 address space has been the motivating factor for moving to IPv6. As Africa, Asia and other areas of the world become more connected to the Internet, there are not enough IPv4 addresses to accommodate this growth. As shown in the figure, four out of the five Regional Internet Registries (RIRs) have run out of IPv4 addresses.

IPv4 has a theoretical maximum of 4.3 billion addresses. Private addresses in combination with Network Address Translation (NAT) have been instrumental in slowing the depletion of IPv4 address space. However, NAT breaks many applications and has limitations that severely impede peer-to-peer communications.

Note NAT is discussed in more detail later in the chapter.

Refer to
Online Course
for Illustration

4.2.6.2 IPv6 Size and Representation

IPv6 is designed to be the successor to IPv4. IPv6 has a 128-bit address space, providing for 340 undecillion addresses. (That is the number 340, followed by 36 zeroes.) However, IPv6 is more than just a bigger pool of addresses. When the Internet Engineering Task Force (IETF) began its development of a successor to IPv4, it used this opportunity to fix the limitations of IPv4 and include additional enhancements. One example is Internet Control Message Protocol version 6 (ICMPv6), which includes address resolution and address auto-configuration not found in ICMP for IPv4 (ICMPv4).

IPv6 addresses are written as a string of hexadecimal values. Every 4 bits is represented by a single hexadecimal digit; for a total of 32 hexadecimal values. IPv6 addresses are not case-sensitive and can be written in either lowercase or uppercase.

As shown in the figure, the format for writing an IPv6 address is x:x:x:x:x:x:x:x, with each "x" consisting of four hexadecimal values. When referring to 8 bits of an IPv4 address we use the term octet. In IPv6, a hextet is the unofficial term used to refer to a segment of 16 bits or four hexadecimal values. Each "x" is a single hextet, 16 bits or four hexadecimal digits.

Refer to
Online Course
for Illustration

4.2.6.3 IPv6 Address Formatting

It is no problem for computers to read the new 128-bit IPv6 addressing. IPv6 just adds more ones and zeros to the source and destination addresses in the packet. For humans, though, the change from a 32-bit address written in dotted decimal notation to an IPv6 address written as a series of 32 hexadecimal digits can be quite an adjustment. Techniques have been developed to compress the written IPv6 address into a more manageable format.

Compressing IPv6 Addresses

IPv6 addresses are written as a string of hexadecimal values. Every 4 bits is represented by a single hexadecimal digit for a total of 32 hexadecimal values. The figure shows a fully expanded IPv6 address and two methods of making it more easily readable. There are two rules that help reduce the number of digits needed to represent an IPv6 address.

Rule 1 - Omit Leading Zeros

The first rule to help reduce the notation of IPv6 addresses is to omit any leading 0s (zeros) in any 16-bit section. For example:

- 0DB8 can be represented as DB8
- 0000 can be represented as 0
- 0200 can be represented as 200

Rule 2 - Omit One "all zeros" Segment

The second rule to help reduce the notation of IPv6 addresses is that a double colon (::) can replace any group of consecutive segments that contain only zeros. The double colon (::) can only be used once within an address, otherwise there would be more than one possible resulting address.

Refer to **Online Course** for Illustration

4.2.6.4 IPv6 Prefix Length

Recall that the prefix, or network portion, of an IPv4 address, can be identified by a dotted-decimal subnet mask or prefix length (slash notation). For example, an IPv4 address of 192.168.1.10 with dotted-decimal subnet mask 255.255.255.0 is equivalent to 192.168.1.10/24.

IPv6 uses the prefix length to represent the prefix portion of the address. IPv6 does not use the dotted-decimal subnet mask notation. The prefix length is used to indicate the network portion of an IPv6 address using the IPv6 address/prefix length.

The prefix length can range from 0 to 128. A typical IPv6 prefix length for LANs and most other types of networks is /64, as shown in the figure. This means the prefix or network portion of the address is 64 bits in length, leaving another 64 bits for the interface ID (host portion) of the address.

Refer to **Interactive Graphic** in online course

4.2.6.5 Activity - IPv6 Address Notation

Refer to **Video** in online course

4.2.6.6 Video Tutorial - Layer 2 and Layer 3 Addressing

Click Play for a review of Layer 2 and Layer 3 addressing.

Click here to read the transcript of this video.

Click here to download the Packet Tracer file used in the video.

4.3 Connectivity Verification

4.3.1 ICMP

Refer to **Interactive Graphic** in online course

4.3.1.1 ICMPv4 Messages

Although IP is only a best-effort protocol, the TCP/IP suite does provide for messages to be sent in the event of certain errors. These messages are sent using the services of ICMP. The purpose of these messages is to provide feedback about issues related to the processing of IP packets under certain conditions, not to make IP reliable. ICMP messages are not required and are often not allowed within a network for security reasons.

ICMP is available for both IPv4 and IPv6. ICMPv4 is the messaging protocol for IPv4. ICMPv6 provides these same services for IPv6 but includes additional functionality. In this course, the term ICMP will be used when referring to both ICMPv4 and ICMPv6.

The types of ICMP messages and the reasons why they are sent, are extensive. We will discuss some of the more common messages.

ICMP messages common to both ICMPv4 and ICMPv6 include:

- Host confirmation
- Destination or Service Unreachable
- Time exceeded
- Route redirection

Host Confirmation

An ICMP Echo Message can be used to determine if a host is operational. The local host sends an ICMP Echo Request to a host. If the host is available, the destination host responds with an Echo Reply. Click Play in the figure to see an animation of the ICMP Echo Request/Echo Reply. This use of the ICMP Echo messages is the basis of the ping utility.

Destination or Service Unreachable

When a host or gateway receives a packet that it cannot deliver, it can use an ICMP Destination Unreachable message to notify the source that the destination or service is unreachable. The message will include a code that indicates why the packet could not be delivered.

These are some of the Destination Unreachable codes for ICMPv4:

- **0** - Net unreachable
- **1** - Host unreachable
- **2** - Protocol unreachable
- **3** - Port unreachable

Note   ICMPv6 has similar but slightly different codes for Destination Unreachable messages.

Time Exceeded

An ICMPv4 Time Exceeded message is used by a router to indicate that a packet cannot be forwarded because the Time to Live (TTL) field of the packet was decremented to 0. If a router receives a packet and decrements the TTL field in the IPv4 packet to zero, it discards the packet and sends a Time Exceeded message to the source host.

ICMPv6 also sends a Time Exceeded message if the router cannot forward an IPv6 packet because the packet has expired. IPv6 does not have a TTL field; it uses the hop limit field to determine if the packet has expired.

Refer to
Interactive Graphic
in online course

4.3.1.2   ICMPv6 RS and RA Messages

The informational and error messages found in ICMPv6 are very similar to the control and error messages implemented by ICMPv4. However, ICMPv6 has new features and improved functionality not found in ICMPv4. ICMPv6 messages are encapsulated in IPv6.

ICMPv6 includes four new protocols as part of the Neighbor Discovery Protocol (ND or NDP).

Messaging between an IPv6 router and an IPv6 device:

- Router Solicitation (RS) message
- Router Advertisement (RA) message

Messaging between IPv6 devices:

- Neighbor Solicitation (NS) message
- Neighbor Advertisement (NA) message

Note ICMPv6 ND also includes the redirect message, which has a similar function to the redirect message used in ICMPv4.

Figure 1 shows an example of a PC and router exchanging Solicitation and Router Advertisement messages. Click each message for more information.

Neighbor Solicitation and Neighbor Advertisement messages are used for Address resolution and Duplicate Address Detection (DAD).

Address Resolution

Address resolution is used when a device on the LAN knows the IPv6 unicast address of a destination but does not know its Ethernet MAC address. To determine the MAC address for the destination, the device will send an NS message to the solicited node address. The message will include the known (targeted) IPv6 address. The device that has the targeted IPv6 address will respond with an NA message containing its Ethernet MAC address. Figure 2 shows two PCs exchanging NS and NA messages. Click each message for more information.

Duplicate Address Detection

When a device is assigned a global unicast or link-local unicast address, it is recommended that DAD is performed on the address to ensure that it is unique. To check the uniqueness of an address, the device will send an NS message with its own IPv6 address as the targeted IPv6 address, shown in Figure 3. If another device on the network has this address, it will respond with an NA message. This NA message will notify the sending device that the address is in use. If a corresponding NA message is not returned within a certain period of time, the unicast address is unique and acceptable for use.

Note DAD is not required, but RFC 4861 recommends that DAD is performed on unicast addresses.

4.3.2   Ping and Traceroute Utilities

Refer to
Online Course
for Illustration

4.3.2.1   Ping - Testing the Local Stack

Ping is a testing utility that uses ICMP echo request and echo reply messages to test connectivity between hosts. Ping works with both IPv4 and IPv6 hosts.

To test connectivity to another host on a network, an echo request is sent to the host address using the ping command. If the host at the specified address receives the echo request, it responds with an echo reply. As each echo reply is received, ping provides feedback on the time between when the request was sent and when the reply was received. This can be a measure of network performance.

Ping has a timeout value for the reply. If a reply is not received within the timeout, ping provides a message indicating that a response was not received. This usually indicates that there is a problem, but could also indicate that security features blocking ping messages have been enabled on the network.

After all the requests are sent, the ping utility provides a summary that includes the success rate and average round-trip time to the destination.

Pinging the Local Loopback

There are some special testing and verification cases for which we can use ping. One case is for testing the internal configuration of IPv4 or IPv6 on the local host. To perform this test, we ping the local loopback address of 127.0.0.1 for IPv4 (::1 for IPv6). Testing the IPv4 loopback is shown in the figure.

A response from 127.0.0.1 for IPv4, or ::1 for IPv6, indicates that IP is properly installed on the host. This response comes from the network layer. This response is not, however, an indication that the addresses, masks, or gateways are properly configured. Nor does it indicate anything about the status of the lower layer of the network stack. This simply tests IP down through the network layer of IP. An error message indicates that TCP/IP is not operational on the host.

Refer to
Online Course
for Illustration

4.3.2.2 Ping - Testing Connectivity to the Local LAN

You can also use ping to test the ability of a host to communicate on the local network. This is generally done by pinging the IP address of the gateway of the host. A ping to the gateway indicates that the host and the router interface serving as the gateway are both operational on the local network.

For this test, the gateway address is most often used because the router is normally always operational. If the gateway address does not respond, a ping can be sent to the IP address of another host on the local network that is known to be operational.

If either the gateway or another host responds, then the local host can successfully communicate over the local network. If the gateway does not respond but another host does, this could indicate a problem with the router interface serving as the gateway.

One possibility is that the wrong gateway address has been configured on the host. Another possibility is that the router interface may be fully operational but have security applied to it that prevents it from processing or responding to ping requests.

Refer to
Interactive Graphic
in online course

4.3.2.3 Ping - Testing Connectivity to Remote Host

Ping can also be used to test the ability of a local host to communicate across an internetwork. The local host can ping an operational IPv4 host of a remote network, as shown in the figure.

If this ping is successful, the operation of a large piece of the internetwork can be verified. A successful ping across the internetwork confirms communication on the local network. It also confirms the operation of the router serving as the gateway, and the operation of all other routers that might be in the path between the local network and the network of the remote host.

Additionally, the functionality of the remote host can be verified. If the remote host could not communicate outside of its local network, it would not have responded.

Note   For security reasons, many network administrators limit or prohibit the entry of ICMP messages into the corporate network; therefore, the lack of a ping response could be due to security restrictions.

Refer to **Interactive Graphic** in online course

4.3.2.4   Traceroute - Testing the Path

Ping is used to test connectivity between two hosts but does not provide information about the details of devices between the hosts. Traceroute (tracert) is a utility that generates a list of hops that were successfully reached along the path. This list can provide important verification and troubleshooting information. If the data reaches the destination, then the trace lists the interface of every router in the path between the hosts. If the data fails at some hop along the way, the address of the last router that responded to the trace can provide an indication of where the problem is, or where security restrictions are found.

Round Trip Time (RTT)

Using traceroute provides round trip time for each hop along the path and indicates if a hop fails to respond. The round trip time is the time a packet takes to reach the remote host and for the response from the host to return. An asterisk (*) is used to indicate a lost or unacknowledged packet.

This information can be used to locate a problematic router in the path. If the display shows high response times or data losses from a particular hop, this is an indication that the resources of the router or its connections may be overloaded.

IPv4 TTL and IPv6 Hop Limit

Traceroute makes use of a function of the TTL field in IPv4 and the Hop Limit field in IPv6 in the Layer 3 headers, along with the ICMP time exceeded message.

Click Play in the figure to see an animation of how Traceroute takes advantage of TTL.

The first sequence of messages sent from traceroute will have a TTL field value of 1. This causes the TTL to time out the IPv4 packet at the first router. This router then responds with an ICMPv4 message. Traceroute now has the address of the first hop.

Traceroute then progressively increments the TTL field (2, 3, 4...) for each sequence of messages. This provides the trace with the address of each hop as the packets timeout further down the path. The TTL field continues to be increased until the destination is reached, or it is incremented to a predefined maximum.

After the final destination is reached, the host responds with either an ICMP port unreachable message or an ICMP echo reply message instead of the ICMP time exceeded message.

Refer to **Online Course** for Illustration

4.3.2.5   ICMP Packet Format

ICMP is encapsulated directly into IP packets. In this sense, it is almost like a transport layer protocol, because it is encapsulated into a packet, however it is considered to be a Layer 3 protocol. ICMP acts as a data payload within the IP packet. It has a special header data field, as shown in the figure.

ICMP uses message codes to differentiate between different types of ICMP messages. These are some common message codes:

- **0** - Echo reply (response to a ping)

- **3** - Destination Unreachable

- **5** - Redirect (use another route to your destination)

- **8** - Echo request (for ping)

- **11** - Time Exceeded (TTL became 0)

As you will see later in the course, a cybersecurity analyst knows that the optional ICMP payload field can be used in an attack vector to exfiltrate data.

4.4   Address Resolution Protocol

4.4.1   MAC and IP

Refer to
Online Course
for Illustration

4.4.1.1   Destination on Same Network

There are two primary addresses assigned to a device on an Ethernet LAN:

- **Physical address (the MAC address) -** This is used for Ethernet NIC to Ethernet NIC communications on the same network.

- **Logical address (the IP address) -** This is used to send the packet from the original source to the final destination.

IP addresses are used to identify the address of the original source device and the final destination device. The destination IP address may be on the same IP network as the source or may be on a remote network.

Note   Most applications use DNS (Domain Name System) to determine the IP address when given a domain name such as www.cisco.com. DNS is discussed in a later chapter.

Layer 2 or physical addresses, like Ethernet MAC addresses, have a different purpose. These addresses are used to deliver the data link frame with the encapsulated IP packet from one NIC to another NIC on the same network. If the destination IP address is on the same network, the destination MAC address will be that of the destination device.

The figure shows the Ethernet MAC addresses and IP address for PC-A sending an IP packet to the file server on the same network.

The Layer 2 Ethernet frame contains:

- **Destination MAC address -** This is the MAC address of the file server's Ethernet NIC.

- **Source MAC address -** This is the MAC address of PC-A's Ethernet NIC.

The Layer 3 IP packet contains:

■ **Source IP address** - This is the IP address of the original source, PC-A.

■ **Destination IP address** - This is the IP address of the final destination, the file server.

Refer to
Online Course
for Illustration

4.4.1.2   Destination on Remote Network

When the destination IP address is on a remote network, the destination MAC address will be the address of the host's default gateway, which is the router's NIC, as shown in the figure. Using a postal analogy, this would be similar to a person taking a letter to their local post office. All they need to do is take the letter to the post office and then it becomes the responsibility of the post office to forward the letter on towards its final destination.

The figure shows the Ethernet MAC addresses and IPv4 addresses for PC-A sending an IP packet to a file server on a remote network. Routers examine the destination IPv4 address to determine the best path to forward the IPv4 packet. This is similar to how the postal service forwards mail based on the address of the recipient.

When the router receives the Ethernet frame, it de-encapsulates the Layer 2 information. Using the destination IP address, it determines the next-hop device, and then encapsulates the IP packet in a new data link frame for the outgoing interface. Along each link in a path, an IP packet is encapsulated in a frame specific to the particular data link technology associated with that link, such as Ethernet. If the next-hop device is the final destination, the destination MAC address will be that of the device's Ethernet NIC.

How are the IPv4 addresses of the IPv4 packets in a data flow associated with the MAC addresses on each link along the path to the destination? This is done through a process called Address Resolution Protocol (ARP).

4.4.2   ARP

Refer to
Online Course
for Illustration

4.4.2.1   Introduction to ARP

Recall that every device with an IP address on an Ethernet network also has an Ethernet MAC address. When a device sends an Ethernet frame, it contains these two addresses:

■ **Destination MAC address** - The MAC address of the Ethernet NIC, which will be either the MAC address of the final destination device or the router.

■ **Source MAC address** - The MAC address of the sender's Ethernet NIC.

To determine the destination MAC address, the device uses ARP. ARP resolves IPv4 addresses to MAC addresses, and maintains a table of mappings.

Refer to
Interactive Graphic
in online course

4.4.2.2   ARP Functions

When a packet is sent to the data link layer to be encapsulated into an Ethernet frame, the device refers to a table in its memory to find the MAC address that is mapped to the IPv4 address. This table is called the ARP table or the ARP cache. The ARP table is stored in the RAM of the device.

The sending device will search its ARP table for a destination IPv4 address and a corresponding MAC address. If the packet's destination IPv4 address is on the same network as the source IPv4 address, the device will search the ARP table for the destination IPv4 address. If the destination IPv4 address is on a different network than the source IPv4 address, the device will search the ARP table for the IPv4 address of the default gateway.

In both cases, the search is for an IPv4 address and a corresponding MAC address for the device.

Each entry, or row, of the ARP table binds an IPv4 address with a MAC address. We call the relationship between the two values a map. It simply means that you can locate an IPv4 address in the table and discover the corresponding MAC address. The ARP table temporarily saves (caches) the mapping for the devices on the LAN.

If the device locates the IPv4 address, its corresponding MAC address is used as the destination MAC address in the frame. If no entry is found, then the device sends an ARP request. Click Play in the figure to view an animation of the ARP request process.

Refer to **Video** in online course

4.4.2.3   Video - ARP Operation - ARP Request

An ARP request is sent when a device needs a MAC address associated with an IPv4 address, and it does not have an entry for the IPv4 address in its ARP table.

ARP messages are encapsulated directly within an Ethernet frame. There is no IPv4 header. The ARP request message includes:

- **Target IPv4 address** - This is the IPv4 address that requires a corresponding MAC address.

- **Target MAC address** - This is the unknown MAC address and will be empty in the ARP request message.

The ARP request is encapsulated in an Ethernet frame using the following header information:

- **Destination MAC address** - This is a broadcast address requiring all Ethernet NICs on the LAN to accept and process the ARP request.

- **Source MAC address** - This is the sender of the ARP request's MAC address.

- **Type** - ARP messages have a type field of 0×806. This informs the receiving NIC that the data portion of the frame needs to be passed to the ARP process.

Because ARP requests are broadcasts, they are flooded out all ports by the switch except the receiving port. All Ethernet NICs on the LAN process broadcasts. Every device must process the ARP request to see if the target IPv4 address matches its own. A router will not forward broadcasts out other interfaces.

Only one device on the LAN will have an IPv4 address that matches the target IPv4 address in the ARP request. All other devices will not reply.

Click Play in the figure to view a demonstration of an ARP request for a destination IPv4 address that is on the local network.

Click here to download video slides from the demonstration.

Click here to read the transcript of this video.

Refer to **Video**
in online course

4.4.2.4   Video - ARP Operation - ARP Reply

Only the device with an IPv4 address associated with the target IPv4 address in the ARP request will respond with an ARP reply. The ARP reply message includes:

- **Sender's IPv4 address** - This is the IPv4 address of the sender, the device whose MAC address was requested.

- **Sender's MAC address** - This is the MAC address of the sender. It is the MAC address that was asked for in the original ARP request message.

The ARP reply is encapsulated in an Ethernet frame using the following header information:

- **Destination MAC address** - This is the MAC address of the original sender of the ARP request.

- **Source MAC address** - This is the ARP reply's MAC address.

- **Type** - ARP messages have a type field of 0×806. This informs the receiving NIC that the data portion of the frame needs to be passed to the ARP process.

Only the device that originally sent the ARP request will receive the unicast ARP reply. After the ARP reply is received, the device will add the IPv4 address and the corresponding MAC address to its ARP table. Packets destined for that IPv4 address can now be encapsulated in frames using its corresponding MAC address.

Click Play in the figure to view a demonstration of an ARP reply.

Click here to download video slides from the demonstration.

If no device responds to the ARP request, the packet is dropped because a frame cannot be created.

Entries in the ARP table are time stamped. If a device does not receive a frame from a particular device by the time the timestamp expires, the entry for this device is removed from the ARP table.

Additionally, static map entries can be entered in an ARP table, but this is rarely done. Static ARP table entries do not expire over time and must be manually removed.

Note   IPv6 uses a similar process to ARP. It is called ICMPv6 neighbor discovery. ICMPv6 uses neighbor solicitation and neighbor advertisement messages, similar to IPv4 ARP requests and ARP replies.

Click here to read the transcript of this video.

Refer to **Video**
in online course

4.4.2.5   Video - ARP Role in Remote Communication

When the destination IPv4 address is not on the same network as the source IPv4 address, the source device needs to send the frame to its default gateway. This is the interface of the local router. Whenever a source device has a packet with an IPv4 address on another network, it will encapsulate that packet in a frame using the destination MAC address of the router.

The IPv4 address of the default gateway address is stored in the IPv4 configuration of the hosts. When a host creates a packet for a destination, it compares the destination IPv4 address and its own IPv4 address to determine if the two IPv4 addresses are located on the same Layer 3 network. If the destination host is not on its same network, the source checks its ARP table for an entry with the IPv4 address of the default gateway. If there is not an entry, it uses the ARP process to determine a MAC address of the default gateway.

Click Play to view a demonstration of an ARP request and ARP reply associated with the default gateway.

Click here to download video slides from the demonstration.

Click here to read the transcript of this video.

Refer to
Online Course
for Illustration

4.4.2.6   Removing Entries from an ARP Table

For each device, an ARP cache timer removes ARP entries that have not been used for a specified period of time. The times differ depending on the device's operating system. For example, some Windows operating systems store ARP cache entries for 2 minutes, as shown in the figure.

Commands may also be used to manually remove all or some of the entries in the ARP table. After an entry has been removed, the process for sending an ARP request and receiving an ARP reply must occur again to enter the map in the ARP table.

Refer to
Online Course
for Illustration

4.4.2.7   ARP Tables on Networking Devices

Network hosts and routers keep ARP tables. ARP information is held in memory on these devices in what is commonly called the ARP cache. The table entries are held for a period of time until they "age out" and are automatically removed from the ARP cache. This ensures the accuracy of the mappings. Holding ARP tables in memory helps to improve network efficiency by decreasing ARP traffic.

The ARP table on a Windows PC can be displayed using the arp -a command, as shown in the figure.

Refer to
Lab Activity
for this chapter

4.4.2.8   Lab - Using Wireshark to Examine Ethernet Frames

In this lab, you will complete the following objectives:

- Part 1: Examine the Header Fields in an Ethernet II Frame
- Part 2: Use Wireshark to Capture and Analyze Ethernet Frames

4.4.3   ARP Issues

Refer to
Online Course
for Illustration

4.4.3.1   ARP Broadcasts

As a broadcast frame, an ARP request is received and processed by every device on the local network. On a typical business network, these broadcasts would probably have minimal impact on network performance. However, if a large number of devices were to be powered up and all start accessing network services at the same time, there could briefly be some reduction in performance, as shown in the figure. After the devices send out the initial ARP broadcasts and have learned the necessary MAC addresses, any impact on the network will be minimized.

Refer to
Online Course
for Illustration

4.4.3.2 ARP Spoofing

In some cases, the use of ARP can lead to a potential security risk known as ARP spoofing or ARP poisoning. This is a technique used by an attacker to reply to an ARP request for an IPv4 address belonging to another device, such as the default gateway, as shown in the figure. The attacker sends an ARP reply with its own MAC address. The receiver of the ARP reply will add the wrong MAC address to its ARP table and send these packets to the attacker.

ARP vulnerabilities will be discussed in more detail later in the course.

4.5 The Transport Layer

4.5.1 Transport Layer Characteristics

Refer to
Interactive Graphic
in online course

4.5.1.1 Transport Layer Protocol Role in Network Communication

The transport layer is responsible for establishing a temporary communication session between two applications and delivering data between them. An application generates data that is sent from an application on a source host to an application on a destination host. This is without regard to the destination host type, the type of media over which the data must travel, the path taken by the data, the congestion on a link, or the size of the network. As shown in Figure 1, the transport layer is the link between the application layer and the lower layers that are responsible for network transmission.

Tracking Individual Conversations

At the transport layer, each set of data flowing between a source application and a destination application is known as a conversation (Figure 2). A host may have multiple applications that are communicating across the network simultaneously. Each of these applications communicates with one or more applications on one or more remote hosts. It is the responsibility of the transport layer to maintain and track these multiple conversations.

Segmenting Data and Reassembling Segments

Data must be prepared to be sent across the media in manageable pieces. Most networks have a limitation on the amount of data that can be included in a single packet. Transport layer protocols have services that segment the application data into blocks that are an appropriate size, as shown in Figure 3. This service includes the encapsulation required on each piece of data. A header, used for reassembly, is added to each block of data. This header is used to track the data stream.

At the destination, the transport layer must be able to reconstruct the pieces of data into a complete data stream that is useful to the application layer. The protocols at the transport layer describe how the transport layer header information is used to reassemble the data pieces into streams to be passed to the application layer.

Identifying the Applications

To pass data streams to the proper applications, the transport layer must identify the target application (Figure 4). To accomplish this, the transport layer assigns each application an identifier called a port number. Each software process that needs to access the network is assigned a port number unique to that host.

Refer to
Interactive Graphic
in online course

4.5.1.2   Transport Layer Mechanisms

Sending some types of data (for example, a streaming video) across a network, as one complete communication stream, can consume all of the available bandwidth. This will then prevent other communications from occurring at the same time. It would also make error recovery and retransmission of damaged data difficult.

Figure 1 shows that segmenting the data into smaller chunks enables many different communications, from many different users, to be interleaved (multiplexed) on the same network.

To identify each segment of data, the transport layer adds a header containing binary data organized into several fields. It is the values in these fields that enable various transport layer protocols to perform different functions in managing data communication.

The transport layer is also responsible for managing reliability requirements of a conversation. Different applications have different transport reliability requirements.

IP is concerned only with the structure, addressing, and routing of packets. IP does not specify how the delivery or transportation of the packets takes place. Transport protocols specify how to transfer messages between hosts. TCP/IP provides two transport layer protocols, Transmission Control Protocol (TCP) and User Datagram Protocol (UDP), as shown in Figure 2. IP uses these transport protocols to enable hosts to communicate and transfer data.

TCP is considered a reliable, full-featured transport layer protocol, which ensures that all of the data arrives at the destination. However, this requires additional fields in the TCP header which increases the size of the packet and also increases delay. In contrast, UDP is a simpler transport layer protocol that does not provide for reliability. It therefore has fewer fields and is faster than TCP.

Refer to
Interactive Graphic
in online course

4.5.1.3   TCP Local and Remote Ports

The transport layer must be able to separate and manage multiple communications with different transport requirement needs. Users expect to be able to simultaneously receive and send email and instant messages, view websites, and conduct a VoIP phone call. Each of these applications is sending and receiving data over the network at the same time, despite different reliability requirements. Additionally, data from the phone call is not directed to the web browser, and text from an instant message does not appear in an email.

TCP and UDP manage these multiple simultaneous conversations by using header fields that can uniquely identify these applications. These unique identifiers are the port numbers.

The source port number is associated with the originating application on the local host, as shown in Figure 1. The destination port number is associated with the destination application on the remote host.

Source Port

The source port number is dynamically generated by the sending device to identify a conversation between two devices. This process allows multiple conversations to occur simultaneously. It is common for a device to send multiple HTTP service requests to a web server at the same time. Each separate HTTP conversation is tracked based on the source ports.

Destination Port

The client places a destination port number in the segment to tell the destination server what service is being requested, as shown in Figure 2. For example, when a client specifies port 80 in the destination port, the server that receives the message knows that web services are being requested. A server can offer more than one service simultaneously such as web services on port 80 at the same time that it offers File Transfer Protocol (FTP) connection establishment on port 21.

Refer to
Online Course
for Illustration

4.5.1.4   Socket Pairs

The source and destination ports are placed within the segment. The segments are then encapsulated within an IP packet. The IP packet contains the IP address of the source and destination. The combination of the source IP address and source port number, or the destination IP address and destination port number is known as a socket. The socket is used to identify the server and service being requested by the client. A client socket might look like this, with 1099 representing the source port number: 192.168.1.5:1099

The socket on a web server might be: 192.168.1.7:80

Together, these two sockets combine to form a socket pair: 192.168.1.5:1099, 192.168.1.7:80

Sockets enable multiple processes, running on a client, to distinguish themselves from each other, and multiple connections to a server process to be distinguished from each other.

The source port number acts as a return address for the requesting application. The transport layer keeps track of this port and the application that initiated the request so that when a response is returned, it can be forwarded to the correct application.

Refer to
Interactive Graphic
in online course

4.5.1.5   TCP vs UDP

For some applications, segments must arrive in a very specific sequence to be processed successfully. With other applications, all data must be fully received before any is considered useful. In both of these instances, TCP is used as the transport protocol. Application developers must choose which transport protocol type is appropriate based on the requirements of the applications.

For example, applications such as databases, web browsers, and email clients, require that all data that is sent arrives at the destination in its original condition. Any missing data could cause a corrupt communication that is either incomplete or unreadable. These applications are designed to use TCP.

TCP transport is analogous to sending packages that are tracked from source to destination. If a shipping order is broken up into several packages, a customer can check online to see the order of the delivery.

With TCP, there are three basic operations of reliability:

- Numbering and tracking data segments transmitted to a specific host from a specific application
- Acknowledging received data
- Retransmitting any unacknowledged data after a certain period of time

Click Play in Figure 1 to see how TCP segments and acknowledgments are transmitted between sender and receiver.

In other cases, an application can tolerate some data loss during transmission over the network, but delays in transmission are unacceptable. UDP is the better choice for these applications because less network overhead is required. There is a trade-off between the value of reliability and the burden it places on network resources. Adding overhead to ensure reliability for some applications could reduce the usefulness of the application and can even be detrimental. In such cases, UDP is a better transport protocol. UDP is preferable for applications such as streaming live audio, live video, and Voice over IP (VoIP). Acknowledgments and retransmission would slow down delivery.

For example, if one or two segments of a live video stream fail to arrive, it creates a momentary disruption in the stream. This may appear as distortion in the image or sound, but may not be noticeable to the user. If the destination device had to account for lost data, the stream could be delayed while waiting for retransmissions, therefore causing the image or sound to be greatly degraded. In this case, it is better to render the best media possible with the segments received, and forego reliability.

UDP provides the basic functions for delivering data segments between the appropriate applications, with very little overhead and data checking. UDP is known as a best-effort delivery protocol. In the context of networking, best-effort delivery is referred to as unreliable because there is no acknowledgment that the data is received at the destination. With UDP, there are no transport layer processes that inform the sender of a successful delivery.

UDP is similar to placing a regular, non-registered, letter in the mail. The sender of the letter is not aware of the availability of the receiver to receive the letter. Nor is the post office responsible for tracking the letter or informing the sender if the letter does not arrive at the final destination.

Click Play in Figure 2 to see an animation of UDP segments being transmitted from sender to receiver.

Figure 3 provides an overview and comparison of the features of TCP and UDP.

Note Applications that stream stored audio and video use TCP. For example, if your network suddenly cannot support the bandwidth needed to watch an on-demand movie, the application pauses the playback. During the pause, you might see a "buffering..." message while TCP works to re-establish the stream. When all the segments are in order and a minimum level of bandwidth is restored, your TCP session resumes and the movie continues to play.

Refer to
Interactive Graphic
in online course

4.5.1.6 TCP and UDP Headers

TCP is a stateful protocol. A stateful protocol is a protocol that keeps track of the state of the communication session. To track the state of a session, TCP records which information it has sent and which information has been acknowledged. The stateful session begins with the session establishment and ends when closed with the session termination.

As shown in Figure 1, each TCP segment has 20 bytes of overhead in the header encapsulating the application layer data:

- **Source Port (16 bits) and Destination Port (16 bits)** - This is used to identify the application.

- **Sequence number (32 bits)** - This is used for data reassembly purposes.

- **Acknowledgment number (32 bits)** - This indicates the data that has been received.

requesting server, the server temporarily stores the numbered address in the event that the same name is requested again.

The DNS Client service on Windows PCs also stores previously resolved names in memory. The **ipconfig /displaydns** command displays all of the cached DNS entries.

Refer to
Online Course
for Illustration

4.6.2.5   Dynamic DNS

DNS requires registrars to accept and distribute DNS mappings from organizations that wish to register domain name and IP address mappings. After the initial mapping has been created, a process which can take 24 hours or more, changes to the IP address that is mapped to the domain name can be made by contacting the registrar or using an online form to the make the change. However, because of the time it takes for this process to occur and the new mapping to be distributed in domain name system, the change can take hours before the new mapping is available to resolvers. In situations in which an ISP is using DHCP to provide addresses to a domain, it is possible that the address that is mapped to the domain could expire and a new address be granted by the ISP. This would result in a disruption of connectivity to the domain through DNS. A new approach was necessary to allow organizations to make fast changes to the IP address that is mapped to a domain.

Dynamic DNS (DDNS) allows a user or organization to register an IP address with a domain name as in DNS. However, when the IP address of the mapping changes, the new mapping can be propagated through the DNS almost instantaneously. For this to occur, a user obtains a subdomain from a DDNS provider. That subdomain is mapped to the IP address of the user's server, or home router connection to the Internet. Client software runs on either the router or a host PC that detects a change in the Internet IP address of the user. When a change is detected, the DDNS provider is immediately informed of the change and the mapping between the user's subdomain and the Internet IP address is immediately updated, as shown in the figure. DDNS does not use a true DNS entry for a user's IP address. Instead, it acts as an intermediary. The DDNS provider's domain is registered with the DNS, but the subdomain is mapped to a totally different IP address. The DDNS provider service supplies that IP address to the resolver's second level DNS server. That DNS server, either at the organization or ISP, provides the DDNS IP address to the resolver.

Refer to
Online Course
for Illustration

4.6.2.6   The WHOIS Protocol

WHOIS is a TCP-based protocol that is used to identify the owners of Internet domains through the DNS system. When an Internet domain is registered and mapped to an IP address for the DNS system, the registrant must supply information regarding who is registering the domain. The WHOIS application uses a query, in the form of a FQDN. The query is issued through a WHOIS service or application. The official ownership registration record is returned to the user by the WHOIS service. This can be useful for identifying the destinations that have been accessed by hosts on a network. WHOIS has limitations, and hackers have ways of hiding their identities. However, WHOIS is a starting point for identifying potentially dangerous Internet locations that may have been reached through the network. An Internet-based WHOIS service is maintained by ICANN and can be reached at https://whois.icann.org/. Other WHOIS services are maintained by regional Internet registries such as RIPE and APNIC.

Refer to
Lab Activity
for this chapter

4.6.2.7   Lab - Using Wireshark to Examine a UDP DNS Capture

In this lab, you will communicate with a DNS server by sending a DNS query using the UDP transport protocol. You will use Wireshark to examine the DNS query and response exchanges with the same server.

4.6.3   NAT

Refer to
Interactive Graphic
in online course

4.6.3.1   NAT Overview

There are not enough public IPv4 addresses to assign a unique address to each device connected to the Internet. Networks are commonly implemented using private IPv4 addresses, as defined in RFC 1918. Figure 1 shows the range of addresses included in RFC 1918. It is very likely that the computer that you use to view this course is assigned a private address.

These private addresses are used within an organization or site to allow devices to communicate locally. However, because these addresses do not identify any single company or organization, private IPv4 addresses cannot be routed over the Internet. To allow a device with a private IPv4 address to access devices and resources outside of the local network, the private address must first be translated to a public address, as shown in Figure 2.

Refer to
Online Course
for Illustration

4.6.3.2   NAT-Enabled Routers

NAT-enabled routers can be configured with one or more valid public IPv4 addresses. These public addresses are known as the NAT pool. When an internal device sends traffic out of the network, the NAT-enabled router translates the internal IPv4 address of the device to a public address from the NAT pool. To outside devices, all traffic entering and exiting the network appears to have a public IPv4 address from the provided pool of addresses.

A NAT router typically operates at the border of a stub network. A stub network is a network that has a single connection to its neighboring network, one way in and one way out of the network. In the example in the figure, R2 is a border router. As seen from the ISP, R2 forms a stub network.

When a device inside the stub network wants to communicate with a device outside of its network, the packet is forwarded to the border router. The border router performs the NAT process, translating the internal private address of the device to a public, outside, routable address.

Note   The connection to the ISP may use a private address or a public address that is shared among customers. For the purposes of this chapter, a public address is shown.

Refer to
Interactive Graphic
in online course

4.6.3.3   Port Address Translation

NAT is can be implemented as one-to-one static mappings of private addresses to public addresses, or many internal addresses can be mapped to a single public address. This is known as Port Address Translation (PAT). PAT is quite commonly used in home networks when an ISP provides a single public IP address to the home router. In most homes, multiple devices will require Internet access. PAT allows all of the network devices within the home network to share the single IP address that is provided by the ISP. In larger networks, PAT can be used to map many internal addresses to several public addresses as well.

With PAT, multiple addresses can be mapped to one or to a few addresses, because each private address is also tracked by a port number. When a device initiates a TCP/IP session, it generates a TCP or UDP source port value or a specially assigned query ID for ICMP, to uniquely identify the session. When the NAT router receives a packet from the client, it uses its source port number to uniquely identify the specific NAT translation. The PAT process also validates that the incoming packets were requested, thus adding a degree of security to the session.

Click the Play and Pause buttons in the figure to control the animation. The animation illustrates the PAT process. PAT adds unique source port numbers to the inside global address to distinguish between translations.

As R2 processes each packet, it uses a port number (1331 and 1555, in this example) to identify the device from which the packet originated. The source address (SA) is the inside local address with the TCP/IP assigned port number added. The destination address (DA) is the outside local address with the service port number added. In this example, the service port is 80, which is HTTP.

For the source address, R2 translates the private address (known as an inside local address) to an outside global public address with the port number added. The destination address is not changed, but is now referred to as the outside global IPv4 address. When the web server replies, the path is reversed.

NAT/PAT can complicate cyber-operations because it can hide addressing information in the log files created by network security and monitoring devices.

4.6.4   File Transfer and Sharing Services

Refer to **Online Course** for Illustration

4.6.4.1   FTP and TFTP

File Transfer Protocol (FTP)

FTP is another commonly used application layer protocol. FTP was developed to allow for data transfers between a client and a server. An FTP client is an application that runs on a computer that is used to push and pull data from an FTP server.

As Figure 1 illustrates, to successfully transfer data, FTP requires two connections between the client and the server, one for commands and replies, the other for the actual file transfer:

1. The client establishes the first connection to the server for control traffic using TCP port 21, consisting of client commands and server replies.

2. The client establishes the second connection to the server for the actual data transfer using TCP port 20. This connection is created every time there is data to be transferred.

The data transfer can happen in either direction. The client can download (pull) data from the server, or the client can upload (push) data to the server.

FTP was not designed to be a secure application layer protocol. For this reason, SSH File Transfer Protocol, which is a secure form of FTP that uses Secure Shell protocol to provide a secure channel, is the preferred file transfer implementation.

Trivial File Transfer Protocol (TFTP)

TFTP is a simplified file transfer protocol that uses well-known UDP port number 69. It lacks many of the features of FTP, such as the file management operations of listing, deleting, or renaming files. Because of its simplicity, TFTP has a very low network overhead and is popular for non-critical file transfer applications. It is fundamentally insecure however, because it has no login or access control features. For this reason, TFTP needs to implemented carefully, and only when absolutely necessary.

Refer to
Interactive Graphic
in online course

4.6.4.2   SMB

The Server Message Block (SMB) is a client/server file sharing protocol that describes the structure of shared network resources, such as directories, files, printers, and serial ports, as shown in Figure 1. It is a request-response protocol. All SMB messages share a common format. This format uses a fixed-sized header, followed by a variable-sized parameter and data component.

SMB messages can start, authenticate, and terminate sessions, control file and printer access, and allow an application to send or receive messages to or from another device.

SMB file sharing and print services have become the mainstay of Microsoft networking, as shown in Figure 2.

Refer to
Lab Activity
for this chapter

4.6.4.3   Lab - Using Wireshark to Examine TCP and UDP Captures

In this lab, you will complete the following objectives:

- Identify TCP Header Fields and Operation Using a Wireshark FTP Session Capture
- Identify UDP Header Fields and Operation Using a Wireshark TFTP Session Capture

4.6.5   Email

Refer to
Online Course
for Illustration

4.6.5.1   Email Overview

Email is an essential network application. To run on a computer or other end device, it requires several applications and services, as shown in the figure. Email is a store-and-forward method of sending, storing, and retrieving electronic messages across a network. Email messages are stored in databases on mail servers.

Email clients communicate with mail servers to send and receive email. Mail servers communicate with other mail servers to transport messages from one domain to another. An email client does not communicate directly with another email client when sending email. Instead, both clients rely on the mail server to transport messages.

Email supports three separate protocols for operation: Simple Mail Transfer Protocol (SMTP), Post Office Protocol version 3 (POP3), and IMAP. The application layer process that sends mail uses SMTP. A client retrieves email, however, using one of the two application layer protocols: POP3 or IMAP.

Refer to
Online Course
for Illustration

4.6.5.2   SMTP

SMTP message formats require a message header and a message body. While the message body can contain any amount of text, the message header must have a properly formatted recipient email address and a sender address.

When a client sends email, the client SMTP process connects with a server SMTP process on well-known port 25. After the connection is made, the client attempts to send the email to the server across the connection. When the server receives the message, it either places the message in a local account, if the recipient is local, or forwards the message to another mail server for delivery, as shown in the figure.

The destination email server may not be online or may be busy when email messages are sent. Therefore, SMTP spools messages to be sent at a later time. Periodically, the server checks the queue for messages and attempts to send them again. If the message is still not delivered after a predetermined expiration time, it is returned to the sender as undeliverable.

Refer to
Online Course
for Illustration

4.6.5.3 POP3

POP3 is used by an application to retrieve mail from a mail server. With POP3, mail is downloaded from the server to the client and then deleted on the server, as shown in the figure.

The server starts the POP3 service by passively listening on TCP port 110 for client connection requests. When a client wants to make use of the service, it sends a request to establish a TCP connection with the server. When the connection is established, the POP3 server sends a greeting. The client and POP3 server then exchange commands and responses until the connection is closed or aborted.

With POP3, email messages are downloaded to the client and removed from the server, so there is no centralized location where email messages are kept. Because POP3 does not store messages, it is undesirable for a small business that needs a centralized backup solution.

Refer to
Online Course
for Illustration

4.6.5.4 IMAP

IMAP is another protocol that describes a method to retrieve email messages, as shown in the figure. Unlike POP3, when the user connects to an IMAP-capable server, copies of the messages are downloaded to the client application. The original messages are kept on the server until manually deleted. Users view copies of the messages in their email client software.

Users can create a file hierarchy on the server to organize and store mail. That file structure is duplicated on the email client as well. When a user decides to delete a message, the server synchronizes that action and deletes the message from the server.

Click here to learn more about email protocols.

4.6.6 HTTP

Refer to
Interactive Graphic
in online course

4.6.6.1 HTTP Overview

To better understand how the web browser and web server interact, we can examine how a web page is opened in a browser. For this example, use the URL http://www.cisco.com, as shown in Figure 1.

First, the browser interprets the three parts of the URL:

- **http** (the protocol or scheme)
- **www.cisco.com** (the server name)
- **index.html** (the default home page is requested)

Note Web servers typically display the home page, index.html, as the default page if no other page is specified. You do not need to enter the full path including the /index.html. If fact, you can simply enter cisco.com. Regardless of whether you enter cisco.com, www.cisco.com, or www.cisco.com/index.html, the web server will display the same home page, index.html.

As shown in Figure 2, the browser then checks with a name server to convert www.cisco.com into a numeric IP address, which it uses to connect to the server. Using HTTP requirements, the browser sends a GET request to the server and asks for the index.html file. The server, as shown in Figure 3, sends the HTML code for this web page to the browser. Finally, as shown in Figure 4, the browser deciphers the HTML code and formats the page for the browser window.

Refer to **Online Course** for Illustration

4.6.6.2 The HTTP URL

HTTP URLs can also specify the port on the server that should handle the HTTP methods. In addition, it can specify a query string and fragment. The query string typically contains information that is not handled by the HTTP server process itself, but is instead handled by another process that is running on the server. Query strings are preceded by a "?" character and typically consist of a series of name and value pairs. A fragment is preceded by a "#" character. It refers to a subordinate part of the resource that is requested in the URL. For example, a fragment could refer to a named anchor in an HTML document. The URL will access the document and then move to the part of the document specified by the fragment if a matching named anchor link exists in the document. An HTTP URL that includes these parts is shown in the figure.

Refer to **Online Course** for Illustration

4.6.6.3 The HTTP Protocol

HTTP is a request/response protocol that uses TCP port 80, although other ports can be used. When a client, typically a web browser, sends a request to a web server, it will use one of five methods that are specified by the HTTP protocol.

- **GET** - A client request for data. A client (web browser) sends the GET message to the web server to request HTML pages, as shown in the figure.

- **POST** - Submits data to be processed by a resource.

- **PUT** - Uploads resources or content to the web server such as an image.

- **DELETE** - Deletes the resource specified.

- **OPTIONS** - Returns the HTTP methods that the server supports.

- **CONNECT** - Requests that an HTTP proxy server forwards the HTTP TCP session to the desired destination.

Although HTTP is remarkably flexible, it is not a secure protocol. The request messages send information to the server in plaintext that can be intercepted and read. The server responses, typically HTML pages, are also unencrypted.

Securing HTTP

For secure communication across the Internet, the HTTP Secure (HTTPS) protocol is used. HTTPS uses TCP port 443. HTTPS uses authentication and encryption to secure data as it travels between the client and server. HTTPS uses the same client request-server response process as HTTP, but the data stream is encrypted with Secure Socket Layer (SSL), or Transport Layer Security (TLS), before being transported across the network. Although SSL is the predecessor to TLS, both protocols are often referred to as SSL.

Much confidential information, such as passwords, credit card information, and medical information are transmitted over the Internet using HTTPS.

Refer to
Online Course
for Illustration

4.6.6.4   HTTP Status Codes

The HTTP server responses are identified with various status codes that inform the host application of the outcome of client requests to the server. The codes are organized into five groups. The codes are numeric, with the first number in the code indicating the type of message. The five status code groups are:

- **1xx** - Informational
- **2xx** - Success
- **3xx** - Redirection
- **4xx** - Client Error
- **5xx** - Server Error

An explanation of some common status codes is shown in the figure. Click here for a detailed list of all status codes with explanations.

Refer to
Lab Activity
for this chapter

4.6.6.5   Lab - Using Wireshark to Examine HTTP and HTTPS Traffic

In this lab, you will complete the following objectives:

- Capture and view HTTP traffic
- Capture and view HTTPS traffic

4.7   Summary

4.7.1   Conclusion

Refer to
Online Course
for Illustration

4.7.1.1   Chapter 4: Network Protocols and Services

In this chapter, you learned the basic operation of network protocols and services. Networks come in all sizes, from small, home office networks to the Internet. Protocols are the rules for how traffic is sent across networks. Networking engineers use two models to understand and communicate the operation of protocols: the OSI model and the TCP/IP model. Regardless of the model used, the process of encapsulation describes how data is formatted for transmission across the network so that the destination can receive and de-encapsulate the data.

Ethernet operates at Layer 2 of the OSI model. Ethernet is responsible for encapsulating the upper layer data in a frame, which includes source and destination MAC addresses. MAC addresses are used on the LAN to locate either the destination or the default gateway.

IP operates at Layer 3 of the OSI model. IP comes in two versions: IPv4 and IPv6. Although IPv4 is being replaced by IPv6, IPv4 is still prevalent on today's networks. IPv4 uses a 32-bit address space represented in dotted decimal format, such as 192.168.1.1. IPv6 uses a 128-bit address space represented in hexadecimal format. In IPv6, you can omit leading zeros in each hextet and omit one "all zeros" segment, such as 2001:0DB8:0000: 1111:0000:0000:0000:0200 represented as 2001:DB8:0:1111::200.

ICMP is used primarily for testing end-to-end connectivity from source to destination. ICMP for IPv4 is different than ICMP for IPv6. ICMP for IPv6 includes router solicitation, router advertisements, and duplicate address detection. The ping and traceroute utilities both use a feature of ICMP. Ping is used to test connectivity between two hosts but does not provide information about the details of devices between the hosts. Traceroute (tracert) is a utility that generates a list of hops that were successfully reached along the path.

ARP operates between Layer 2 and Layer 3, mapping MAC addresses to IP addresses. Before a host can send traffic to a remote network, it must know the MAC address for the default gateway. The host already knows the IP address for the default gateway. For example, a host with an IP address 192.168.1.10 might have a default gateway configured of 192.168.1.1. The host uses an ARP request to ask "Who is 192.168.1.1?" The default gateway will reply with its own MAC address. At that point, the host has mapped the IP address to the default gateway's MAC address and can now construct the frame to send data to a remote network.

The transport layer is responsible for separating the data from the application layer into segments that can be sent down to the network layer. TCP is the transport layer protocol used when all the data must arrive at the destination in the correct order. UDP is the transport layer protocol used when the application can tolerate some data loss during transmission.

At the application, there are several important network services that the cybersecurity analysts should be aware of:

- **DHCP** - This automates the assignment of IPv4 addresses, subnet masks, gateways, and other IPv4 networking parameters.

- **DNS** - This provides a reliable means of managing and providing domain names and their associated IP addresses.

- **NAT** - This translates between private and public IPv4 addresses.

- **File Transfer** - Applications such as FTP, TFTP, and SMB can be used to transfer files from one host to another.

- **Email** - his requires several applications and services including POP3, IMAP, and SMTP.

- **HTTP** - This protocol is used to send and receive web pages.

Go to the online course to take the quiz and exam.

Chapter 4 Quiz

This quiz is designed to provide an additional opportunity to practice the skills and knowledge presented in the chapter and to prepare for the chapter exam. You will be allowed multiple attempts and the grade does not appear in the gradebook.

Chapter 4 Exam

The chapter exam assesses your knowledge of the chapter content.

Your Chapter Notes

Stage 2: Authentication

Figure 3 provides a simple overview of the authentication process. However, in most shared key authentication installations, the exchange is as follows:

1. The wireless client sends an authentication frame to the AP.

2. The AP responds with a challenge text to the client.

3. The client encrypts the message using its shared key and returns the encrypted text back to the AP.

4. The AP then decrypts the encrypted text using its shared key.

5. If the decrypted text matches the challenge text, the AP authenticates the client. If the messages do not match, the wireless client is not authenticated and wireless access is denied.

After a wireless client has been authenticated, the AP proceeds to the association stage.

Stage 3: Association

The association stage finalizes settings and establishes the data link between the wireless client and the AP, as shown in Figure 4.

As part of this stage:

1. The wireless client forwards an Association Request frame that includes its MAC address.

2. The AP responds with an Associate Response that includes the AP BSSID, which is the AP MAC address.

3. The AP maps a logical port known as the association identifier (AID) to the wireless client. The AID is equivalent to a port on a switch and allows the infrastructure switch to keep track of frames destined for the wireless client to be forwarded.

Refer to **Interactive Graphic** in online course

5.1.2.5   Activity - Order the Steps in the Client and AP Association Process

Refer to **Online Course** for Illustration

5.1.2.6   Wireless Devices - AP, LWAP, WLC

A common wireless data implementation is enabling devices to connect wirelessly via a LAN. In general, a wireless LAN requires wireless access points and clients that have wireless NICs. Home and small business wireless routers integrate the functions of a router, switch, and access point into one device, as shown in the figure. Note that in small networks, the wireless router may be the only AP because only a small area requires wireless coverage. In larger networks, there can be many APs.

All of the control and management functions of the APs on a network can be centralized into a Wireless LAN Controller (WLC). When using a WLC, the APs no longer act autonomously, but instead act as lightweight APs (LWAPs). LWAPs only forward data between the wireless LAN and the WLC. All management functions, such as defining SSIDs and authentication are conducted on the centralized WLC rather than on each individual AP. A major benefit of centralizing the AP management functions in the WLC is simplified configuration and monitoring of numerous access points, among many other benefits.

Refer to **Interactive Graphic** in online course

5.1.2.7   Activity - Identify the LAN Device

5.2 Network Security Infrastructure

5.2.1 Security Devices

Refer to **Video** in online course

5.2.1.1 Video Tutorial - Security Devices

Click Play to view a video tutorial on security devices in a sample network.

Click here to read the transcript of this video.

Click here to download the Packet Tracer file used in the video.

Refer to **Interactive Graphic** in online course

5.2.1.2 Firewalls

A firewall is a system, or group of systems, that enforces an access control policy between networks. Click Play in the figure to view a firewall. All firewalls share some common properties:

- Firewalls are resistant to network attacks.
- Firewalls are the only transit point between internal corporate networks and external networks because all traffic flows through the firewall.
- Firewalls enforce the access control policy.

There are several benefits of using a firewall in a network:

- They prevent the exposure of sensitive hosts, resources, and applications to untrusted users.
- They sanitize protocol flow, which prevents the exploitation of protocol flaws.
- They block malicious data from servers and clients.
- They reduce security management complexity by off-loading most of the network access control to a few firewalls in the network.

Firewalls also present some limitations:

- A misconfigured firewall can have serious consequences for the network, such as becoming a single point of failure.
- The data from many applications cannot be passed over firewalls securely.
- Users might proactively search for ways around the firewall to receive blocked material, which exposes the network to potential attack.
- Network performance can slow down.
- Unauthorized traffic can be tunneled or hidden as legitimate traffic through the firewall.

Refer to **Online Course** for Illustration

5.2.1.3 Firewall Type Descriptions

It is important to understand the different types of firewalls and their specific capabilities so that the right firewall is used for each situation.

- **Packet filtering (stateless) firewall -** Typically a router with the capability to filter some packet content, such as Layer 3 and sometimes Layer 4 information according to a set of configured rules (Figure 1).

- **Stateful firewall** - A stateful inspection firewall allows or blocks traffic based on state, port, and protocol. It monitors all activity from the opening of a connection until it is closed. Filtering decisions are made based on both administrator-defined rules as well as context, which refers to using information from previous connections and packets belonging to the same connection (Figure 2).

- **Application gateway firewall (proxy firewall)** - Filters information at Layers 3, 4, 5, and 7 of the OSI reference model. Most of the firewall control and filtering is done in software. When a client needs to access a remote server, it connects to a proxy server. The proxy server connects to the remote server on behalf of the client. Therefore, the server only sees a connection from the proxy server (Figure 3).

Other methods of implementing firewalls include:

- **Host-based (server and personal) firewall** - A PC or server with firewall software running on it.

- **Transparent firewall** - Filters IP traffic between a pair of bridged interfaces.

- **Hybrid firewall** - A combination of the various firewall types. For example, an application inspection firewall combines a stateful firewall with an application gateway firewall.

Refer to **Online Course** for Illustration

5.2.1.4   Packet Filtering Firewalls

Packet filtering firewalls are usually part of a router firewall, which permits or denies traffic based on Layer 3 and Layer 4 information. They are stateless firewalls that use a simple policy table look-up that filters traffic based on specific criteria, as shown in the figure. For example, SMTP servers listen to port 25 by default. An administrator can configure the packet filtering firewall to block port 25 from a specific workstation to prevent it from broadcasting an email virus.

Refer to **Online Course** for Illustration

5.2.1.5   Stateful Firewalls

Stateful firewalls are the most versatile and the most common firewall technologies in use. Stateful firewalls provide stateful packet filtering by using connection information maintained in a state table. Stateful filtering is a firewall architecture that is classified at the network layer. It also analyzes traffic at OSI Layer 4 and Layer 5, as shown in the figure.

Refer to **Online Course** for Illustration

5.2.1.6   Next-Generation Firewalls

Next-generation firewalls go beyond stateful firewalls by providing:

- Standard firewall capabilities like stateful inspection
- Integrated intrusion prevention
- Application awareness and control to see and block risky apps
- Upgrade paths to include future information feeds
- Techniques to address evolving security threats

Refer to
Interactive Graphic
in online course

5.2.1.7   Activity - Identify the Type of Firewall

Refer to
Online Course
for Illustration

5.2.1.8   Intrusion Protection and Detection Devices

A networking architecture paradigm shift is required to defend against fast-moving and evolving attacks. This must include cost-effective detection and prevention systems, such as intrusion detection systems (IDS) or the more scalable intrusion prevention systems (IPS). The network architecture integrates these solutions into the entry and exit points of the network.

When implementing IDS or IPS, it is important to be familiar with the types of systems available, host-based and network-based approaches, the placement of these systems, the role of signature categories, and possible actions that a Cisco IOS router can take when an attack is detected.

IDS and IPS technologies share several characteristics, as shown in the figure. IDS and IPS technologies are both deployed as sensors. An IDS or IPS sensor can be in the form of several different devices:

- A router configured with Cisco IOS IPS software

- A device specifically designed to provide dedicated IDS or IPS services

- A network module installed in an adaptive security appliance (ASA), switch, or router

IDS and IPS technologies use signatures to detect patterns in network traffic. A signature is a set of rules that an IDS or IPS uses to detect malicious activity. Signatures can be used to detect severe breaches of security, to detect common network attacks, and to gather information. IDS and IPS technologies can detect atomic signature patterns (single-packet) or composite signature patterns (multi-packet).

Refer to
Online Course
for Illustration

5.2.1.9   Advantages and Disadvantages of IDS and IPS

IDS Advantages and Disadvantages

A list of the advantages and disadvantages of IDS and IPS is shown in the figure.

A primary advantage of an IDS platform is that it is deployed in offline mode. Because the IDS sensor is not inline, it has no impact on network performance. It does not introduce latency, jitter, or other traffic flow issues. In addition, if a sensor fails it does not affect network functionality. It only affects the ability of the IDS to analyze the data.

However, there are many disadvantages of deploying an IDS platform. An IDS sensor is primarily focused on identifying possible incidents, logging information about the incidents, and reporting the incidents. The IDS sensor cannot stop the trigger packet and is not guaranteed to stop a connection. The trigger packet alerts the IDS to a potential threat. IDS sensors are also less helpful in stopping email viruses and automated attacks, such as worms.

Users deploying IDS sensor response actions must have a well-designed security policy and a good operational understanding of their IDS deployments. Users must spend time tuning IDS sensors to achieve expected levels of intrusion detection.

Finally, because IDS sensors are not inline, an IDS implementation is more vulnerable to network security evasion techniques in the form of various network attack methods.

IPS Advantages and Disadvantages

An IPS sensor can be configured to perform a packet drop to stop the trigger packet, the packets associated with a connection, or packets from a source IP address. Additionally, because IPS sensors are inline, they can use stream normalization. Stream normalization is a technique used to reconstruct the data stream when the attack occurs over multiple data segments.

A disadvantage of IPS is that (because it is deployed inline) errors, failure, and overwhelming the IPS sensor with too much traffic can have a negative effect on network performance. An IPS sensor can affect network performance by introducing latency and jitter. An IPS sensor must be appropriately sized and implemented so that time-sensitive applications, such as VoIP, are not adversely affected.

Deployment Considerations

Using one of these technologies does not negate the use of the other. In fact, IDS and IPS technologies can complement each other. For example, an IDS can be implemented to validate IPS operation because the IDS can be configured for deeper packet inspection offline. This allows the IPS to focus on fewer but more critical traffic patterns inline.

Deciding which implementation to use is based on the security goals of the organization as stated in their network security policy.

Refer to **Online Course** for Illustration

5.2.1.10   Types of IPS

There are two primary kinds of IPSs available: host-based and network-based.

Host-based IPS

Host-based IPS (HIPS) is software installed on a single host to monitor and analyze suspicious activity. A significant advantage of HIPS is that it can monitor and protect operating system and critical system processes that are specific to that host. With detailed knowledge of the operating system, HIPS can monitor abnormal activity and prevent the host from executing commands that do not match typical behavior. This suspicious or malicious behavior might include unauthorized registry updates, changes to the system directory, executing installation programs, and activities that cause buffer overflows. Network traffic can also be monitored to prevent the host from participating in a denial-of-service (DoS) attack or being part of an illicit FTP session.

HIPS can be thought of as a combination of antivirus software, antimalware software, and firewall. Combined with a network-based IPS, HIPS is an effective tool in providing additional protection for the host.

A disadvantage of HIPS is that it operates only at a local level. It does not have a complete view of the network, or coordinated events that might be happening across the network. To be effective in a network, HIPS must be installed on every host and have support for every operating system. The advantages and disadvantages of HIPS are shown in Figure 1.

Network-based IPS

A network-based IPS can be implemented using a dedicated or non-dedicated IPS device. Network-based IPS implementations are a critical component of intrusion prevention. There are host-based IDS/IPS solutions, but these must be integrated with a network-based IPS implementation to ensure a robust security architecture.

Sensors detect malicious and unauthorized activity in real time and can take action when required. Sensors are deployed at designated network points (Figure 2) that enable security managers to monitor network activity while it is occurring, regardless of the location of the attack target.

Refer to
Online Course
for Illustration

5.2.1.11 Specialized Security Appliances

Cisco Advanced Malware Protection (AMP) is an enterprise-class advanced malware analysis and protection solution. It provides comprehensive malware protection for organizations before, during, and after an attack:

- Before an attack, AMP strengthens defenses and protects against known and emerging threats.

- During an attack, AMP identifies and blocks policy-violating file types, exploit attempts, and malicious files from infiltrating the network.

- After an attack, or after a file is initially inspected, AMP goes beyond point-in-time detection capabilities and continuously monitors and analyzes all file activity and traffic, regardless of disposition, searching for any indications of malicious behavior. If a file with an unknown or previously deemed "good" disposition starts behaving badly, AMP will detect it and instantly alert security teams with an indication of compromise. It then provides visibility into where the malware originated, what systems were affected, and what the malware is doing.

AMP accesses the collective security intelligence of the Cisco Talos Security Intelligence and Research Group. Talos detects and correlates threats in real time using the largest threat-detection network in the world.

Cisco Web Security Appliance (WSA) is a secure web gateway that combines leading protections to help organizations address the growing challenges of securing and controlling web traffic. WSA protects the network by automatically blocking risky sites and testing unknown sites before allowing users to access them. WSA provides malware protection, application visibility and control, acceptable use policy controls, insightful reporting and secure mobility.

Cisco Cloud Web Security (CWS). While WSA protects the network from malware intrusion, it does not provide protection for users who want to connect to the Internet directly outside of the protected network, such as at a public Wi-Fi service. In this instance, the user's PC can be infected with malware which can then spread to other networks and devices. To help protect user PCs from these types of malware infections there is Cisco Cloud Web Security (CWS).

CWS together with WSA provides comprehensive protection against malware and the associated impacts. The Cisco CWS solution enforces secure communication to and from the Internet and provides remote workers the same level of security as onsite employees when using a laptop issued by Cisco. Cisco CWS incorporates two main functions, web filtering and web security, and both are accompanied by extensive, centralized reporting.

Cisco Email Security Appliance (ESA)/ Cisco Cloud Email Security help to mitigate email-based threats. The Cisco ESA defends mission-critical email systems. The Cisco ESA is constantly updated by real-time feeds from the Cisco Talos, which detects and correlates threats using a worldwide database monitoring system. These are some of the main features of ESA:

- **Global threat intelligence** - Cisco Talos provides a 24-hour view into global traffic activity. It analyzes anomalies, uncovers new threats, and monitors traffic trends.

- **Spam blocking** - A multilayered defense combines an outer layer of filtering based on the reputation of the sender and an inner layer of filtering that performs a deep analysis of the message.

- **Advanced malware protection** – Includes AMP that takes advantage of the vast cloud security intelligence network of Sourcefire. It delivers protection across the attack continuum before, during, and after an attack.

- **Outbound message control** - Controls outbound messages to help ensure that important messages comply with industry standards and are protected in transit.

A group of Cisco security appliances is shown in the figure.

Refer to
Interactive Graphic
in online course

5.2.1.12   Activity - Compare IDS and IPS Characteristics

5.2.2   Security Services

Refer to **Video**
in online course

5.2.2.1   Video Tutorial - Security Services

Click Play to view a tutorial on security services in the network.

Click here to read the transcript of this video.

Click here to download the Packet Tracer file used in the video.

Refer to
Online Course
for Illustration

5.2.2.2   Traffic Control with ACLs

An Access Control List (ACL) is a series of commands that control whether a device forwards or drops packets based on information found in the packet header. When configured, ACLs perform the following tasks:

- They limit network traffic to increase network performance. For example, if corporate policy does not allow video traffic on the network, ACLs that block video traffic could be configured and applied. This would greatly reduce the network load and increase network performance.

- They provide traffic flow control. ACLs can restrict the delivery of routing updates to ensure that the updates are from a known source.

- They provide a basic level of security for network access. ACLs can allow one host to access a part of the network and prevent another host from accessing the same area. For example, access to the Human Resources network can be restricted to authorized users.

- They filter traffic based on traffic type. For example, an ACL can permit email traffic, but block all Telnet traffic.

- They screen hosts to permit or deny access to network services. ACLs can permit or deny a user to access file types, such as FTP or HTTP.

In addition to either permitting or denying traffic, ACLs can be used for selecting types of traffic to be analyzed, forwarded, or processed in other ways. For example, ACLs can be used to classify traffic to enable priority processing. This capability is similar to having a VIP pass at a concert or sporting event. The VIP pass gives selected guests privileges not offered to general admission ticket holders, such as priority entry or being able to enter a restricted area.

The figure shows a sample topology with ACLs applied to routers R1, R2, and R3.

Refer to **Online Course** for Illustration

5.2.2.3 ACLs: Important Features

Two types of Cisco IPv4 ACLs are standard and extended. Standard ACLs can be used to permit or deny traffic only from source IPv4 addresses. The destination of the packet and the ports involved are not evaluated.

Extended ACLs filter IPv4 packets based on several attributes that include:

- Protocol type
- Source IPv4 address
- Destination IPv4 address
- Source TCP or UDP ports
- Destination TCP or UDP ports
- Optional protocol type information for finer control

Standard and extended ACLs can be created using either a number or a name to identify the ACL and its list of statements.

Using numbered ACLs is an effective method for determining the ACL type on smaller networks with more homogeneously defined traffic. However, a number does not provide information about the purpose of the ACL. For this reason, a name can be used to identify a Cisco ACL.

By configuring ACL logging, an ACL message can be generated and logged when traffic meets the permit or deny criteria defined in the ACL.

Cisco ACLs can also be configured to only allow TCP traffic that has an ACK or RST bit set, so that only traffic from an established TCP session is permitted. This can be used to deny any TCP traffic from outside the network that is trying to establish a new TCP session.

Refer to **Packet Tracer Activity** for this chapter

5.2.2.4 Packet Tracer - ACL Demonstration

In this activity, you will observe how an access control list (ACL) can be used to prevent a ping from reaching hosts on remote networks. After removing the ACL from the configuration, the pings will be successful.

Refer to **Online Course** for Illustration

5.2.2.5 SNMP

Simple Network Management Protocol (SNMP) allows administrators to manage end devices such as servers, workstations, routers, switches, and security appliances, on an IP network. It enables network administrators to monitor and manage network performance, find and solve network problems, and plan for network growth.

SNMP is an application layer protocol that provides a message format for communication between managers and agents. The SNMP system consists of three elements:

- SNMP manager that runs SNMP management software.

- SNMP agents which are the nodes being monitored and managed.

- Management Information Base (MIB) which is a database on the agent that stores data and operational statistics about the device.

Refer to
Online Course
for Illustration

5.2.2.6   NetFlow

NetFlow is a Cisco IOS technology that provides statistics on packets flowing through a Cisco router or multilayer switch. While SNMP attempts to provide a very wide range of network management features and options, NetFlow is focused on providing statistics on IP packets flowing through network devices.

NetFlow provides data to enable network and security monitoring, network planning, traffic analysis to include identification of network bottlenecks, and IP accounting for billing purposes. For example, in the figure, PC 1 connects to PC 2 using an application such as HTTPS. NetFlow can monitor that application connection, tracking byte and packet counts for that individual application flow. It then pushes the statistics over to an external server called a NetFlow collector.

NetFlow technology has seen several generations that provide more sophistication in defining traffic flows, but "original NetFlow" distinguished flows using a combination of seven fields. Should one of these fields vary in value from another packet, the packets could be safely determined to be from different flows:

- Source IP address

- Destination IP address

- Source port number

- Destination port number

- Layer 3 protocol type

- Type of Service (ToS) marking

- Input logical interface

The first four of the fields NetFlow uses to identify a flow should be familiar. The source and destination IP addresses, plus the source and destination ports, identify the connection between source and destination application. The Layer 3 protocol type identifies the type of header that follows the IP header (usually TCP or UDP, but other options include ICMP). The ToS byte in the IPv4 header holds information about how devices should apply quality of service (QoS) rules to the packets in that flow.

Refer to
Online Course
for Illustration

5.2.2.7   Port Mirroring

A packet analyzer (also known as a packet sniffer or traffic sniffer) is typically software that captures packets entering and exiting the network interface card (NIC). It is not always possible or desirable to have the packet analyzer on the device that is being monitored. Sometimes it is better on a separate station designated to capture the packets.

Because network switches can isolate traffic, traffic sniffers or other network monitors, such as IDS, cannot access all the traffic on a network segment. Port mirroring is a feature that allows a switch to make duplicate copies of traffic passing through a switch, and then send it out a port with a network monitor attached. The original traffic is forwarded in the usual manner. An example of port mirroring is illustrated in the figure.

Refer to **Online Course** for Illustration

5.2.2.8 Syslog Servers

When certain events occur on a network, networking devices have trusted mechanisms to notify the administrator with detailed system messages. These messages can be either non-critical or significant. Network administrators have a variety of options for storing, interpreting, and displaying these messages, and for being alerted to those messages that could have the greatest impact on the network infrastructure.

The most common method of accessing system messages is to use a protocol called syslog.

Many networking devices support syslog, including routers, switches, application servers, firewalls, and other network appliances. The syslog protocol allows networking devices to send their system messages across the network to syslog servers as shown in the figure.

The syslog logging service provides three primary functions:

- The ability to gather logging information for monitoring and troubleshooting
- The ability to select the type of logging information that is captured
- The ability to specify the destination of captured syslog messages

Refer to **Online Course** for Illustration

5.2.2.9 NTP

It is important to synchronize the time across all devices on the network because all aspects of managing, securing, troubleshooting, and planning networks require accurate and consistent timestamping. When the time is not synchronized between devices, it will be impossible to determine the order of the events that have occurred in different parts of the network.

Typically, the date and time settings on a network device can be set using one of two methods:

- Manual configuration of the date and time
- Configuring the Network Time Protocol (NTP)

As a network grows, it becomes difficult to ensure that all infrastructure devices are operating with synchronized time. Even in a smaller network environment, the manual method is not ideal. If a device reboots, how will it get an accurate date and timestamp?

A better solution is to configure the NTP on the network. This protocol allows routers on the network to synchronize their time settings with an NTP server. A group of NTP clients that obtain time and date information from a single source have more consistent time settings. When NTP is implemented in the network, it can be set up to synchronize to a private master clock or it can synchronize to a publicly available NTP server on the Internet.

NTP networks use a hierarchical system of time sources. Each level in this hierarchical system is called a stratum. The stratum level is defined as the number of hop counts from the authoritative source. The synchronized time is distributed across the network using NTP. The figure displays a sample NTP network.

NTP servers are arranged in three levels known as strata:

- **Stratum 0** - An NTP network gets the time from authoritative time sources. These authoritative time sources, also referred to as stratum 0 devices, are high-precision timekeeping devices assumed to be accurate and with little or no delay associated with them.

- **Stratum 1** - The stratum 1 devices are directly connected to the authoritative time sources. They act as the primary network time standard.

- **Stratum 2 and Lower** - The stratum 2 servers are connected to stratum 1 devices through network connections. Stratum 2 devices, such as NTP clients, synchronize their time using the NTP packets from stratum 1 servers. They could also act as servers for stratum 3 devices.

Smaller stratum numbers indicate that the server is closer to the authorized time source than larger stratum numbers. The larger the stratum number, the lower the stratum level. The max hop count is 15. Stratum 16, the lowest stratum level, indicates that a device is unsynchronized. Time servers on the same stratum level can be configured to act as a peer with other time servers on the same stratum level for backup or verification of time.

5.2.2.10 AAA Servers

Refer to **Online Course** for Illustration

AAA is an architectural framework for configuring a set of three independent security functions:

- **Authentication** - Users and administrators must prove that they are who they say they are. Authentication can be established using username and password combinations, challenge and response questions, token cards, and other methods. For example: "I am user 'student' and I know the password to prove it." AAA authentication provides a centralized way to control access to the network.

- **Authorization** - After the user is authenticated, authorization services determine which resources the user can access and which operations the user is allowed to perform. An example is "User 'student' can access host serverXYZ using SSH only."

- **Accounting and auditing** - Accounting records what the user does, including what is accessed, the amount of time the resource is accessed, and any changes that were made. Accounting keeps track of how network resources are used. An example is "User 'student' accessed host serverXYZ using SSH for 15 minutes."

Terminal Access Controller Access-Control System Plus (TACACS+) and Remote Authentication Dial-In User Service (RADIUS) are both authentication protocols that are used to communicate with AAA servers. Whether TACACS+ or RADIUS is selected depends on the needs of the organization.

While both protocols can be used to communicate between a router and AAA servers, TACACS+ is considered the more secure protocol. This is because all TACACS+ protocol exchanges are encrypted, while RADIUS only encrypts the user's password. RADIUS does not encrypt user names, accounting information, or any other information carried in the RADIUS message. The figure shows differences between the two protocols.

Refer to
Online Course
for Illustration

5.2.2.11   VPN

A VPN is a private network that is created over a public network, usually the Internet, as shown in Figure 1. Instead of using a dedicated physical connection, a VPN uses virtual connections routed through the Internet from the organization to the remote site. The first VPNs were strictly IP tunnels that did not include authentication or encryption of the data. For example, Generic Routing Encapsulation (GRE) is a tunneling protocol developed by Cisco that can encapsulate a wide variety of network layer protocol packet types inside IP tunnels. This creates a virtual point-to-point link to Cisco routers at remote points over an IP internetwork.

A VPN is virtual in that it carries information within a private network, but that information is actually transported over a public network. A VPN is private in that the traffic is encrypted to keep the data confidential while it is transported across the public network.

A VPN is a communications environment in which access is strictly controlled to permit peer connections within a defined community of interest. Confidentiality is achieved by encrypting the traffic within the VPN. Today, a secure implementation of VPN with encryption is what is generally equated with the concept of virtual private networking.

In the simplest sense, a VPN connects two endpoints, such as a remote office to a central office, over a public network, to form a logical connection. The logical connections can be made at either Layer 2 or Layer 3. Common examples of Layer 3 VPNs are GRE, Multiprotocol Label Switching (MPLS), and IPsec. Layer 3 VPNs can be point-to-point site connections, such as GRE and IPsec, or they can establish any-to-any connectivity to many sites using MPLS.

IPsec is a suite of protocols developed with the backing of the IETF to achieve secure services over IP packet-switched networks, as shown in Figure 2. IPsec services allow for authentication, integrity, access control, and confidentiality. With IPsec, the information exchanged between remote sites can be encrypted and verified. Both remote-access and site-to-site VPNs can be deployed using IPsec.

Refer to
Interactive Graphic
in online course

5.2.2.12   Activity - Identify the Network Security Device or Service

5.3   Network Representations

5.3.1   Network Topologies

Refer to
Online Course
for Illustration

5.3.1.1   Overview of Network Components

The path that a message takes from source to destination can be as simple as a single cable connecting one computer to another, or as complex as a collection of networks that literally spans the globe. This network infrastructure provides the stable and reliable channel over which these communications occur.

The network infrastructure contains three categories of network components:

- Devices (Figure 1)
- Media (Figure 2)
- Services (Figure 3)

Devices and media are the physical elements, or hardware, of the network. Hardware is often the visible components of the network platform such as a laptop, PC, switch, router, wireless access point, or the cabling used to connect the devices.

Services include many of the common network applications people use every day, like email hosting services and web hosting services. Processes provide the functionality that directs and moves the messages through the network. Processes are less obvious to us but are critical to the operation of networks.

Refer to **Online Course** for Illustration

5.3.1.2   Physical and Logical Topologies

The topology of a network is the arrangement or relationship of the network devices and the interconnections between them. LAN and Wide Area Networks (WAN) topologies can be viewed in two ways:

- **Physical topology** - Refers to the physical connections and identifies how end devices and infrastructure devices such as routers, switches, and wireless access points are interconnected (Figure 1).

- **Logical topology** - Refers to the way a network transfers frames from one node to the next. This arrangement consists of virtual connections between the nodes of a network. These logical signal paths are defined by data link layer protocols. The logical topology of point-to-point links is relatively simple, while shared media offers different access control methods (Figure 2).

The data link layer "sees" the logical topology of a network when controlling data accesses the media. It is the logical topology that influences the type of network framing and media access control used.

Refer to **Online Course** for Illustration

5.3.1.3   WAN Topologies

WANs are commonly interconnected using the following physical topologies:

- **Point-to-Point** - This is the simplest topology. It consists of a permanent link between two endpoints. For this reason, this is a very popular WAN topology.

- **Hub and Spoke** - A WAN version of the star topology in which a central site interconnects branch sites using point-to-point links.

- **Mesh** - This topology provides high availability, but requires that every end system be interconnected to every other system. Therefore, the administrative and physical costs can be significant. Each link is essentially a point-to-point link to the other node.

The three common physical WAN topologies are illustrated in the figure.

A hybrid is a variation or combination of any of the above topologies. For example, a partial mesh is a hybrid topology in which some, but not all, end devices are interconnected.

Refer to **Online Course** for Illustration

5.3.1.4   LAN Topologies

Physical topology defines how the end systems are physically interconnected. In shared media LANs, end devices can be interconnected using the following physical topologies:

- **Star** - End devices are connected to a central intermediate device. Early star topologies interconnected end devices using Ethernet hubs. However, star topologies now use Ethernet switches. The star topology is easy to install, very scalable (easy to add and remove end devices), and easy to troubleshoot.

- **Extended Star** - In an extended star topology, additional Ethernet switches interconnect other star topologies. An extended star is an example of a hybrid topology.

- **Bus** - All end systems are chained to each other and terminated in some form on each end. Infrastructure devices such as switches are not required to interconnect the end devices. Bus topologies using coaxial cables were used in legacy Ethernet networks because it was inexpensive and easy to set up.

- **Ring** - End systems are connected to their respective neighbors, forming a ring. Unlike the bus topology, the ring does not need to be terminated. Ring topologies were used in legacy Fiber Distributed Data Interface (FDDI) and Token Ring networks.

The figure illustrates how end devices are interconnected on LANs.

Refer to **Online Course** for Illustration

5.3.1.5   The Three-Layer Network Design Model

The campus wired LAN uses a hierarchical design model to break the design up into modular groups or layers. Breaking the design up into layers allows each layer to implement specific functions, which simplifies the network design and therefore, the deployment and management of the network.

The campus wired LAN enables communications between devices in a building or group of buildings, as well as interconnection to the WAN and Internet edge at the network core.

A hierarchical LAN design includes the following three layers, as shown in Figure 1:

- Access layer
- Distribution layer
- Core layer

Each layer is designed to meet specific functions.

The access layer provides endpoints and users direct access to the network. The distribution layer aggregates access layers and provides connectivity to services. Finally, the core layer provides connectivity between distribution layers for large LAN environments. User traffic is initiated at the access layer and passes through the other layers if the functionality of those layers is required.

Even though the hierarchical model has three layers, some smaller enterprise networks may implement a two-tier hierarchical design. In a two-tier hierarchical design, the core and distribution layers are collapsed into one layer, reducing cost and complexity, as shown in Figure 2.

In flat or meshed network architectures, changes tend to affect a large number of systems. Hierarchical design helps constrain operational changes to a subset of the network, which makes it easy to manage as well as improve resiliency. Modular structuring of the network into small, easy-to-understand elements also facilitates resiliency via improved fault isolation.

Refer to **Video** in online course

5.3.1.6   Video Tutorial - Three-Layer Network Design

Click Play to view a tutorial about three-layer network design.

Click here to read the transcript of this video.

Click here to download the Packet Tracer file used in the video.

Refer to
Online Course
for Illustration

5.3.1.7 Common Security Architectures

Firewall design is primarily about device interfaces permitting or denying traffic based on the source, the destination, and the type of traffic. Some designs are as simple as designating an outside network and inside network, which are determined by two interfaces on a firewall. As shown in Figure 1, the public network (or outside network) is untrusted, and the private network (or inside network) is trusted. Typically, a firewall with two interfaces is configured as follows:

■ Traffic originating from the private network is permitted and inspected as it travels toward the public network. Inspected traffic returning from the public network and associated with traffic that originated from the private network is permitted.

■ Traffic originating from the public network and traveling to the private network is generally blocked.

A demilitarized zone (DMZ) is a firewall design where there is typically one inside interface connected to the private network, one outside interface connected to the public network, and one DMZ interface, as shown in Figure 2.

■ Traffic originating from the private network is inspected as it travels toward the public or DMZ network. This traffic is permitted with little or no restriction. Inspected traffic returning from the DMZ or public network to the private network is permitted.

■ Traffic originating from the DMZ network and traveling to the private network is usually blocked.

■ Traffic originating from the DMZ network and traveling to the public network is selectively permitted based on service requirements.

■ Traffic originating from the public network and traveling toward the DMZ is selectively permitted and inspected. This type of traffic is typically email, DNS, HTTP, or HTTPS traffic. Return traffic from the DMZ to the public network is dynamically permitted.

■ Traffic originating from the public network and traveling to the private network is blocked.

Zone-based policy firewalls (ZPFs) use the concept of zones to provide additional flexibility. A zone is a group of one or more interfaces that have similar functions or features. Zones help you specify where a Cisco IOS firewall rule or policy should be applied. In Figure 3, security policies for LAN 1 and LAN 2 are similar and can be grouped into a zone for firewall configurations. By default, the traffic between interfaces in the same zone is not subject to any policy and passes freely. However, all zone-to-zone traffic is blocked. In order to permit traffic between zones, a policy allowing or inspecting traffic must be configured.

The only exception to this default deny any policy is the router self zone. The self zone is the router itself and includes all the router interface IP addresses. Policy configurations that include the self zone would apply to traffic destined to and sourced from the router. By default, there is no policy for this type of traffic. Traffic that should be considered when designing a policy for the self zone includes management plane and control plane traffic, such as SSH, SNMP, and routing protocols.

Refer to **Interactive Graphic** in online course

5.3.1.8   Activity - Identify the Network Topology

5.3.1.9   Activity - Identify the Network Design Terminology

Refer to **Interactive Graphic** in online course

5.3.1.10   Packet Tracer - Identify Packet Flow

Refer to **Packet Tracer Activity** for this chapter

In this Packet Tracer activity, you will observe packet flow in a LAN and WAN topology. You will also observe how the packet flow path may change when there is a change in the network topology.

5.4   Summary

5.4.1   Conclusion

Refer to **Online Course** for Illustration

5.4.1.1   Chapter 5: Network Infrastructure

In this chapter, you learned the basic operation of the network infrastructure. Routers are network layer devices and use the process of routing to forward data packets between networks or subnetworks. Switches segment a LAN into separate collision domains, one for each switch port. A switch makes forwarding decisions based on Ethernet MAC addresses. Multilayer switches (also known as Layer 3 switches) not only perform Layer 2 switching, but also forward frames based on Layer 3 and 4 information. Wireless networking devices, such as an AP or WLC, use the 802.11 standard instead of the 802.3 standard to connect wireless devices to the network.

Various types of firewalls enable network security including:

- **Packet filtering (stateless) firewall** - This provides Layer 3 and sometimes Layer 4 filtering.

- **Stateful firewall** - A stateful inspection firewall allows or blocks traffic based on state, port, and protocol.

- **Application gateway firewall (proxy firewall)** - This filters information at Layers 3, 4, 5, and 7.

Network security services enhance network security through the use of the following:

- **ACLs -** These are a series of commands that control whether a device forwards or drops packets based on information found in the packet header.

- **SNMP -** This service enables network administrators to monitor and manage network performance, find and solve network problems, and plan for network growth.

- **NetFlow -** This provides statistics on packets flowing through a Cisco router or multilayer switch.

- **Port mirroring -** This is a feature that allows a switch to make duplicate copies of traffic passing through a switch, and then send it out a port with a network monitor attached.

- **Syslog server -** Use these to access the system messages generated by networking devices.

- **NTP -** his will synchronize the time across all devices on the network to ensure accurate and consistent timestamping of system messages.

- **AAA -** This is a framework for configuring user authentication, authorization, and accounting services.

- **VPN -** This is a private network created between two endpoints across a public network.

Network topologies are typically represented as physical networks and logical networks. A physical network topology refers to the physical connections and identifies how end devices are connected. A logical topology refers to the standards and protocols that devices use to communicate. Most topologies are a combination of both, showing how devices are physically and logically connected.

When looking at a topology that has access to outside or public networks, you should be able to determine the security architecture. Some designs are as simple as designating an outside network and inside network, which are determined by two interfaces on a firewall. Networks that require public access to services will often include a DMZ that the public can access, while strictly blocking access to the inside network. ZPFs use the concept of zones to provide additional flexibility. A zone is a group of one or more interfaces that have similar functions or features.

Go to the online course to take the quiz and exam.

Chapter 5 Quiz

This quiz is designed to provide an additional opportunity to practice the skills and knowledge presented in the chapter and to prepare for the chapter exam. You will be allowed multiple attempts and the grade does not appear in the gradebook.

Chapter 5 Exam

The chapter exam assesses your knowledge of the chapter content.

Your Chapter Notes

Principles of Network Security

6.0 Introduction

6.0.1 Welcome

Refer to
Online Course
for Illustration

6.0.1.1 Chapter 6: Principles of Network Security

The motivation for attacking networks can be financial gain, corporate- or state-sponsored espionage, activism, or simply malicious intent. The people and groups that engage in attacks on our network infrastructures are commonly referred to as threat actors.

This chapter covers the variety of tools and methods threat actors use to launch network attacks.

6.1 Attackers and Their Tools

6.1.1 Who is Attacking Our Network?

Refer to
Online Course
for Illustration

6.1.1.1 Threat, Vulnerability, and Risk

We are under attack and attackers want access to our assets. Assets are anything of value to an organization such as data and other intellectual property, servers, computers, smart phones, tablets, and more.

To better understand any discussion of network security, it is important to know the following terms:

- **Threat** - A potential danger to an asset such as data or the network itself.

- **Vulnerability and Attack Surface** - A weakness in a system or its design that could be exploited by a threat. An attack surface is the total sum of the vulnerabilities in a given system that is accessible to an attacker. The attack surface describes different points where an attacker could get into a system, and where they could get data out of the system. For example, your operating system and web browser could both need security patches. They are each vulnerable to attacks. Together, they create an attack surface the threat actor can exploit.

- **Exploit** - The mechanism that is used to leverage a vulnerability to compromise an asset. Exploits may be remote or local. A remote exploit is one that works over the network without any prior access to the target system. The attacker does not need an account in the end system to exploit the vulnerability. In a local exploit, the threat actor has some type of user or administrative access to the end system. A local exploit does not necessarily mean that the attacker has physical access to the end system.

- **Risk** - The likelihood that a particular threat will exploit a particular vulnerability of an asset and result in an undesirable consequence.

Risk management is the process that balances the operational costs of providing protective measures with the gains achieved by protecting the asset. There are four common ways to manage risk:

- **Risk acceptance** - This is when the cost of risk management options outweighs the cost of the risk itself. The risk is accepted without action.

- **Risk avoidance** - This is an action that avoids any exposure to the risk. This is usually the most expensive risk mitigation option.

- **Risk limitation** - This limits a company's risk exposure by taking some action. It is a strategy employing a bit of risk acceptance along with a bit of risk avoidance. It is the most commonly used risk mitigation strategy.

- **Risk transfer** - The risk is transferred to a willing third party such as an insurance company.

Other commonly used network security terms include:

- **Countermeasure** - The **protection** solution that mitigates a threat or risk.

- **Impact** - The resulting damage to the organization that is caused by the threat.

Note   A local exploit requires inside network access such as a user with an account on the network. A remote exploit does not require an account on the network to exploit that network's vulnerability.

Refer to
Interactive Graphic
in online course

6.1.1.2   Hacker vs. Threat Actor

As we know, "hacker" is a common term used to describe a threat actor. However, the term "hacker" has a variety of meanings:

- A clever programmer capable of developing new programs and coding changes to existing programs to make them more efficient.

- A network professional that uses sophisticated programming skills to ensure that networks are not vulnerable to attack.

- A person who tries to gain unauthorized access to devices on the Internet.

- Individuals who run programs to prevent or slow network access to a large number of users, or corrupt or wipe out data on servers.

As shown in the figure, the terms white hat hacker, black hat hacker, and grey hat hacker are often used to describe hackers.

Good or bad, hacking is an important aspect of network security. In this course, the term threat actor is used when referring to those individuals or groups that could be classified as gray or black hat hackers.

Refer to
Interactive Graphic
in online course

6.1.1.3   Evolution of Threat Actors

Hacking started in the 1960s with phone freaking, or phreaking, which refers to using various audio frequencies to manipulate phone systems. At that time, telephone switches used various tones, or tone dialing, to indicate different functions. Early threat actors realized that by mimicking a tone using a whistle, they could exploit the phone switches to make free long-distance calls.

In the mid-1980s, computer dial-up modems were used to connect computers to networks. Threat actors wrote "war dialing" programs which dialed each telephone number in a given area in search of computers, bulletin board systems, and fax machines. When a phone number was found, password-cracking programs were used to gain access. Since then, general threat actor profiles and motives have changed quite a bit.

The figure displays modern threat actor terms and a brief description of each.

Refer to
Interactive Graphic
in online course

6.1.1.4   Cybercriminals

Cybercriminals are threat actors who are motivated to make money using any means necessary. While sometimes cybercriminals work independently, they are more often financed and sponsored by criminal organizations. It is estimated that globally, cybercriminals steal billions of dollars from consumers and businesses every year.

Cybercriminals operate in an underground economy where they buy, sell, and trade exploits and tools. They also buy and sell the private information and intellectual property they steal from victims. Cybercriminals target small businesses and consumers, as well as large enterprises and industries.

Refer to
Interactive Graphic
in online course

6.1.1.5   Cybersecurity Tasks

Threat actors do not discriminate. They target the vulnerable end devices of home users and small-to-medium sized businesses, as well as large public and private organizations.

To make the Internet and networks safer and more secure, we must all develop good cybersecurity awareness. Cybersecurity is a shared responsibility which all users must practice. For example, we must report cybercrime to the appropriate authorities, be aware of potential threats in email and the web, and guard important information from theft.

Organizations must take action and protect their assets, users, and customers. They must develop and practice cybersecurity tasks such as those listed in the figure.

Refer to
Interactive Graphic
in online course

6.1.1.6   Cyber Threat Indicators

Many network attacks can be prevented by sharing information about attack indicators. Each attack has unique identifiable attributes. These are known as **cyber threat indicators** or simply **attack indicators**.

For instance, a user receives an email claiming they have won a big prize (Figure 1). Clicking on the link in the email results in an attack. The attack indicators could include the fact the user did not enter that contest, the IP address of the sender, the email subject line, the included link to click, or an attachment to download, among others.

Governments are now actively promoting cybersecurity. For instance, the U.S. Department of Homeland Security (DHS) and United States Computer Emergency Readiness Team (US-CERT) are leading efforts to automate the sharing of cybersecurity information with public and private organizations at no cost. DHS and US-CERT use a system called Automated Indicator Sharing (AIS). AIS enables the sharing of attack indicators between the US government and the private sector as soon as the threat is verified.

Click here for more information on AIS.

The DHS also promotes cybersecurity to all users. For instance, they have an annual campaign in October called "Cybersecurity Awareness Month". This campaign was developed to promote and raise awareness about cybersecurity. As shown in Figure 2, the DHS also promotes the "Stop. Think. Connect." campaign to encourage all citizens to be safer and more secure online. The campaign provides material on a wide variety of security topics including:

- Best Practices for Creating a Password
- Best Practices for Using Public Wi-Fi
- Five Every Day Steps Towards Online Safety
- How to Recognize and Prevent Cybercrime
- Five Steps to Protecting Your Digital Home

Click here for a complete list of topics made available by the DHS "Stop. Think. Connect." Campaign.

Refer to **Interactive Graphic** in online course

6.1.1.7   Activity - What Color is my Hat?

6.1.2   Threat Actor Tools

Refer to **Interactive Graphic** in online course

6.1.2.1   Introduction of Attack Tools

To exploit a vulnerability, an attacker must have a technique or tool that can be used. Over the years, attack tools have become more sophisticated, and highly automated, requiring less technical knowledge to use them than in the past.

In the figure, drag the white circle across the timeline to view the relationship between the sophistication of attack tools versus the technical knowledge required to use them.

Refer to **Interactive Graphic** in online course

6.1.2.2   Evolution of Security Tools

Ethical hacking involves many different types of tools to test and keep the network and its data secure. To validate the security of a network and its systems, many network penetration testing tools have been developed. However, many of these tools can also be used by threat actors for exploitation.

Threat actors have also created various hacking tools. These tools are explicitly written for nefarious reasons. Cybersecurity personnel must also know how to use these tools when performing network penetration tests.

Figures 1 and 2 highlight categories of common network penetration testing tools. Notice how some tools are used by white hats and black hats. Keep in mind that the list is not exhaustive as new tools are continually being developed.

Note   Many of these tools are UNIX or Linux based; therefore, a security professional should have a strong UNIX and Linux background.

The Social Engineering Toolkit (SET) was designed by TrustedSec to help white hat hackers and other network security professionals create social engineering attacks to test their own networks.

Click here to learn more about SET.

Refer to
Online Course
for Illustration

6.2.2.8   Strengthening the Weakest Link

Cybersecurity is only as strong as its weakest link. Since computers and other Internet-connected devices have become an essential part of our lives, they no longer seem new or different. People have become very casual in their use of these devices and rarely think about network security. The weakest link in cybersecurity can be the personnel within an organization, with social engineering as a major security threat. Because of this, one of the most effective security measures that an organization can take is to train its personnel and create a "security-aware culture." Read this article from Cisco regarding this essential approach to network security.

Refer to
Lab Activity
for this chapter

6.2.2.9   Lab - Social Engineering

In this lab, you will research examples of social engineering and identify ways to recognize and prevent it.

Refer to
Interactive Graphic
in online course

6.2.2.10   Denial of Service Attacks

Denial-of-Service (DoS) attacks are highly publicized network attacks. A DoS attack results in some sort of interruption of service to users, devices, or applications.

There are two major sources of DoS attacks:

- **Overwhelming Quantity of Traffic** - This is when a network, host, or application is unable to handle an enormous quantity of data, causing the system to crash or become extremely slow.

- **Maliciously Formatted Packets** - This is when maliciously formatted packets are forwarded to a host or application and the receiver is unable to handle an unexpected condition. A buffer overflow attack is a method used in this type of DoS attack. For example, a threat actor forwards packets containing errors that cannot be identified by the application, or forwards improperly formatted packets. This causes the receiving device to crash or run very slowly.

Click Play in the figure to view a simple animation of a DoS attack.

DoS attacks are considered a major risk because they can easily interrupt business processes or essential network services, and cause significant loss. These attacks are relatively simple to conduct, even by an unskilled threat actor.

Refer to
Online Course
for Illustration

6.2.2.11   DDoS Attacks

If threat actors can compromise many hosts, they can perform a Distributed DoS Attack (DDoS). DDoS attacks are similar in intent to DoS attacks, except that a DDoS attack increases in magnitude because it originates from multiple, coordinated sources, as shown in the figure. A DDoS attack can use hundreds or thousands of sources, as in IoT-based DDoS attacks.

The following terms are used to describe components of a DDoS attack:

- **Zombies** - Refers to a group of compromised hosts (i.e., agents). These hosts run malicious code referred to as robots (i.e., bots). The zombie malware continually attempts to self-propagate like a worm.

- **Bots** - Bots are malware that are designed to infect a host and communicate with a handler system. Bots can also log keystrokes, gather passwords, capture and analyze packets, and more.

- **Botnet** - Refers to a group of zombies that have been infected using self-propagating malware (i.e., bots) and are controlled by handlers.

- **Handlers** - Refers to a master **command-and-control (CnC or C2)** server controlling groups of zombies. The originator of a botnet can use Internet Relay Chat (IRC) or a web server on the C2 server to remotely control the zombies.

- **Botmaster** - This is the threat actor in control of the botnet and handlers.

Note   There is an underground economy where botnets can be bought (and sold) for a nominal fee. This can provide threat actors with botnets of infected hosts ready to launch a DDoS attack.

> Refer to
> **Interactive Graphic**
> in online course

6.2.2.12   Example DDoS Attack

As an example, a DDoS attack could proceed as follows:

1. The threat actor builds or purchases a botnet of zombie hosts.

2. Zombie computers continue to scan and infect more targets to create more zombies.

3. When ready, the botmaster uses the handler systems to make the botnet of zombies carry out the DDoS attack on the chosen target.

Click Play in the figure to view an animation of a DDoS attack.

> Refer to
> **Interactive Graphic**
> in online course

6.2.2.13   Buffer Overflow Attack

The goal of a threat actor when using a buffer overflow DoS attack is to find a system memory-related flaw on a server and exploit it. Exploiting the buffer memory by overwhelming it with unexpected values usually renders the system inoperable, creating a DoS attack.

For example, a threat actor enters input that is larger than expected by the application running on a server. The application accepts the large amount of input and stores it in memory. The result is that it may consume the associated memory buffer and potentially overwrite adjacent memory, eventually corrupting the system and causing it to crash.

An early example of using malformed packets was the **Ping of Death**. In this legacy attack, the threat actor sent a ping of death, which was an echo request in an IP packet larger than the maximum packet size of 65,535 bytes. The receiving host would not be able to handle a packet of that size and it would crash.

Buffer overflow attacks are continually evolving. For instance, a remote denial of service attack vulnerability was recently discovered in Microsoft Windows 10. Specifically, a threat actor created malicious code to access out-of-scope memory. When this code is accessed by the Windows AHCACHE.SYS process, it attempts to trigger a system crash, denying service to the user. Click here to read the Talos blog on this attack.

Note   It is estimated that one third of malicious attacks are the result of buffer overflows.

Refer to
Online Course
for Illustration

6.2.2.14   Evasion Methods

Threat actors learned long ago that "to hide is to thrive". This means their malware and attack methods are most effective when they are undetected. For this reason, many attacks use stealthy evasion techniques to disguise an attack payload. Their goal is to prevent detection by network and host defenses.

Some of the evasion methods used by threat actors include:

- **Encryption and tunneling** - This evasion technique uses tunneling to hide the content, or encryption to scramble its contents, making it difficult for many security detection techniques to detect and identify the malware.

- **Resource exhaustion** - This evasion technique keeps the host too busy to properly use security detection techniques.

- **Traffic fragmentation** - This evasion technique splits a malicious payload into smaller packets to bypass network security detection. After the fragmented packets bypass the security detection system, the malware is reassembled and may begin sending sensitive data out of the network.

- **Protocol-level misinterpretation** - This evasion technique occurs when network defenses do not properly handle features of a PDU like a checksum or TTL value. This can trick a firewall into ignoring packets that it should check.

- **Traffic substitution** - In this evasion technique, the threat actor attempts to trick the IPS by obfuscating the data in the payload. This is done by encoding it in a different format. For example, the threat actor could use encoded traffic in Unicode instead of ASCII. The IPS does not recognize the true meaning of the data, but the target end system can read the data.

- **Traffic insertion** - Similar to traffic substitution, but the threat actor inserts extra bytes of data in a malicious sequence of data. The IPS rules miss the malicious data, accepting the full sequence of data.

- **Pivoting** - This technique assumes the threat actor has compromised an inside host and wants to expand their access further into the compromised network. An example is a threat actor who has gained access to the administrator password on a compromised host and is attempting to login to another host using the same credentials.

- **Rootkits** - A rootkit is a complex attacker tool used by experienced threat actors. It integrates with the lowest levels of the operating system. When a program attempts to list files, processes, or network connections, the rootkit presents a sanitized version of the output, eliminating any incriminating output. The goal of the rootkit is to completely hide the activities of the attacker on the local system.

New attack methods are constantly being developed. Network security personnel must be aware of the latest attack methods in order to detect them.

Refer to
Interactive Graphic
in online course

6.2.2.15   Activity - Identify the Types of Network Attack

Refer to
Interactive Graphic
in online course

6.2.2.16   Activity - Components of a DDoS Attack

6.3 Summary

6.3.1 Conclusion

Refer to
Online Course
for Illustration

6.3.1.1 Chapter 6: Principles of Network Security

In this chapter, you learned how networks are attacked. You learned the types of threats and attacks used by threat actors. Threat actors are gray or black hat hackers that attempt to gain unauthorized access to our networks. They may also run programs that prevent or slow network access for others. Cybercriminals are threat actors that are motivated solely by financial gain.

Threat actors use a variety of tools including:

- Password crackers
- Wireless hacking tools
- Network scanning and hacking tools
- Packet crafting tools
- Packet sniffers
- Rootkit detectors
- Forensic tools
- Debuggers
- Hacking operating systems
- Encryption tools
- Vulnerability exploitation tools
- Vulnerability scanners

These tools can be used to launch a variety of attacks including:

- Eavesdropping
- Data modification
- IP address spoofing
- Password cracking
- Denial of service
- Man-in-the-middle
- Compromised key
- Network sniffing

Malware, or malicious code, is software that is specifically designed to damage, disrupt, steal, or generally inflict some other "bad" or illegitimate action on data, hosts, or networks. The three most common types of malware are viruses, worms, and Trojan horses:

- A virus is a type of malware that propagates by inserting a copy of itself into another program.

- Worms are similar to viruses because they replicate and can cause the same type of damage. Whereas a virus requires a host program to run, worms can run by themselves.

- A Trojan horse is software that appears to be legitimate, but it contains malicious code which exploits the privileges of the user that runs it.

Malware continues to evolve. The most dominate attack currently is ransomware. Ransomware is malware that denies access to the infected computer system or its data until the owner pays the cybercriminal.

All the various types of tools threat actors use to launch network attacks can be classified as one or more of the following:

- **Reconnaissance** - This is unauthorized discovery and mapping of systems, services, or vulnerabilities.

- **Access attacks** - These exploit known vulnerabilities to gain entry to web accounts, confidential databases, and other sensitive information.

- **Social engineering** - This is an attempt to manipulate individuals into performing actions or divulging confidential information such as passwords and usernames.

- **Denial of Service** - This occurs by overwhelming the network with a large quantity of traffic, or maliciously formatting packets that the receiver is unable to handle causing the device to run very slowly or even crash.

- **Buffer overflow** - This uses a system memory-related flaw on a server to overwhelm it with unexpected values. The goal is to render it inoperable.

To stay hidden and continue their attack, threat actors use a variety of evasion methods including:

- Encryption and tunneling

- Resource exhaustion

- Traffic fragmentation

- Protocol-level misinterpretation

- Traffic substitution

- Traffic insertion

- Pivoting

- Rootkits

Go to the online course to take the quiz and exam.

Chapter 6 Quiz

This quiz is designed to provide an additional opportunity to practice the skills and knowledge presented in the chapter and to prepare for the chapter exam. You will be allowed multiple attempts and the grade does not appear in the gradebook.

Chapter 6 Exam

The chapter exam assesses your knowledge of the chapter content.

Your Chapter Notes

Network Attacks: A Deeper Look

7.0 Introduction

7.0.1 Welcome

Refer to
Online Course
for Illustration

7.0.1.1 Chapter 7: Network Attacks: A Deeper Look

Cybersecurity analysts use a variety of tools to identify attacks. A solid understanding of protocol vulnerabilities is essential to using these tools.

This chapter covers the importance of traffic monitoring and how it is conducted. This is followed by an in-depth discussion of the vulnerabilities to network protocols and services including IP, TCP, UDP, ARP, DNS, DHCP, HTTP, and email.

Refer to
Lab Activity
for this chapter

7.0.1.2 Class Activity - What's Going On?

In this activity, you will identify the processes running on a computer, the protocol they are using, and their local and remote port addresses.

7.1 Attackers and Their Tools

7.1.1 Who is Attacking Our Network?

Refer to
Online Course
for Illustration

7.1.1.1 Network Security Topology

"All networks are targets" is a common adage used to describe the current landscape of network security. Therefore, to mitigate threats, all networks must be secured and protected as best as possible.

This requires a defense-in-depth approach. It requires using proven methods and secure infrastructure consisting of firewalls, intrusion detection systems (IDSs)/intrusion prevention systems (IPSs), and endpoint security software. These methods and technologies are used to introduce automated monitoring to the network, creating alerts or even automatically blocking offensive devices when something goes wrong.

However, for large networks, an extra layer of protection must be added. Devices such as firewalls and IPSs operate based on pre-configured rules. They monitor traffic and compare it against the configured rules. If there is a match, the traffic is handled according to the rule. This works relatively seamlessly but sometimes, legitimate traffic is mistaken for unauthorized traffic. Called false positives, these situations require human eyes to see and evaluate them before they can be validated. An important part of the job of the security analyst is to review all alerts generated by network devices and validate their nature. Was that file downloaded by user X really malware? Is that website visited by user Y really malicious? Is the printer on the third floor really compromised because it is trying to connect to a server that is out on the Internet? All these questions are commonly asked by security analysts daily. It is their job to determine the correct answers.

Refer to **Online Course** for Illustration

7.1.1.2 Monitoring the Network

The day-to-day operation of a network consists of common patterns of traffic flow, bandwidth usage, and resource access. Together, these patterns identify the normal network behavior. Security analysts must be intimately familiar with the normal network behavior because abnormal network behavior typically indicates a problem.

To discover the normal network behavior, network monitoring must be implemented. Various tools are used to help discover normal network behavior including IDS, packet analyzers, SNMP, NetFlow, and others.

Some of these tools require captured network data. There are two common methods used to capture traffic and send it to network monitoring devices:

- Network Test Access Points (TAPs)

- Traffic mirroring using Switch Port Analyzer (SPAN)

Both of these methods are discussed in this chapter.

Refer to **Online Course** for Illustration

7.1.1.3 Network Taps

A network TAP is typically a passive splitting device implemented inline between a device of interest and the network. A TAP forwards all traffic including physical layer errors to an analysis device.

The figure displays a sample topology displaying a TAP installed between a network firewall and the internal router. Notice how the TAP simultaneously sends both the transmit (TX) data stream from the internal router and the receive (RX) data stream to the internal router on separate, dedicated channels. This ensures that all data arrives at the monitoring device in real time. Therefore, network performance is not affected or degraded by monitoring the connection.

TAPs are also typically fail-safe, which means if it fails or loses power, traffic between the firewall and internal router is not affected.

Click here for information on NetScout TAPs for copper UTP Ethernet, fiber Ethernet, and serial links.

Refer to **Online Course** for Illustration

7.1.1.4 Traffic Mirroring and SPAN

Network switches segment the network by design, limiting the amount of traffic visible by the network monitoring device. Because data capturing for network monitoring requires all traffic to be captured, special techniques must be employed to bypass the network segmentation imposed by network switches. Port mirroring is one of these techniques. Supported by many enterprise switches, port mirroring enables the switch to copy frames of one or more ports to a Switch Port Analyzer (SPAN) port connected to an analysis device.

SPAN terminology includes:

- **Ingress traffic** - Traffic that enters the switch.

- **Egress traffic** - Traffic that leaves the switch.

- **Source (SPAN) port** - Source ports are monitored as traffic entering them is replicated (mirrored) to the destination ports.

- **Destination (SPAN) port** - A port that mirrors source ports. Destination SPAN ports often connect to analysis devices such as a packet analyzer or an IDS.

The figure displays a sample topology that shows a switch interconnecting two hosts. The switch will forward ingress traffic on F0/1 and egress traffic on F0/2 to the destination SPAN port G0/1 connecting to an IDS.

The association between source ports and a destination port is called a SPAN session. In a single session, one or multiple ports can be monitored. On some Cisco switches, session traffic can be copied to more than one destination port. Alternatively, a source VLAN can be specified in which all ports in the source VLAN become sources of SPAN traffic. Each SPAN session can have ports or VLANs as sources, but not both.

Note   A variation of SPAN called Remote SPAN (RSPAN) enables a network administrator to use the flexibility of VLANs to monitor traffic on remote switches.

7.1.2   Introduction to Network Monitoring Tools

Refer to Online Course for Illustration

7.1.2.1   Network Security Monitoring Tools

Common tools used for network security monitoring include:

- Network protocol analyzers (Wireshark and Tcpdump)

- Netflow

- Security Information and Event Management Systems (SIEM)

It is also common for security analysts to rely on log files and Simple Network Management Protocol (SNMP) for network normal behavior discovery.

Practically all systems generate log files to communicate and record their operations. By closely monitoring log files, a security analyst can gather extremely valuable information.

SNMP allows analysts to ask and receive information about the operation of network devices, and is another good tool for monitoring the behavior of a network.

Security analysts must be familiar with all of these tools.

Refer to Interactive Graphic in online course

7.1.2.2   Network Protocol Analyzers

Network protocol analyzers (or "packet sniffer" applications) are programs used to capture traffic. Often including a graphical interface, protocol analyzers show what is happening on the network. Analysts can use these applications to see network exchanges down to the packet level. If a computer has been infected with malware and is currently attacking other computers in the network, the analyst can see that clearly by capturing real-time network traffic and analyzing the packets.

Not only used for security analysis, network protocol analyzers are also very useful for network troubleshooting, software and protocol development, and education. For instance, in security forensics, a security analyst may attempt to reconstruct an incident from relevant packet captures.

Wireshark, shown in Figure 1, has become a very popular network protocol analyzer tool that is used in Windows, Linux, and Mac OS environments. Captured frames are saved in a PCAP file. PCAP files contain the frame information, interface information, packet length, and time stamps.

Performing a long-term packet capture produces large PCAP files.

Wireshark can also open files that contain captured traffic from other software such as the **tcpdump** utility. Popular among UNIX-like systems such as Linux, tcpdump is a powerful utility with numerous command-line options. The example in Figure 2 displays a sample tcpdump capture of ping packets.

Note   **windump** is a Microsoft Windows variant of tcpdump.

Note   **tshark** is Wireshark command line tool similar to tcpdump.

7.1.2.3   NetFlow

Refer to
Online Course
for Illustration

NetFlow is a Cisco IOS technology that provides 24×7 statistics on packets flowing through a Cisco router or multilayer switch. NetFlow is the standard for collecting IP operational data in IP networks. NetFlow is now supported on non-Cisco platforms.

NetFlow can be used for network and security monitoring, network planning, and traffic analysis. It provides a complete audit trail of basic information about every IP flow forwarded on a device. This information includes the source and destination device IP information, the time of the communication, and the amount of data transferred. NetFlow does not capture the actual content on the flow. NetFlow functionality is often compared to a telephone bill. The bill identifies the destination number, the time and duration of the call. However, it does not display the content of the telephone conversation.

Although NetFlow stores flow information in a local cache on the device, it should always be configured to forward data to a NetFlow collector such as Cisco StealthWatch.

For example, in the figure, PC1 connects to PC2 using an application such as HTTPS. NetFlow can monitor that application connection, tracking byte and packet counts for that individual application flow. It then pushes the statistics over to an external server called a NetFlow collector.

NetFlow collectors like Cisco Stealthwatch can also perform advanced functions including:

■ **Flow stitching:** It groups individual entries into flows.

■ **Flow deduplication:** It filters duplicate incoming entries from multiple NetFlow clients.

■ **NAT stitching:** It simplifies flows with NAT entries.

Cisco StealthWatch has many more features than just NetFlow. Click here to see a short video on Cisco StealthWatch.

Refer to
Online Course
for Illustration

7.3.1.4   DNS Tunneling

Botnets have become a popular attack method of threat actors. Most often, botnets are used to spread malware or launch DDoS and phishing attacks.

DNS in the enterprise is sometimes overlooked as a protocol which can be used by botnets. Because of this, when DNS traffic is determined to be part of an incident, the attack is already over. It is necessary for the security analyst to be able to detect when an attacker is using DNS tunneling to steal data, and prevent and contain the attack. To accomplish this, the security analyst must implement a solution that can block the outbound communications from the infected hosts.

Threat actors who use DNS tunneling place non-DNS traffic within DNS traffic. This method often circumvents security solutions. For the threat actor to use DNS tunneling, the different types of DNS records such as TXT, MX, SRV, NULL, A, or CNAME are altered. For example, the TXT record can store the most commands for sending to the infected hosts over DNS replies. A DNS tunneling attack using TXT works like this:

- The data is split into multiple encoded chunks.

- Each chunk is placed into a lower level domain name label of the DNS query.

- Because there is no response from the local or networked DNS for the query, the request is sent to the ISP's recursive DNS servers.

- The recursive DNS service will forward the query to the attacker's authoritative name server.

- The process is repeated until all of the queries containing the chunks are sent.

- When the attacker's authoritative name server receives the DNS queries from the infected devices, it sends responses for each DNS query, which contains the encapsulated, encoded commands.

- The malware on the compromised host recombines the chunks and executes the commands hidden within.

To be able to stop DNS tunneling, a filter that inspects DNS traffic must be used. Pay particular attention to DNS queries that are longer than average, or those that have a suspicious domain name. Also, DNS solutions, like Cisco OpenDNS, block much of the DNS tunneling traffic by identifying suspicious domains.

Click here to learn more about Cisco OpenDNS.

Refer to
Interactive Graphic
in online course

7.3.1.5   DHCP

DHCP servers dynamically provide IP configuration information including IP address, subnet mask, default gateway, DNS servers, and more to clients. The typical sequence of DHCP message exchange between client and server is displayed in Figure 1.

DHCP is vulnerable to DHCP spoofing attacks. A DHCP spoofing attack occurs when a rogue DHCP server is connected to the network and provides false IP configuration parameters to legitimate clients. A rogue server can provide a variety of misleading information:

- **Wrong default gateway** - Threat actor provides an invalid gateway or the IP address of its host to create a MITM attack. This may go entirely undetected as the intruder intercepts the data flow through the network.

■ **Wrong DNS server** - Threat actor provides an incorrect DNS server address pointing the user to a malicious website.

■ **Wrong IP address** - Threat actor provides an invalid IP address, invalid default gateway IP address, or both invalid IP address and default gateway. The threat actor then creates a DoS attack on the DHCP client.

Figures 2 through 5 illustrate a DHCP spoofing attack. Assume a threat actor has successfully connected a rogue DHCP server to a switch port on the same subnet as the target clients. The goal of the rogue server is to provide clients with false IP configuration information.

In Figure 2, a legitimate client connects to the network and requires IP configuration parameters. Therefore, the client broadcasts a DHCP Discover request looking for a response from a DHCP server. Both servers will receive the message. Figure 3 illustrates how the legitimate and rogue DHCP servers each respond with valid IP configuration parameters. The client will reply to the first offer received.

In this scenario, the client received the rogue offer first. It broadcasts a DHCP request accepting the parameters from the rogue server as shown in Figure 4. The legitimate and rogue server will receive the request. However, as shown in Figure 5, only the rogue server unicasts a reply to the client to acknowledge its request. The legitimate server will cease communicating with the client.

DHCP is also vulnerable to a DHCP starvation attack. The goal of this attack is to create a DoS for connecting clients. DHCP starvation attacks require an attack tool such as Gobbler. Gobbler forwards DHCP discovery messages with bogus MAC addresses in an attempt to lease the entire pool of addresses.

Refer to
Lab Activity
for this chapter

7.3.1.6   Lab - Exploring DNS Traffic

In this lab, you will complete the following objectives:

■ Capture DNS Traffic

■ Explore DNS Query Traffic

■ Explore DNS Response Traffic

7.3.2   Enterprise Services

Refer to
Interactive Graphic
in online course

7.3.2.1   HTTP and HTTPS

Internet browsers are used by almost everyone. Blocking web browsing completely is not an option because businesses need access to the web, without undermining web security.

To investigate web-based attacks, security analysts must have a good understanding of how a standard web-based attack works. These are the common stages of a typical web attack:

■ The victim unknowingly visits a web page that has been compromised by malware.

■ The compromised web page redirects the user, often through many compromised servers, to a site containing malicious code.

- The user visits this site with malicious code and their computer becomes infected. This is known as drive-by-downloads. When the user visits the site, an exploit kit scans the software running on the victim's computer including the OS, Java, or Flash player looking for an exploit in the software. The exploit kit is often a PHP script and provides the attacker with a management console to manage the attack.

- After identifying a vulnerable software package running on the victim's computer, the exploit kit contacts the exploit kit server to download code that can use the vulnerability to run malicious code on the victim's computer.

- After the victim's computer has been compromised, it connects to the malware server and downloads a payload. This could be malware, or a file download service that downloads other malware.

- The final malware package is run on the victim's computer.

Independent of the type of attack being used, the main goal of the threat actor is to ensure the victim's web browser ends up on the threat actor's web page, which then serves out the malicious exploit to the victim.

Some malicious sites take advantage of vulnerable plugins or browser vulnerabilities to compromise the client's system. Larger networks rely on IDSs to scan downloaded files for malware. If detected, the IDS issue alerts and records the event to log files for later analysis.

Server connection logs can often reveal information about the type of scan or attack. The different types of connection status codes are listed here:

- **Informational 1xx** - A provisional response, consisting only of the Status-Line and optional headers. It is terminated by an empty line. There are no required headers for this class of status code. Servers MUST NOT send a 1xx response to an HTTP/1.0 client except under experimental conditions.

- **Successful 2xx** - The client's request was successfully received, understood, and accepted.

- **Redirection 3xx** - Further action must be taken by the user agent to fulfill the request. A client SHOULD detect infinite redirection loops, because these loops generate network traffic for each redirection.

- **Client Error 4xx** - For cases in which the client seems to have erred. Except when responding to a HEAD request, the server SHOULD include an entity containing an explanation of the situation, and if it is temporary. User agents SHOULD display any included entity to the user.

- **Server Error 5xx** - For cases where the server is aware that it has erred, or it cannot perform the request. Except when responding to a HEAD request, the server SHOULD include an entity containing an explanation of the error situation, and if it is temporary. User agents SHOULD display any included entity to the user.

Click here for more information about all of the connection status codes.

To defend against web-based attacks, the following countermeasures should be used:

- Always update the OS and browsers with current patches and updates.

- Use a web proxy like Cisco Cloud Web Security or Cisco Web Security Appliance to block malicious sites.

- Use the best security practices from the Open Web Application Security Project (OWASP) when developing web applications.

- Educate end users by showing them how to avoid web-based attacks.

Click here and here to learn more about Cisco Web Security.

Click here to learn more about OWASP.

Malicious iFrames

Threat actors often make use of malicious inline frames (iFrames). An iFrame is an HTML element that allows the browser to load another web page from another source. iFrame attacks have become very common, as they are often used to insert advertisements from other sources into the page. In some instances, the iFrame page that is loaded consists of only a few pixels. This makes it very hard for the user to see. Because the iFrame is run in the page, it can be used to deliver a malicious exploit.

These are some of the ways to prevent or reduce malicious iFrames:

- Use a web proxy like Cisco Cloud Web Security or Cisco Web Security Appliance to block malicious sites.

- Because attackers often change the source of the iFrame in a compromised web site, make sure web developers do not use iFrames to isolate any content from third parties from a web site.

- Use a service such as Cisco OpenDNS to prevent users from navigating to web sites that are known to be malicious.

- Make sure the end user understands what an Iframe is and that threat actors have been using this method often in web-based attacks.

HTTP 302 Cushioning

Another type of HTTP attack is the HTTP 302 cushioning attack. Threat actors use the 302 Found HTTP response status code to direct the user's web browser to the new location. Threat actors often use legitimate HTTP functions such as HTTP redirects to carry out their attacks. HTTP allows servers to redirect a client's HTTP request to a different server. HTTP redirection is used, for example, when web content has moved to a different URL or domain name. This allows old URLs and bookmarks to continue to function. Therefore, security analysts should understand how a function such as HTTP redirection works and how it can be used during attacks.

When the response from the server is a 302 Found status, it also provides the URL in the location field. The browser believes that the new location is the URL provided in the header. The browser is invited to request this new URL. This redirect function can be used multiple times until the browser finally lands on the page that contains the exploit. The redirects may be difficult to detect due to the fact that legitimate redirects frequently occur on the network.

These are some ways to prevent or reduce HTTP 302 cushioning attacks:

- Use a web proxy like Cisco Cloud Web Security or Cisco Web Security Appliance to block malicious sites.

- Use a service such as Cisco OpenDNS to prevent users from navigating to web sites that are known to be malicious.

- Make sure the end user understands how the browser is redirected through a series of HTTP 302 redirections.

Domain Shadowing

When a threat actor wishes to create a domain shadowing attack, they must first compromise a domain. Then they must create multiple subdomains of that domain to be used for the attacks. Hijacked domain registration logins are then used to create the many subdomains needed. After these subdomains have been created, attackers can use them as they wish even if they are found out to be malicious domains. They can simply make more from the parent domain. The following sequence is typically used by threat actors:

- Website becomes compromised

- HTTP 302 cushioning is used

- Domain shadowing is used

- An exploit kit landing page is created

- Malware is spread through its payload

These are some ways to prevent or reduce Domain shadowing attacks

- Secure all domain owner accounts. Use strong passwords and use two-factor authentication to secure these powerful accounts.

- Use a web proxy like Cisco Cloud Web Security or Cisco Web Security Appliance to block malicious sites.

- Use a service such as Cisco OpenDNS to prevent users from navigating to web sites that are known to be malicious.

- Make sure that domain owners validate their registration accounts and look for any subdomains that they have not authorized.

Refer to Interactive Graphic in online course

7.3.2.2   Email

Over the past 25 years, email has evolved from a tool used primarily by technical and research professionals to become the backbone of corporate communications. Each day, more than 100 billion corporate email messages are exchanged. As the level of use rises, security becomes a greater priority. The way that users access email today also increases the opportunity for the threat of malware to be introduced. It used to be that corporate users accessed text-based email from a corporate server. The corporate server was on a workstation that was protected by the company's firewall. Today, HTML messages are accessed from many different devices that are often not protected by the company's firewall. HTML allows more attacks because of the amount of access that can sometimes bypass different security layers.

The following are examples of email threats:

- **Attachment-based attacks** - Threat actors embed malicious content in business files such as an email from the IT department. Legitimate users open malicious content. Malware is used in broad attacks often targeting a specific business vertical to seem legitimate, enticing users working in that vertical to open attachments, or click embedded links.

- **Email spoofing** - Threat actors create email messages with a forged sender address that is meant to fool the recipient into providing money or sensitive information. For example, a bank sends you an email asking you to update your credentials. When this email displays the identical bank logo as mail you have previously opened that was legitimate, it has a higher chance of being opened, having attachments opened and links clicked. The spoofed email may even ask you to verify your credentials so that the bank is assured that you are you, exposing your login information.

- **Spam email** - Threat actors send unsolicited email containing advertisements or malicious files. This type of email is sent most often to solicit a response, telling the threat actor that the email is valid and a user has opened the spam.

- **Open mail relay server** - Threat actors take advantage of enterprise servers that are misconfigured as open mail relays to send large volumes of spam or malware to unsuspecting users. The open mail relay is an SMTP server that allows anybody on the Internet to send mail. Because anyone can use the server, they are vulnerable to spammers and worms. Very large volumes of spam can be sent by using an open mail relay. It is important that corporate email servers are never set up as an open relay. This will considerably reduce the amount of unsolicited emails.

- **Homoglyphs** - Threat actors can use text characters that are very similar or even identical to legitimate text characters. These can be used in phishing emails to make them look very convincing. In DNS, these characters are very different from the real thing. When the DNS record is searched, a completely different URL is found when the link with the homoglyph is used in the search.

Just like any other service that is listening to a port for incoming connections, SMTP servers also may have vulnerabilities. Always keep SMTP software up to date with security and software patches and updates. To further prevent threat actors from completing their task of fooling the end user, implement countermeasures. Use a security appliance specific to email such as the Cisco Email Security Appliance. This will help to detect and block many known types of threats such as phishing, spam, and malware. Also, educate the end user. When attacks make it by the security measures in place, and they will sometimes, the end user is the last line of defense. Teach them how to recognize spam, phishing attempts, suspicious links and URLs, homoglyphs, and to never open suspicious attachments.

Refer to **Online Course** for Illustration

7.3.2.3 Web-Exposed Databases

Web applications commonly connect to a relational database to access data. Because relational databases often contain sensitive data, databases are a frequent target for attacks.

Command Injection

Attackers are able to execute commands on a web server's OS through a web application that is vulnerable. This might occur if the web application provides input fields to the attacker for entering malicious data. The attacker's commands that are executed through the web application have the same permissions as the web application. This type of attack is used because often there is insufficient validation of input. SQL injection and XSS are two different types of command injection.

SQL Injection

SQL is the language used to query a relational database. Threat actors use SQL injections to breach the relational database, create malicious SQL queries, and obtain sensitive data from the relational database.

One of the most common database attacks is the SQL injection attack. The SQL injection attack consists of inserting a SQL query via the input data from the client to the application. A successful SQL injection exploit can read sensitive data from the database, modify database data, execute administration operations on the database, and, sometimes, issue commands to the operating system.

Unless an application uses strict input data validation, it will be vulnerable to the SQL injection attack. If an application accepts and processes user-supplied data without any input data validation, a threat actor could submit a maliciously crafted input string to trigger the SQL injection attack.

Security analysts should be able to recognize suspicious SQL queries in order to detect if the relational database has been subjected to SQL injection attacks. They need to be able to determine which user ID was used by the threat actor to log in, then identify any information or further access the threat actor could have leveraged after a successful login.

Cross-Site Scripting

Not all attacks are initiated from the server side. Cross-Site Scripting (XSS) is where web pages that are executed on the client-side, within their own web browser, are injected with malicious scripts. These scripts can be used by Visual Basic, JavaScript, and others to access a computer, collect sensitive information, or deploy more attacks and spread malware. As with SQL injection, this is often due to the attacker posting content to a trusted website with a lack of input validation. Future visitors to the trusted web site will be exposed to the content provided by the attacker.

These are the two main types of XSS:

- **Stored (persistent)** - This is permanently stored on the infected server and is received by all visitors to the infected page.

- **Reflected (non-persistent)** - This only requires that the malicious script is located in a link and visitors must click the infected link to become infected.

These are some ways to prevent or reduce command injection attacks:

- Use the items listed in the OWASP XSS prevention cheat sheet for web application developers:

- Use an IPS implementation to detect and prevent malicious scripts.

- Use a web proxy like Cisco Cloud Web Security or Cisco Web Security Appliance to block malicious sites.

- Use a service such as Cisco OpenDNS to prevent users from navigating to web sites that are known to be malicious.

- As with all other security measures, be sure to educate end users. Teach them to identify phishing attacks and notify infosec personnel when they are suspicious of anything security-related.

Refer to
Lab Activity
for this chapter

7.3.2.4 Lab - Attacking a MySQL Database

In this lab, you will view a PCAP file from a previous attack against a SQL database.

Refer to
Lab Activity
for this chapter

7.3.2.5 Lab - Reading Server Logs

In this lab, you will complete the following objectives:

- Reading Log Files with Cat, More, and Less

- Log Files and Syslog

- Log Files and Journalctl

Refer to
Lab Activity
for this chapter

7.3.2.6 Lab - Reading Server Logs

In this lab, you will complete the following objectives:

- Reading Log Files with Cat, More, and Less

- Log Files and Syslog

- Log Files and Journalctl

7.4 Summary

7.4.1 Conclusion

Refer to
Online Course
for Illustration

7.4.1.1 Chapter 7: Network Attacks: A Deeper Look

In this chapter, you learned the importance of network monitoring and the tools used by cybersecurity analysts. These tools include port mirroring, protocol analyzers, and SIEMs.

You also learned about the inherent vulnerabilities in network protocols and services.

IP is vulnerable to a variety of attacks including:

- ICMP attacks

- DoS attacks

- DDoS attacks

- Address spoofing attacks

- Man-in-the-middle attack (MITM)

- Session hijacking

TCP is also vulnerable to TCP SYN flood attacks, TCP reset attacks, and TCP session hijacking attacks. UDP is vulnerable to checksum modification attacks and UDP flood attacks.

IP services have a several of vulnerabilities including:

- ARP cache poisoning

- DNS attacks including poisoning, amplification and reflection, resource utilization, and stealth attacks

- DNS tunneling for botnets and other malicious activity

- DHCP spoofing and starvation attacks

- Web attacks through unsecure HTTP, iFrames, and HTTP 302 cushioning

- SQL injection attacks

- Cross-site scripting attacks

Go to the online course to take the quiz and exam.

Chapter 7 Quiz

This quiz is designed to provide an additional opportunity to practice the skills and knowledge presented in the chapter and to prepare for the chapter exam. You will be allowed multiple attempts and the grade does not appear in the gradebook.

Chapter 7 Exam

The chapter exam assesses your knowledge of the chapter content.

Your Chapter Notes

Protecting the Network

8.0 Introduction

8.0.1 Welcome

Refer to
Online Course
for Illustration

8.0.1.1 Chapter 8: Protecting the Network

Protecting our networks will continue to be a challenge. Millions of new devices are joining our networks every year as the Internet of Things (IoT) continues to expand. In addition, with wireless capabilities those devices can be almost anywhere. Threat actors will continue to look for vulnerabilities that can be exploited.

We use a variety of methods to protect our networks, devices, and data. This chapter covers approaches to network security defense, access control methods, and the various sources cybersecurity analysts rely on for threat intelligence.

8.1 Understanding Defense

8.1.1 Defense-in-Depth

Refer to
Interactive Graphic
in online course

8.1.1.1 Assets, Vulnerabilities, Threats

Cybersecurity analysts must prepare for any type of attack. It is their job to secure the assets of the organization's network. To do this, cybersecurity analysts must first identify:

- **Assets** - Anything of value to an organization that must be protected including servers, infrastructure devices, end devices, and the greatest asset, data.

- **Vulnerabilities** - A weakness in a system or its design that could be exploited by a threat.

- **Threats** - Any potential danger to an asset.

Refer to
Interactive Graphic
in online course

8.1.1.2 Identify Assets

As an organization grows, so do its assets. Consider the number of assets a large organization would have to protect. It may also acquire other assets through mergers with other companies. The result is that many organizations only have a general idea of the assets that need to be protected.

The collection of all the devices and information owned or managed by the organization are the assets. The assets constitute the attack surface that threat actors could target. These assets must be inventoried and assessed for the level of protection needed to thwart potential attacks.

Asset management consists of inventorying all assets, and then developing and implementing policies and procedures to protect them. This task can be daunting considering many organizations must protect internal users and resources, mobile workers, and cloud-based and virtual services.

Further, organizations need to identify where critical information assets are stored, and how access is gained to that information. Information assets vary, as do the threats against them. For example, a retail business may store customer credit card information. An engineering firm will store competition-sensitive designs and software. A bank will store customer data, account information, and other sensitive financial information. Each of these assets can attract different threat actors who have different skill-levels and motivations.

Refer to
Online Course
for Illustration

8.1.1.3   Identify Vulnerabilities

Threat identification provides an organization with a list of likely threats for a particular environment. When identifying threats, it is important to ask several questions:

- What are the possible vulnerabilities of a system?

- Who may want to exploit those vulnerabilities to access specific information assets?

- What are the consequences if system vulnerabilities are exploited and assets are lost?

For example, as highlighted in the figure, threat identification for an e-banking system would include:

- **Internal system compromise** - The attacker uses the exposed e-banking servers to break into an internal bank system.

- **Stolen customer data** - An attacker steals the personal and financial data of bank customers from the customer database.

- **Phony transactions from an external server** - An attacker alters the code of the e-banking application and makes transactions by impersonating a legitimate user.

- **Phony transactions using a stolen customer PIN or smart card** - An attacker steals the identity of a customer and completes malicious transactions from the compromised account.

- **Insider attack on the system** - A bank employee finds a flaw in the system from which to mount an attack.

- **Data input errors** - A user inputs incorrect data or makes incorrect transaction requests.

- **Data center destruction** - A cataclysmic event severely damages or destroys the data center.

Identifying vulnerabilities on a network requires an understanding of the important applications that are used, as well as the different vulnerabilities of that application and hardware. This can require a significant amount of research on the part of the network administrator.

Refer to
Online Course
for Illustration

8.1.1.4   Identify Threats

Organizations must use a defense-in-depth approach to identify threats and secure vulnerable assets. This approach uses multiple layers of security at the network edge, within the network, and on network endpoints.

For example, the figure displays a simple topology of a defense-in-depth approach:

- **Edge router** - The first line of defense is known as an edge router (R1 in the figure). The edge router has a set of rules specifying which traffic it allows or denies. It passes all connections that are intended for the internal LAN to the firewall.

- **Firewall** - A second line of defense is the firewall. The firewall is a checkpoint device that performs additional filtering and tracks the state of the connections. It denies the initiation of connections from the outside (untrusted) networks to the inside (trusted) network while enabling internal users to establish two-way connections to the untrusted networks. It can also perform user authentication (authentication proxy) to grant external remote users access to internal network resources.

- **Internal router** - Another line of defense is the internal router (R2 in the figure). It can apply final filtering rules on the traffic before it is forwarded to its destination.

Routers and firewalls are not the only devices that are used in a defense-in-depth approach. Other security devices include Intrusion Prevention Systems (IPS), advanced malware protection (AMP), web and email content security systems, identity services, network access controls and more.

In the layered defense-in-depth security approach, the different layers work together to create a security architecture in which the failure of one safeguard does not affect the effectiveness of the other safeguards.

Refer to
Interactive Graphic
in online course

8.1.1.5   Security Onion and Security Artichoke Approaches

A common analogy used to describe a defense-in-depth approach is called the "security onion." As illustrated in Figure 1, a threat actor would have to peel away at a network's defense mechanisms in a manner similar to peeling an onion.

However, the changing landscape of networking, such as the evolution of borderless networks, has changed this analogy to the "security artichoke", which benefits the threat actor. As illustrated in Figure 2, threat actors no longer have to peel away each layer. They only need to remove certain "artichoke leaves." The bonus is that each "leaf" of the network may reveal sensitive data that is not well secured. For example, it's easier for a threat actor to compromise a mobile device than it is to compromise an internal computer or server that is protected by layers of defense. Each mobile device is a leaf. And leaf after leaf, it all leads the hacker to more data. The heart of the artichoke is where the most confidential data is found. Each leaf provides a layer of protection while simultaneously providing a path to attack.

Not every leaf needs to be removed in order to get at the heart of the artichoke. The hacker chips away at the security armor along the perimeter to get to the "heart" of the enterprise.

While Internet-facing systems are usually very well protected and boundary protections are typically solid, persistent hackers, aided by a mix of skill and luck, do eventually find a gap in that hard-core exterior through which they can enter and go where they please.

Note   The security onion described on this page is a way of visualizing defense-in-depth. This is not to be confused with the Security Onion suite of network security tools.

8.1.2   Security Policies

Refer to
Interactive Graphic
in online course

8.1.2.1   Business Policies

Business policies are the guidelines developed by an organization to govern its actions. The policies define standards of correct behavior for the business and its employees. In networking, policies define the activities that are allowed on the network. This sets a baseline of acceptable use. If behavior that violates business policy is detected on the network, it is possible that a security breach has occurred.

An organization may have several guiding policies:

- **Company policies** - These policies establish the rules of conduct and the responsibilities of both employees and employers. Policies protect the rights of workers as well as the business interests of employers. Depending on the needs of the organization, various policies and procedures establish rules regarding employee conduct, attendance, dress code, privacy and other areas related to the terms and conditions of employment.

- **Employee policies** - These policies are created and maintained by human resources staff to identify employee salary, pay schedule, employee benefits, work schedule, vacations, and more. They are often provided to new employees to review and sign.

- **Security policies** - These policies identify a set of security objectives for a company, define the rules of behavior for users and administrators, and specify system requirements. These objectives, rules, and requirements collectively ensure the security of a network and the computer systems in an organization. Much like a continuity plan, a security policy is a constantly evolving document based on changes in the threat landscape, vulnerabilities, and business and employee requirements.

Refer to
Online Course
for Illustration

8.1.2.2   Security Policy

A comprehensive security policy has a number of benefits:

- Demonstrates an organization's commitment to security

- Sets the rules for expected behavior

- Ensures consistency in system operations, software and hardware acquisition and use, and maintenance

- Defines the legal consequences of violations

- Gives security staff the backing of management

Security policies are used to inform users, staff, and managers of an organization's requirements for protecting technology and information assets. A security policy also specifies the mechanisms that are needed to meet security requirements and provides a baseline from which to acquire, configure, and audit computer systems and networks for compliance.

As shown in the figure, a security policy may include the following:

- **Identification and authentication policy** - Specifies authorized persons that can have access to network resources and identity verification procedures.

- **Password policies** - Ensures passwords meet minimum requirements and are changed regularly.

- **Acceptable use policy (AUP)** - Identifies network applications and uses that are acceptable to the organization. It may also identify ramifications if this policy is violated.

- **Remote access policy** - Identifies how remote users can access a network and what is accessible via remote connectivity.

- **Network maintenance policy** - Specifies network device operating systems and end user application update procedures.

- **Incident handling procedures** - Describes how security incidents are handled.

One of the most common security policy components is an acceptable use policy (AUP). This can also be referred to as an appropriate use policy. This component defines what users are allowed and not allowed to do on the various system components. This includes the type of traffic that is allowed on the network. The AUP should be as explicit as possible to avoid misunderstanding. For example, an AUP might list specific websites, newsgroups, or bandwidth intensive applications that are prohibited from being accessed by company computers or from the company network. Every employee should be required to sign an AUP, and the signed AUPs should be retained for the duration of employment.

8.1.2.3   BYOD Policies

Refer to **Online Course** for Illustration

Many organizations must now also support Bring Your Own Device (BYOD). This enables employees to use their own mobile devices to access company systems, software, networks, or information. BYOD provides several key benefits to enterprises, including increased productivity, reduced IT and operating costs, better mobility for employees, and greater appeal when it comes to hiring and retaining employees.

However, these benefits also bring an increased information security risk, because BYOD can lead to data breaches and greater liability for the organization.

A BYOD security policy should be developed to accomplish the following:

- Specify the goals of the BYOD program.

- Identify which employees can bring their own devices.

- Identify which devices will be supported.

- Identify the level of access employees are granted when using personal devices.

- Describe the rights to access and activities permitted to security personnel on the device.

- Identify which regulations must be adhered to when using employee devices.

- Identify safeguards to put in place if a device is compromised.

The following BYOD security best practices help mitigate BYOD risks:

■ **Password protect access** - Use unique passwords for each device and account.

■ **Manually control wireless connectivity** - Turn off Wi-Fi and Bluetooth connectivity when not in use. Connect only to trusted networks.

■ **Keep updated** - Always keep the device OS and other software updated. Updated software often contains security patches to mitigate against the latest threats or exploits.

■ **Back up data** - Enable backup of the device in case it is lost or stolen.

■ **Enable "Find my Device"** - Subscribe to a device locator service with remote wipe feature.

■ **Provide antivirus software** - Provide antivirus software for approved BYOD devices.

■ **Use Mobile Device Management (MDM) software** - MDM software enables IT teams to implement security settings and software configurations on all devices that connect to company networks.

Refer to
Interactive Graphic
in online course

8.1.2.4   Regulatory and Standard Compliance

There are also external regulations regarding network security. Network security professionals must be familiar with the laws and codes of ethics that are binding on Information Systems Security (INFOSEC) professionals.

Many organizations are mandated to develop and implement security policies. Compliance regulations define what organizations are responsible for providing and the liability if they fail to comply. The compliance regulations that an organization is obligated to follow depend on the type of organization and the data that the organization handles. Specific compliance regulations will be discussed later in the course.

8.2   Access Control

8.2.1   Access Control Concepts

Refer to
Online Course
for Illustration

8.2.1.1   Communications Security: CIA

Information security deals with protecting information and information systems from unauthorized access, use, disclosure, disruption, modification, or destruction.

As shown in the figure, the CIA triad consists of three components of information security:

■ **Confidentiality** - Only authorized individuals, entities, or processes can access sensitive information.

■ **Integrity** - Refers to the protection of data from unauthorized alteration.

■ **Availability** - Authorized users must have uninterrupted access to important resources and data.

Network data can be encrypted (made unreadable to unauthorized users) using various cryptography applications. The conversation between two IP phone users can be encrypted. The files on a computer can also be encrypted. These are just a few examples. Cryptography can be used almost anywhere that there is data communication. In fact, the trend is toward all communication being encrypted.

Refer to
Online Course
for Illustration

8.2.1.2   Access Control Models

An organization must implement proper access controls to protect its network resources, information system resources, and information.

A security analyst should understand the different basic access control models to have a better understanding of how attackers can break the access controls.

- **Mandatory access control (MAC)** - Applies the strictest access control and is typically used in military or mission critical applications. It assigns security level labels to information and enables users with access based on their security level clearance.

- **Discretionary access control (DAC)** - It allows users to control access to their data as owners of that data. DAC may use ACLs or other methods to specify which users or groups of users have access to the information.

- **Non-Discretionary access control** - Access decisions are based on an individual's roles and responsibilities within the organization, also known as role-based access control (RBAC).

- **Attribute-based access control (ABAC)** - Allows access based on attributes of the object (resource) be to accessed, the subject (user) accessing the resource, and environmental factors regarding how the object is to be accessed, such as time of day.

Another access control model is the principle of least privilege, which specifies a limited, as-needed approach to granting user and process access rights to specific information and tools. The principle of least privilege states that users should be granted the minimum amount of access required to perform their work function.

A common exploit is known as privilege escalation. In this exploit, vulnerabilities in servers or access control systems are exploited to grant an unauthorized user, or software process, higher levels of privilege than they should have. After the privilege is granted, the threat actor can access sensitive information or take control of a system.

Refer to
Interactive Graphic
in online course

8.2.1.3   Activity - Identify the Access Control Model

8.2.2   AAA Usage and Operation

Refer to
Online Course
for Illustration

8.2.2.1   AAA Operation

A network must be designed to control who is allowed to connect to it and what they are allowed to do when they are connected. These design requirements are identified in the network security policy. The policy specifies how network administrators, corporate users, remote users, business partners, and clients access network resources. The network security policy can also mandate the implementation of an accounting system that tracks who logged in and when and what they did while logged in. Some compliance regulations may specify that access must be logged and the logs retained for a set period of time.

The Authentication, Authorization, and Accounting (AAA) protocol provides the necessary framework to enable scalable access security.

Network and administrative AAA security has several functional components:

- **Authentication** - Users and administrators must prove that they are who they say they are. Authentication can be established using username and password combinations, challenge and response questions, token cards, and other methods. For example: "I am user 'student'. I know the password to prove that I am user 'student'."

- **Authorization** - After the user is authenticated, authorization services determine which resources the user can access and which operations the user is allowed to perform. An example is "User 'student' can access host serverXYZ using Telnet only."

- **Accounting and auditing** - Accounting records what the user does and when they do it, including what is accessed, the amount of time the resource is accessed, and any changes that were made. Accounting keeps track of how network resources are used. An example is "User 'student' accessed host serverXYZ using Telnet for 15 minutes."

This concept is similar to the use of a credit card, as indicated by the figure. The credit card identifies who can use it, how much that user can spend, and keeps account of what items the user spent money on.

Refer to **Interactive Graphic** in online course

8.2.2.2   AAA Authentication

AAA Authentication can be used to authenticate users for administrative access or it can be used to authenticate users for remote network access. Cisco provides two common methods of implementing AAA services:

- **Local AAA Authentication** - This method is sometimes known as self-contained authentication because it authenticates users against locally stored usernames and passwords, as shown in Figure 1. Local AAA is ideal for small networks.

- **Server-Based AAA Authentication** - This method authenticates against a central AAA server that contains the usernames and passwords for all users, as shown in Figure 2. Server-based AAA authentication is appropriate for medium-to-large networks.

Centralized AAA is more scalable and manageable than local AAA authentication and therefore, it is the preferred AAA implementation.

A centralized AAA system may independently maintain databases for authentication, authorization, and accounting. It can leverage Active Directory or Lightweight Directory Access Protocol (LDAP) for user authentication and group membership, while maintaining its own authorization and accounting databases.

Devices communicate with the centralized AAA server using either the Remote Authentication Dial-In User Service (RADIUS) or Terminal Access Controller Access Control System (TACACS+) protocols.

The following are specifics of the RADIUS protocol:

- RADIUS uses UDP ports 1812 and 1813, or 1645 and 1646.

- RADIUS combines authentication and authorization.

- RADIUS encrypts only the password in the access-request packet from the client to the server. The remainder of the packet is unencrypted, leaving the username, authorized services, and accounting unprotected.

The following are specifics of the TACACS+ protocol:

- TACACS+ uses TCP port 49.

- TACACS+ separates authentication, authorization, and accounting.

- TACACS+ encrypts the entire body of the packet but leaves a standard TACACS+ header.

Refer to
Online Course
for Illustration

8.2.2.3   AAA Accounting Logs

Centralized AAA also enables the use of the Accounting method. Accounting records from all devices are sent to centralized repositories, enabling simplified auditing of user actions.

AAA Accounting collects and reports usage data in AAA logs. These logs are useful for security auditing. The collected data might include the start and stop connection times, executed commands, number of packets, and number of bytes.

One widely deployed use of accounting is to combine it with AAA authentication. This helps with managing access to internetworking devices by network administrative staff. Accounting provides more security than just authentication. The AAA servers keep a detailed log of exactly what the authenticated user does on the device, as shown in Figure 1. This includes all EXEC and configuration commands issued by the user. The log contains numerous data fields, including the username, the date and time, and the actual command that was entered by the user. This information is useful when troubleshooting devices. It also provides evidence against individuals who perform malicious actions.

Figure 2 displays the various types of accounting information that can be collected.

Refer to
Interactive Graphic
in online course

8.2.2.4   Activity - Identify the Characteristic of AAA

8.3   Threat Intelligence

8.3.1   Information Sources

Refer to
Interactive Graphic
in online course

8.3.1.1   Network Intelligence Communities

To effectively protect a network, security professionals must stay informed and gain network intelligence. There are many security organizations which provide network intelligence. They provide resources, workshops, and conferences to help security professionals. These organizations often have the latest information on threats and vulnerabilities.

Click the logos in the figure to learn more about a few important network security organizations.

To remain effective, a network security professional must:

- **Keep abreast of the latest threats** - This includes subscribing to real-time feeds regarding threats, routinely perusing security-related websites, following security blogs and podcasts, and more.

■ **Continue to upgrade skills** - This includes attending security-related training, workshops, and conferences.

Note Network security has a very steep learning curve and requires a commitment to continuous professional development.

Refer to
Interactive Graphic
in online course

8.3.1.2   Cisco Cybersecurity Reports

A resource to help security professionals stay abreast of the latest threats is the Cisco Annual Cybersecurity Report, and the Mid-Year Cybersecurity Report. These reports provide an update on the state of security preparedness, expert analysis of top vulnerabilities, factors behind the explosion of attacks using adware and spam, and more.

Cybersecurity analysts should subscribe to and read these reports to learn how threat actors are targeting their networks, and what can be done to mitigate these attacks.

Click here to download the latest and past Cisco Cybersecurity Reports.

Refer to
Online Course
for Illustration

8.3.1.3   Security Blogs and Podcasts

Another method for keeping up-to-date on the latest threats is to read blogs and listen to podcasts. Blogs and podcasts also provide advice, research, and recommended mitigation techniques.

There are several security blogs and podcasts available that a cybersecurity analyst should follow to learn about the latest threats, vulnerabilities, and exploits.

As shown in the figure, Cisco provides a downloadable podcast and a blog from the Cisco Talos group.

Click here to read more about Talos security blog and podcast.

8.3.2   Threat Intelligence Services

Refer to
Online Course
for Illustration

8.3.2.1   Cisco Talos

Threat intelligence services allow the exchange of threat information such as vulnerabilities, indicators of compromise (IOC), and mitigation techniques. This information is not only shared with personnel, but also with security systems. As threats emerge, threat intelligence services create and distribute firewall rules and IOCs to the devices that have subscribed to the service.

One such service is the Cisco Talos group. Talos is a world leading threat intelligence team with a goal to help protect enterprise users, data, and infrastructure from active adversaries. The Talos team collects information about active, existing, and emerging threats. Talos then provides comprehensive protection against these attacks and malware to its subscribers.

Cisco Security products can use Talos threat intelligence in real time to provide fast and effective security solutions.

Cisco Talos also provides free software, services, resources, and data.

Click here to learn more about Cisco Talos and emerging security threats and vulnerabilities.

Refer to
Online Course
for Illustration

8.3.2.2   FireEye

FireEye is another security company that offers services to help enterprises secure their networks. FireEye uses a three-pronged approach combining security intelligence, security expertise and technology.

The FireEye Malware Protection System blocks attacks across web and email threat vectors, and latent malware that resides on file shares. It can block advanced malware that easily bypasses traditional signature-based defenses and compromises the majority of enterprise networks. It addresses all stages of an attack lifecycle with a signature-less engine utilizing stateful attack analysis to detect zero-day threats.

Click here to learn more about FireEye and view the security intelligence resources it offers.

Refer to
Online Course
for Illustration

8.3.2.3   Automated Indicator Sharing

The U.S. Department of Homeland Security (DHS) offers a free service called Automated Indicator Sharing (AIS). AIS enables the real-time exchange of cyber threat indicators (e.g., malicious IP addresses, the sender address of a phishing email, etc.) between the U.S. Federal Government and the private sector.

AIS creates an ecosystem where, as soon as a threat is recognized, it is immediately shared with the community to help them protect their networks from that particular threat.

Click here to learn more about the DHS AIS service.

Refer to
Online Course
for Illustration

8.3.2.4   Common Vulnerabilities and Exposures Database

The United States government sponsored the MITRE Corporation to create and maintain a catalog of known security threats called Common Vulnerabilities and Exposures (CVE). The CVE serves as a dictionary of common names (i.e., CVE Identifiers) for publicly known cybersecurity vulnerabilities.

The MITRE Corporation defines unique CVE Identifiers for publicly known information-security vulnerabilities to make it easier to share data.

Click here to learn more about CVE.

Refer to
Online Course
for Illustration

8.3.2.5   Threat Intelligence Communication Standards

Network organizations and professionals must share information to increase knowledge about threat actors and the assets they want to access. Several intelligence sharing open standards have evolved to enable communication across multiple networking platforms. These standards enable the exchange of cyber threat intelligence (CTI) in an automated, consistent, and machine readable format.

Two common threat intelligence sharing standards include:

- **Structured Threat Information Expression (STIX)** - This is a set of specifications for exchanging cyber threat information between organizations. The Cyber Observable Expression (CybOX) standard has been incorporated into STIX.

- **Trusted Automated Exchange of Indicator Information (TAXII)** - This is the specification for an application layer protocol that allows the communication of CTI over HTTPS. TAXII is designed to support STIX.

These open standards provide the specifications that aid in the automated exchange of cyber threat intelligence information in a standardized format.

Click here to learn more about STIX and TAXII.

Refer to
Interactive Graphic
in online course

8.3.2.6   Activity - Identify the Threat Intelligence Information Source

8.4   Summary

8.4.1   Conclusion

Refer to
Online Course
for Illustration

8.4.1.1   Chapter 8: Protecting the Network

In this chapter, you learned the importance of protecting our networks, devices, and data from threat actors.

Organizations must use a defense-in-depth approach to identify threats and secure vulnerable assets. This approach uses multiple layers of security at the network edge, within the network, and on network endpoints.

Organizations must also have a set of policies that define the activities that are allowed on the network. These include business policies, security policies, BYOD policies, and policies that ensure the organization complies with governmental regulations.

Access control methods are used to protect the confidentiality, integrity, and availability of our networks, devices, and data. Access control models include:

- Mandatory access control
- Discretionary access control
- Non-Discretionary access control
- Attribute-based access control

AAA security provides the necessary framework to enable scalable access security:

- **Authentication** - Users and administrators must prove that they are who they say they are.
- **Authorization** - After the user is authenticated, authorization services determine which resources the user can access and which operations the user is allowed to perform.
- **Accounting** - Records what the user does and when they do it, including what is accessed, the amount of time the resource is accessed, and any changes that were made.

Security experts and cybersecurity analysts rely on various information sources to keep abreast of the latest threats and continue to upgrade their skills. Threat intelligences services, such as Cisco Talos, FireEye, DHC AIS, and the CVE database, allow the exchange of threat information such as vulnerabilities, indicators of compromise (IOC), and mitigation techniques. These services are guided by the threat intelligence sharing standards STIX and TAXII.

Go to the online course to take the quiz and exam.

Chapter 8 Quiz

This quiz is designed to provide an additional opportunity to practice the skills and knowledge presented in the chapter and to prepare for the chapter exam. You will be allowed multiple attempts and the grade does not appear in the gradebook.

Chapter 8 Exam

The chapter exam assesses your knowledge of the chapter content.

Your Chapter Notes

Cryptography and the Public Key Infrastructure

9.0 Introduction

9.0.1 Welcome

Refer to
Online Course
for Illustration

9.0.1.1 Chapter 9: Cryptography and the Public Key Infrastructure

When Internet standards were first drafted, no one was thinking that data would need to be protected from threat actors. As you have seen in previous chapters, the protocols of the TCP/IP protocol suite are vulnerable to a variety of attacks.

To address these vulnerabilities, we use a variety of cryptographic technologies to keep our data private and secure. However, cryptography is a double-edge sword in that threat actors can also use it to hide their actions. This chapter covers the impact of cryptography on network security monitoring.

Refer to
Lab Activity
for this chapter

9.0.1.2 Class Activity - Creating Codes

Secret codes have been used for thousands of years. Ancient Greeks and Spartans used a scytale (rhymes with Italy) to encode messages. Romans used a Caesar cipher to encrypt messages. A few hundred years ago, the French used the Vigenère cipher to encode messages. Today, there are many ways that messages can be encoded.

In this lab, you will create and encrypt messages using online tools.

9.1 Cryptography

9.1.1 What is Cryptography?

Refer to
Interactive Graphic
in online course

9.1.1.1 Securing Communications

To ensure secure communications across both public and private networks, the first goal is to secure devices including routers, switches, servers, and hosts.

For example, the topology in Figure 1 displays a number of secure devices indicated by the padlock or red brick firewall icon. Network infrastructure devices and hosts are secured using a variety of techniques:

- Device hardening
- AAA (Authentication, Authorization, and Accounting) access control
- Access Control Lists (ACLs)
- Firewalls

- Monitoring threats using an intrusion prevention system (IPS)

- Securing endpoints using Advanced Malware Protection (AMP)

- Enforcing email and web security using the Cisco Email Security Appliance (ESA) and Cisco Web Security Appliance (WSA)

The next goal is to secure the data as it travels across various links. This may include internal traffic, but of greater concern is protecting the data that travels outside of the organization to branch sites, telecommuter sites, and partner sites.

Secure communications consists of four elements, as summarized in Figure 2:

- **Data Confidentiality** - Guarantees that only authorized users can read the message. If the message is intercepted, it cannot be deciphered within a reasonable amount of time. Data confidentiality is implemented using symmetric and asymmetric encryption algorithms.

- **Data Integrity** - Guarantees that the message was not altered. Any changes to data in transit will be detected. Integrity is ensured by implementing either Message Digest version 5 (MD5) or Secure Hash Algorithm (SHA) hash-generating algorithms.

- **Origin Authentication** - Guarantees that the message is not a forgery and does actually come from whom it states. Many modern networks ensure authentication with protocols, such as hash message authentication code (HMAC).

- **Data Non-Repudiation** - Guarantees that the sender cannot repudiate, or refute, the validity of a message sent. Nonrepudiation relies on the fact that only the sender has the unique characteristics or signature for how that message is treated.

Note MD5, SHA, and HMAC are discussed in more detail later in the chapter.

Refer to
Online Course
for Illustration

9.1.1.2 Cryptology

Cryptology is used to secure communications. Cryptology is the science of making and breaking secret codes.

As shown in the figure, cryptology combines two separate disciplines:

- **Cryptography** - This is the development and use of codes that are used for communicating privately. Specifically, it is the practice and study of techniques to secure communications. Historically, cryptography was synonymous with encryption.

- **Cryptanalysis** - This is the breaking of those codes. Specifically, it is the practice and study of determining and exploiting weaknesses in cryptographic techniques.

There is a symbiotic relationship between the two disciplines because each makes the other one stronger. National security organizations employ practitioners of both disciplines and put them to work against each other.

There have been times when one of the disciplines has been ahead of the other. For example, during the Hundred Years War between France and England, the cryptanalysts were leading the cryptographers. France mistakenly believed that the Vigenère cipher was unbreakable, and then the British cracked it. Some historians believe that the successful cracking of encrypted codes and messages had a major impact on the outcome of World War II.

Click here for an excellent video, or here for a brief synopsis explaining how code breaking helped the U.S. Navy win the Battle of Midway.

Currently, it is believed that cryptographers have the advantage.

Refer to
Interactive Graphic
in online course

9.1.1.3   Cryptography - Ciphers

Over the centuries, various cryptography methods, physical devices, and aids have been used to encrypt and decrypt text. The following historical ciphering examples are in displayed in Figure 1:

- Scytale
- Caesar Cipher
- Vigenère Cipher
- Enigma Machine

Each of these encryption methods uses a specific algorithm, called a cipher. A cipher is an algorithm that consists of a series of well-defined steps that can be followed as a procedure when encrypting and decrypting messages.

The following are types of ciphers that have been used over the years:

- **Substitution cipher** - Substitution ciphers retain the letter frequency of the original message. The Caesar cipher was a simple substitution cipher. For example, refer to the plaintext message in Figure 2. If the key used was 3, the letter A was moved three letters to the right to become D, as shown in Figure 3. The resulting ciphertext is displayed in Figure 4.

- **Transposition cipher** - In transposition ciphers, no letters are replaced; they are simply rearranged. An example is taking the FLANK EAST ATTACK AT DAWN message and reversing it to read NWAD TAKCATTA TSAE KNALF. Another example of a transposition cipher is known as the rail fence cipher. For example, refer to the plaintext message in Figure 5. Figure 6 displays how to transpose the message using a rail fence cipher with a key of three. The key specifies that three lines are required when creating the encrypted code. The resulting ciphertext is displayed in Figure 7.

- **Polyalphabetic ciphers** - Polyalphabetic ciphers are based on substitution, using multiple substitution alphabets. The famous Vigenère cipher is an example shown in Figure 8. That cipher uses a series of different Caesar ciphers that are based on the letters of a keyword. It is a simple form of polyalphabetic substitution and is therefore invulnerable to frequency analysis.

Refer to
Online Course
for Illustration

9.1.1.4   Cryptanalysis - Code Breaking

Cryptanalysis is often used by cyber criminals to decipher encrypted messages. While cryptanalysis is often linked to mischievous purposes, it is actually a necessity.

Cryptanalysis is also used by governments in military and diplomatic surveillance, and by enterprises in testing the strength of security procedures. Enterprises and governments employ the services of mathematicians, scholars, security forensic experts, and cryptanalysts for these purposes.

Cryptanalysts are individuals who perform cryptanalysis to crack secret codes. The sample job description in the figure highlights the need for cryptanalysts.

Several methods are used in cryptanalysis:

■ **Brute-force method** - The cryptanalyst tries every possible key knowing that eventually one of them will work. All algorithms are vulnerable to brute force. If every possible key is tried, one of the keys has to work.

■ **Ciphertext method** - The cryptanalyst has the ciphertext of several encrypted messages but no knowledge of the underlying plaintext.

■ **Known-Plaintext method** - The cryptanalyst has access to the ciphertext of several messages and knows something about the plaintext underlying that ciphertext.

■ **Chosen-Plaintext method** - The cryptanalyst chooses which data the encryption device encrypts and observes the ciphertext output.

■ **Chosen-Ciphertext method** - The cryptanalyst can choose different ciphertext to be decrypted and has access to the decrypted plaintext.

■ **Meet-in-the-Middle method** - The cryptanalyst knows a portion of the plaintext and the corresponding ciphertext.

Note   The actual processes of these cryptanalysis methods are beyond the scope of this course.

No algorithm is unbreakable. It is an ironic fact of cryptography that it is impossible to prove that any algorithm is secure. It can only be proven that it is not vulnerable to known cryptanalytic attacks.

9.1.1.5   Keys

Refer to
Online Course
for Illustration

Authentication, integrity, and data confidentiality are implemented in many ways, using various protocols and algorithms. The choice of protocol and algorithm varies based on the level of security required to meet the goals of the network security policy.

Old encryption algorithms, such as the Caesar cipher or the Enigma machine, were based on the secrecy of the algorithm to achieve confidentiality.

With modern technology, security of encryption lies in the secrecy of the keys, not the algorithm.

Two terms that are used to describe keys are:

■ **Key length** - Also called the key size, this is measured in bits. In this course, we will use the term key length.

■ **Keyspace** - This is the number of possibilities that can be generated by a specific key length.

As key length increases, the keyspace increases exponentially. The keyspace of an algorithm is the set of all possible key values. A key that has n bits produces a keyspace that has 2^n possible key values:

■ A 2-bit (2^2) key length = a keyspace of 4 because there are four possible keys (00, 01, 10, and 11).

■ A 3-bit (2^3) key length = a keyspace of 8, because there are eight possible keys (000, 001, 010, 011, 100, 101, 110, 111).

- A 4-bit (2^4) key length = a keyspace of 16 possible keys.

- A 40-bit (2^40) key length = a keyspace of 1,099,511,627,776 possible keys.

By adding one bit to the key, the keyspace is effectively doubled, as shown in the figure.

Longer keys are more secure. However, they are also more resource intensive. Caution should be exercised when choosing longer keys because handling them could add a significant load to the processor in lower-end products.

Refer to **Lab Activity** for this chapter

9.1.1.6   Lab - Encrypting and Decrypting Data Using OpenSSL

In this lab, you will complete the following objectives:

- Encrypting Messages with OpenSSL

- Decrypting Messages with OpenSSL

Refer to **Lab Activity** for this chapter

9.1.1.7   Lab - Encrypting and Decrypting Data Using a Hacker Tool

In this lab, you will complete the following objectives:

- Setup Scenario

- Create and Encrypt Files

- Recover Encrypted Zip File Passwords

Refer to **Lab Activity** for this chapter

9.1.1.8   Lab - Examining Telnet and SSH in Wireshark

In this lab, you will complete the following objectives:

- Examine a Telnet Session with Wireshark

- Examine a SSH Session with Wireshark

9.1.2   Integrity and Authenticity

Refer to **Interactive Graphic** in online course

9.1.2.1   Cryptographic Hash Functions

Hashes are used to verify and ensure data integrity. Hashing is based on a one-way mathematical function that is relatively easy to compute, but significantly harder to reverse. Grinding coffee is a good analogy of a one-way function. It is easy to grind coffee beans, but it is almost impossible to put all of the tiny pieces back together to rebuild the original beans. The cryptographic hashing function can also be used to verify authentication.

As shown in Figure 1, a hash function takes a variable block of binary data, called the message, and produces a fixed-length, condensed representation, called the hash. The resulting hash is also sometimes called the message digest, digest, or digital fingerprint.

With hash functions, it is computationally infeasible for two different sets of data to come up with the same hash output. Every time the data is changed or altered, the hash value also changes. Because of this, cryptographic hash values are often called digital fingerprints. They can be used to detect duplicate data files, file version changes, and similar applications. These values are used to guard against an accidental or intentional change to the data, or accidental data corruption.

In Figure 2, the config.txt and config-bk.txt files have the same hash value. This means that the content of these files is identical. The cryptographic hash function is applied in many different situations for entity authentication, data integrity, and data authenticity purposes.

Refer to
Online Course
for Illustration

9.1.2.2 Cryptographic Hash Operation

Mathematically, the equation $b = H(x)$ is used to explain how a hash algorithm operates. As shown in the figure, a hash function H takes an input x and returns a fixed-size string hash value h.

The example in the figure summarizes the mathematical process. A cryptographic hash function should have the following properties:

■ The input can be any length.

■ The output has a fixed length.

■ H(x) is relatively easy to compute for any given x.

■ H(x) is one way and not reversible.

■ H(x) is collision free, meaning that two different input values will result in different hash values.

If a hash function is hard to invert, it is considered a one-way hash. Hard to invert means that given a hash value of b, it is computationally infeasible to find an input for x such that $b = H(x)$.

Refer to
Interactive Graphic
in online course

9.1.2.3 MD5 and SHA

Hash functions are used to ensure the integrity of a message. They ensure data has not changed accidentally or intentionally.

In Figure 1, the sender is sending a $100 money transfer to Alex. The sender wants to ensure that the message is not altered on its way to the receiver.

■ The sending device inputs the message into a hashing algorithm and computes its fixed-length hash of 4ehiDx67NMop9.

■ This hash is then attached to the message and sent to the receiver. Both the message and the hash are in plaintext.

■ The receiving device removes the hash from the message and inputs the message into the same hashing algorithm. If the computed hash is equal to the one that is attached to the message, the message has not been altered during transit. If the hashes are not equal, as shown in the figure, then the integrity of the message can no longer be trusted.

There are three well-known hash functions:

■ **MD5 with 128-bit digest** - Developed by Ron Rivest and used in a variety of Internet applications, MD5 is a one-way function that produces a 128-bit hashed message, as shown in Figure 2. MD5 is considered to be a legacy algorithm and should be avoided and used only when no better alternatives are available. It is recommended that SHA-2 be used instead.

- **SHA-1** - Developed by the U.S. National Institute of Standards and Technology (NIST) in 1994 and is very similar to the MD5 hash functions, as shown in Figure 3. Several versions exist. SHA-1 creates a 160 bit hashed message and is slightly slower than MD5. SHA-1 has known flaws and is a legacy algorithm.

- **SHA-2** - Developed by NIST and includes SHA-224 (224 bit), SHA-256 (256 bit), SHA-384 (384 bit), and SHA-512 (512 bit). SHA-256, SHA-384, and SHA-512 are next-generation algorithms and should be used whenever possible.

While hashing can be used to detect accidental changes, it cannot be used to guard against deliberate changes. There is no unique identifying information from the sender in the hashing procedure. This means that anyone can compute a hash for any data, as long as they have the correct hash function.

For example, when the message traverses the network, a potential attacker could intercept the message, change it, recalculate the hash, and append it to the message. The receiving device will only validate against whatever hash is appended.

Therefore, hashing is vulnerable to man-in-the-middle attacks and does not provide security to transmitted data. To provide integrity and origin authentication, something more is required.

Refer to **Interactive Graphic** in online course

9.1.2.4   Hash Message Authentication Code

To add authentication to integrity assurance, a keyed-hash message authentication code (HMAC; also sometimes abbreviated as KHMAC) is used. To add authentication, HMAC uses an additional secret key as input to the hash function.

As shown in Figure 1, an HMAC is calculated using a specific algorithm (i.e., MD5, or SHA-1) that combines a cryptographic hash function with a secret key. Hash functions are the basis of the protection mechanism of HMACs.

Only the sender and the receiver know the secret key, and the output of the hash function now depends on the input data and the secret key. Only parties who have access to that secret key can compute the digest of an HMAC function. This characteristic defeats man-in-the-middle attacks and provides authentication of the data origin.

If two parties share a secret key and use HMAC functions for authentication, a properly constructed HMAC digest of a message that a party has received indicates that the other party was the originator of the message. This is because the other party possesses the secret key.

As shown in Figure 2, the sending device inputs data (such as Terry Smith's pay of $100 and the secret key) into the hashing algorithm and calculates the fixed-length HMAC digest. This authenticated digest is then attached to the message and sent to the receiver.

In Figure 3, the receiving device removes the digest from the message and uses the plaintext message with its secret key as input to the same hashing function. If the digest that is calculated by the receiving device is equal to the digest that was sent, the message has not been altered. Additionally, the origin of the message is authenticated because only the sender possesses a copy of the shared secret key. The HMAC function has ensured the authenticity of the message.

Figure 4 illustrates how HMACs are used by Cisco routers configured to use Open Shortest Path First (OSPF) routing authentication. In the figure, R1 is sending a link state update (LSU) regarding a route to network 10.2.0.0/16.

- R1 calculates the hash value using the LSU message and the secret key.

- The resulting hash value is sent with the LSU to R2.

- R2 calculates the hash value using the LSU and its secret key. R2 accepts the update if the hash values match. Otherwise, R2 discards the update.

Refer to **Lab Activity** for this chapter

9.1.2.5 Lab - Hashing Things Out

In this lab, you will complete the following objectives:

- Creating Hashes with OpenSSL

- Verifying Hashes

9.1.3 Confidentiality

Refer to **Online Course** for Illustration

9.1.3.1 Encryption

There are two classes of encryption used to provide data confidentiality. These two classes differ in how they use keys:

- **Symmetric encryption algorithms** - Encryption algorithms use the same key to encrypt and decrypt data. They are based on the premise that each communicating party knows the pre-shared key.

- **Asymmetric encryption algorithms** - Encryption algorithms use different keys to encrypt and decrypt data. They are based on the assumption that the two communicating parties have not previously shared a secret and must establish a secure method to do so. Asymmetric algorithms are resource intensive and slower to execute.

The figure highlights some differences between each encryption algorithm method.

Refer to **Online Course** for Illustration

9.1.3.2 Symmetric Encryption

Symmetric algorithms use the same pre-shared key to encrypt and decrypt data. A pre-shared key, also called a secret key, is known by the sender and receiver before any encrypted communications can take place.

To help illustrate how symmetric encryption works, consider an example where Alice and Bob live in different locations and want to exchange secret messages with one another through the mail system. In this example, Alice wants to send a secret message to Bob.

In the figure, Alice and Bob have identical keys to a single padlock. These keys were exchanged prior to sending any secret messages. Alice writes a secret message and puts it in a small box that she locks using the padlock with her key. She mails the box to Bob. The message is safely locked inside the box as the box makes its way through the post office system. When Bob receives the box, he uses his key to unlock the padlock and retrieve the message. Bob can use the same box and padlock to send a secret reply back to Alice.

Today, symmetric encryption algorithms are commonly used with VPN traffic. This is because symmetric algorithms use less CPU than asymmetric encryption algorithms, which are discussed later. This allows the encryption and decryption of data to be fast when using a VPN. When using symmetric encryption algorithms, like any other type of encryption, the longer the key, the longer it will take for someone to discover the key. Most encryption keys are between 112 and 256 bits. To ensure that the encryption is safe, a minimum key length of 128 bits should be used. Use a longer key for more secure communications.

Refer to Interactive Graphic in online course

9.1.3.3 Symmetric Encryption Algorithms

Encryption algorithms are often classified as either:

- **Block ciphers -** Block ciphers transform a fixed-length block of plaintext into a common block of ciphertext of 64 or 128 bits, as shown in Figure 1. Common block ciphers include DES with a 64-bit block size and AES with a 128-bit block size.

- **Stream Ciphers -** Stream ciphers encrypt plaintext one byte or one bit at a time, as shown in Figure 2. Stream ciphers are basically a block cipher with a block size of one byte or bit. Stream ciphers are typically faster than block ciphers because data is continuously encrypted. Examples of stream ciphers include RC4 and A5 which is used to encrypt GSM cell phone communications. Data Encryption Standard (DES) can also be used in stream cipher mode.

Well-known symmetric encryption algorithms include:

- **Data Encryption Standard (DES) -** This is an older legacy symmetric encryption algorithm. It can be used in stream cipher mode but usually operates in block mode by encrypting data in 64-bit block size. Figure 3 summarizes DES.

- **3DES (Triple DES) -** This is a newer version of DES, but it repeats the DES algorithm process three times. It is more computationally taxing than DES. The basic algorithm has been well tested in the field for more than 35 years and is therefore considered very trustworthy when implemented using very short key lifetimes. Figure 4 summarizes 3DES.

- **Advanced Encryption Standard (AES) -** Based on the Rijndael cipher, it is a popular and recommended symmetric encryption algorithm. It offers nine combinations of key and block length by using a variable key length of 128-, 192-, or 256-bit key to encrypt data blocks that are 128, 192, or 256 bits long. AES is a secure and more efficient algorithm than 3DES. Figure 5 summarizes AES. AES counter mode (AES-CTR) is the preferred encryption algorithm for SSHv2. It can use any of the AES key lengths, such as AES256-CTR.

- **Software-Optimized Encryption Algorithm (SEAL) -** SEAL is a fast alternative symmetric encryption algorithm to DES, 3DES, and AES. It is a stream cipher that uses a 160-bit encryption key. SEAL has a lower impact on the CPU compared to other software-based algorithms but is still considered unproven. Figure 6 summarizes SEAL.

- **Rivest ciphers (RC)** series algorithms (includes RC2, RC4, RC5, and RC6) - This was developed by Ron Rivest. Several variations have been developed, but RC4 is the most prevalent in use. RC4 is a stream cipher and is used to secure web traffic in SSL and TLS. Figure 7 summarizes the RC algorithms.

Note   There are many other symmetric encryption algorithms, such as Blowfish, Twofish, Threefish, and Serpent. However, these algorithms are beyond the scope of this course.

Refer to **Interactive Graphic** in online course

9.1.3.4   Asymmetric Encryption Algorithms

Asymmetric algorithms, also called public-key algorithms, are designed so that the key that is used for encryption is different from the key that is used for decryption, as shown in Figure 1. The decryption key cannot, in any reasonable amount of time, be calculated from the encryption key and vice versa.

Asymmetric algorithms use a public key and a private key. Both keys are capable of the encryption process, but the complementary paired key is required for decryption. The process is also reversible in that data encrypted with the public key requires the private key to decrypt.

This process enables asymmetric algorithms to achieve confidentiality, authentication, and integrity.

Because neither party has a shared secret, very long key lengths must be used. Asymmetric encryption can use key lengths between 512 to 4,096 bits. Key lengths greater than or equal to 1,024 bits can be trusted while shorter key lengths are considered unreliable.

Examples of protocols that use asymmetric key algorithms include:

- **Internet Key Exchange (IKE)** - This is a fundamental component of IPsec VPNs.
- **Secure Socket Layer (SSL)** - This is now implemented as IETF standard TLS.
- **Secure Shell (SSH)** - This is a protocol that provides a secure remote access connection to network devices.
- **Pretty Good Privacy (PGP)** - This is a computer program that provides cryptographic privacy and authentication. It is often used to increase the security of email communications.

Asymmetric algorithms are substantially slower than symmetric algorithms. Their design is based on computational problems, such as factoring extremely large numbers or computing discrete logarithms of extremely large numbers.

Because they lack speed, asymmetric algorithms are typically used in low-volume cryptographic mechanisms, such as digital signatures and key exchange. However, the key management of asymmetric algorithms tends to be simpler than symmetric algorithms, because usually one of the two encryption or decryption keys can be made public.

Common examples of asymmetric encryption algorithms are described in the table in Figure 2.

Refer to **Interactive Graphic** in online course

9.1.3.5   Asymmetric Encryption - Confidentiality

Asymmetric algorithms are used to provide confidentiality without pre-sharing a password. The confidentiality objective of asymmetric algorithms is initiated when the encryption process is started with the public key.

The process can be summarized using the formula:

Public Key (Encrypt) + Private Key (Decrypt) = Confidentiality

When the public key is used to encrypt the data, the private key must be used to decrypt the data. Only one host has the private key; therefore, confidentiality is achieved.

If the private key is compromised, another key pair must be generated to replace the compromised key.

For example, in Figure 1, Alice requests and obtains Bob's public key. In Figure 2, Alice uses Bob's public key to encrypt a message using an agreed-upon algorithm. Alice sends the encrypted message to Bob. Bob then uses his private key to decrypt the message as shown in Figure 3.

Refer to
Interactive Graphic
in online course

9.1.3.6   Asymmetric Encryption - Authentication

The authentication objective of asymmetric algorithms is initiated when the encryption process is started with the private key.

The process can be summarized using the formula:

Private Key (Encrypt) + Public Key (Decrypt) = Authentication

When the private key is used to encrypt the data, the corresponding public key must be used to decrypt the data. Because only one host has the private key, only that host could have encrypted the message, providing authentication of the sender. Typically, no attempt is made to preserve the secrecy of the public key, so any number of hosts can decrypt the message. When a host successfully decrypts a message using a public key, it is trusted that the private key encrypted the message, which verifies who the sender is. This is a form of authentication.

For example, in Figure 1, Alice encrypts a message using her private key. Alice sends the encrypted message to Bob. Bob needs to authenticate that the message did indeed come from Alice. Therefore, in Figure 2, Bob requests Alice's public key. In Figure 3 Bob uses Alice's public key to decrypt the message.

Refer to
Interactive Graphic
in online course

9.1.3.7   Asymmetric Encryption - Integrity

Combining the two asymmetric encryption processes provides message confidentiality, authentication, and integrity.

The following example will be used to illustrate this process. In this example, a message will be ciphered using Bob's public key and a ciphered hash will be encrypted using Alice's private key to provide confidentiality, authenticity, and integrity.

The process in Figure 1 provides confidentiality. Alice wants to send a message to Bob ensuring that only Bob can read the document. In other words, Alice wants to ensure message confidentiality. Alice uses the public key of Bob to cipher the message. Only Bob will be able to decipher it using his private key.

Alice also wants to ensure message authentication and integrity. Authentication ensures Bob that the document was sent by Alice, and integrity ensures that it was not modified. In Figure 2, Alice uses her private key to cipher a hash of the message. Alice sends the encrypted message with its encrypted hash to Bob.

In Figure 3, Bob uses Alice's public key to verify that the message was not modified. The received hash is equal to the locally determined hash based on Alice's public key. Additionally, this verifies that Alice is definitely the sender of the message because nobody else has Alice's private key.

Finally, in Figure 4, Bob uses his private key to decipher the message.

Refer to
Online Course
for Illustration

9.1.3.8 Diffie-Hellman

Diffie-Hellman (DH) is an asymmetric mathematical algorithm that allows two computers to generate an identical shared secret without having communicated before. The new shared key is never actually exchanged between the sender and receiver. However, because both parties know it, the key can be used by an encryption algorithm to encrypt traffic between the two systems.

Here are three examples of instances when DH is commonly used:

- Data is exchanged using an IPsec VPN

- Data is encrypted on the Internet using either SSL or TLS

- SSH data is exchanged

To help illustrate how DH operates, refer to the figure. The colors in the figure will be used instead of complex long numbers to simplify the DH key agreement process. The DH key exchange begins with Alice and Bob agreeing on an arbitrary common color that does not need to be kept secret. The agreed on color in our example is yellow.

Next, Alice and Bob will each select a secret color. Alice chose red while Bob chose blue. These secret colors will never be shared with anyone. The secret color represents the chosen secret private key of each party.

Alice and Bob now mix the shared common color (yellow) with their respective secret color to produce a private color. Therefore, Alice will mix the yellow with her red color to produce a private color of orange. Bob will mix the yellow and the blue to produce a private color of green.

Alice sends her private color (orange) to Bob and Bob sends his private color (green) to Alice.

Alice and Bob each mix the color they received with their own, original secret color (Red for Alice and blue for Bob.). The result is a final brown color mixture that is identical to the partner's final color mixture. The brown color represents the resulting shared secret key between Bob and Alice.

The security of DH is based on the fact that it uses unbelievably large numbers in its calculations. For example, a DH 1024-bit number is roughly equal to a decimal number of 309 digits. Considering that a billion is 10 decimal digits (1,000,000,000), one can easily imagine the complexity of working with not one, but multiple 309 digit decimal numbers.

Unfortunately, asymmetric key systems are extremely slow for any sort of bulk encryption. This is why it is common to encrypt the bulk of the traffic using a symmetric algorithm, such as 3DES or AES and use the DH algorithm to create keys that will be used by the encryption algorithm.

Refer to
Interactive Graphic
in online course

9.1.3.9 Activity - Classify the Encryption Algorithms

9.2 Public Key Infrastructure

9.2.1 Public Key Cryptography

Refer to
Interactive Graphic
in online course

9.2.1.1 Using Digital Signatures

Digital signatures are a mathematical technique used to provide three basic security services. Click each Plus sign (+) in Figure 1 more information. Digital signatures have specific properties that enable entity authentication and data integrity. Click each Plus sign in Figure 2 more information.

Digital signatures are commonly used in the following two situations:

- **Code signing** - This is used for data integrity and authentication purposes. Code signing is used to verify the integrity of executable files downloaded from a vendor website. It also uses signed digital certificates to authenticate and verify the identity of the site.

- **Digital certificates** - These are similar to a virtual ID card and used to authenticate the identity of system with a vendor website and establish an encrypted connection to exchange confidential data.

There are three Digital Signature Standard (DSS) algorithms that are used for generating and verifying digital signatures:

- **Digital Signature Algorithm (DSA)** - DSA is the original standard for generating public and private key pairs, and for generating and verifying digital signatures. Figure 3 summarizes DSA.

- **Rivest-Shamir Adelman Algorithm (RSA)** - RSA is an asymmetric algorithm that is commonly used for generating and verifying digital signatures. Figure 4 summarizes RSA.

- **Elliptic Curve Digital Signature Algorithm (ECDSA)** - ECDSA is a newer variant of DSA and provides digital signature authentication and non-repudiation with the added benefits of computational efficiency, small signature sizes, and minimal bandwidth.

Diffie-Hellman uses different DH groups to determine the strength of the key that is used in the key agreement process. The higher group numbers are more secure, but require additional time to compute the key. The following identifies the DH groups supported by Cisco IOS Software and their associated prime number value:

- DH Group 1: 768 bits
- DH Group 2: 1024 bits
- DH Group 5: 1536 bits
- DH Group 14: 2048 bits
- DH Group 15: 3072 bits
- DH Group 16: 4096 bits

Note   A DH key agreement can also be based on elliptic curve cryptography. DH groups 19, 20, and 24, based on elliptic curve cryptography, are also supported by Cisco IOS Software.

In the 1990s, RSE Security Inc. started to publish public-key cryptography standards (PKCS). There were 15 PKCS, although 1 has been withdrawn as of the time of this writing. RSE published these standards because they had the patents to the standards and wished to promote them. PKCS are not industry standards, but are well recognized in the security industry and have recently begun to become relevant to standards organizations such as the IETF and PKIX working-group.

Refer to
Interactive Graphic
in online course

9.2.1.2   Digital Signatures for Code Signing

Digital signatures are commonly used to provide assurance of the authenticity and integrity of software code. Executable files are wrapped in a digitally signed envelope, which allows the end user to verify the signature before installing the software.

Digitally signing code provides several assurances about the code:

- The code is authentic and is actually sourced by the publisher.

- The code has not been modified since it left the software publisher.

- The publisher undeniably published the code. This provides nonrepudiation of the act of publishing.

The US Government Federal Information Processing Standard (FIPS) Publication 140-3, specifies that software available for download on the Internet is to be digitally signed and verified. The purpose of digitally signed software is to ensure that the software has not been tampered with, and that it originated from the trusted source as claimed.

Refer to the Figures 1 through 5 to see the properties of a file with a digitally signed certificate.

Refer to
Interactive Graphic
in online course

9.2.1.3   Digital Signatures for Digital Certificates

A digital certificate is equivalent to an electronic passport. They enable users, hosts, and organizations to securely exchange information over the Internet. Specifically, a digital certificate is used to authenticate and verify that users sending a message are who they claim to be. Digital certificates can also be used to provide confidentiality for the receiver with the means to encrypt a reply.

Digital certificates are similar to physical certificates. For example, the paper-based Cisco Certified Network Associate Security (CCNA-S) certificate in Figure 1 identifies who the certificate is issued to, who authorized the certificate, and for how long the certificate is valid. Notice how the digital certificate in Figure 2 also identifies similar elements.

To help understand how a digital certificate is used, refer to Figure 3. In this scenario, Bob is confirming an order with Alice. Click the plus signs (+) to see how Bob's computer sends the digital certificate.

Click the plus signs in Figure 4 to see how Alice will use the digital certificate.

Refer to
Lab Activity
for this chapter

9.2.1.4   Lab - Create a Linux Playground

In this lab, you will install VirtualBox on your personal computer. You will also import a virtual machine into VirtualBox inventory.

9.2.2   Authorities and the PKI Trust System

Refer to
Online Course
for Illustration

9.2.2.1   Public Key Management

Internet traffic consists of traffic between two parties. When establishing an asymmetric connection between two hosts, the hosts will exchange their public key information. There are trusted third parties on the Internet that validate the authenticity of these public keys using digital certificates. The trusted third party does an in-depth investigation prior to the issuance of credentials. After this in-depth investigation, the third party issues credentials (i.e. digital certificate) that are difficult to forge. From that point forward, all individuals who trust the third party simply accept the credentials that the third party issues.

These trusted third parties provide services similar to governmental licensing bureaus. The figure illustrates how a driver's license is analogous to a digital certificate.

The Public Key Infrastructure (PKI) is an example of a trusted third-party system referred to as certificate authority (CA). The CA provides a service similar to governmental licensing bureaus. The PKI is the framework used to securely exchange information between parties. The CA issues digital certificates that authenticate the identity of organizations and users. These certificates are also used to sign messages to ensure that the messages have not been tampered with.

Refer to
Interactive Graphic
in online course

9.2.2.2   The Public Key Infrastructure

PKI is needed to support large-scale distribution and identification of public encryption keys. The PKI framework facilitates a highly scalable trust relationship.

It consists of the hardware, software, people, policies, and procedures needed to create, manage, store, distribute, and revoke digital certificates.

Click the plus signs (+) in Figure 1 to see the main elements of the PKI.

Click the plus signs in Figure 2 to see how these elements interoperate:

- In the example, Bob has received his digital certificate from the CA. This certificate is used whenever Bob communicates with other parties.

- Bob communicates with Alice.

- When Alice receives Bob's digital certificate, she communicates with the trusted CA to validate Bob's identity.

Note   Not all PKI certificates are directly received from a CA. A registration authority (RA) is a subordinate CA and is certified by a root CA to issue certificates for specific uses.

Refer to
Interactive Graphic
in online course

9.2.2.3   The PKI Authorities System

Many vendors provide CA servers as a managed service or as an end-user product. Some of these vendors include Symantec Group (VeriSign), Comodo, Go Daddy Group, GlobalSign, and DigiCert among others.

Organizations may also implement private PKIs using Microsoft Server or Open SSL.

CAs, especially those that are outsourced, issue certificates based on classes which determine how trusted a certificate is.

Figure 1 provides a description of the classes. The class number is determined by how rigorous the procedure was that verified the identity of the holder when the certificate was issued. The higher the class number, the more trusted the certificate. Therefore, a class 5 certificate is trusted much more than a lower class certificate.

For example, a class 1 certificate might require an email reply from the holder to confirm that they wish to enroll. This kind of confirmation is a weak authentication of the holder. For a class 3 or 4 certificate, the future holder must prove identity and authenticate the public key by showing up in person with at least two official ID documents.

Some CA public keys are preloaded, such as those listed in web browsers. Figure 2 displays various VeriSign certificates contained in the certificate store on the host. Any certificates signed by any of the CAs in the list will be seen by the browser as legitimate and will be trusted automatically.

Note   An enterprise can also implement PKI for internal use. PKI can be used to authenticate employees who are accessing the network. In this case, the enterprise is its own CA.

Refer to
Interactive Graphic
in online course

9.2.2.4   The PKI Trust System

PKIs can form different topologies of trust. The simplest is the single-root PKI topology.

As shown in Figure 1, a single CA, called the root CA, issues all the certificates to the end users, which are usually within the same organization. The benefit to this approach is its simplicity. However, it is difficult to scale to a large environment because it requires a strictly centralized administration, which creates a single point of failure.

On larger networks, PKI CAs may be linked using two basic architectures:

- **Cross-certified CA topologies** - As shown in Figure 2, this is a peer-to-peer model in which individual CAs establish trust relationships with other CAs by cross-certifying CA certificates. Users in either CA domain are also assured that they can trust each other. This provides redundancy and eliminates the single-point of failure.

- **Hierarchical CA topologies** - As shown in Figure 3, the highest level CA is called the root CA. It can issue certificates to end users and to a subordinate CA. The sub-CAs could be created to support various business units, domains, or communities of trust. The root CA maintains the established "community of trust" by ensuring that each entity in the hierarchy conforms to a minimum set of practices. The benefits of this topology include increased scalability and manageability. This topology works well in most large organizations. However, it can be difficult to determine the chain of the signing process.

A hierarchical and cross-certification topology can be combined to create a hybrid infrastructure. An example would be when two hierarchical communities want to cross-certify each other in order for members of each community to trust each other.

Refer to
Interactive Graphic
in online course

9.2.2.5   Interoperability of Different PKI Vendors

Interoperability between a PKI and its supporting services, such as Lightweight Directory Access Protocol (LDAP) and X.500 directories, is a concern because many CA vendors have proposed and implemented proprietary solutions instead of waiting for standards to develop.

Note   LDAP and X.500 are protocols that are used to query a directory service, such as Microsoft Active Directory, to verify a username and password.

To address this interoperability concern, the IETF published the Internet X.509 Public Key Infrastructure Certificate Policy and Certification Practices Framework (RFC 2527). The X.509 version 3 (X.509v3) standard defines the format of a digital certificate.

Click the plus signs (+) in the figure for more information about X.509v3 applications. As shown in the figure, the X.509 format is already extensively used in the infrastructure of the Internet.

Refer to
Interactive Graphic
in online course

9.2.2.6   Certificate Enrollment, Authentication, and Revocation

In the CA authentication procedure, the first step when contacting the PKI is to securely obtain a copy of the CA's public key. All systems that leverage the PKI must have the CA's public key, called the self-signed certificate. The CA public key verifies all the certificates issued by the CA and is vital for the proper operation of the PKI.

Note   Only a root CA can issue a self-signed certificate.

For many systems such as web browsers, the distribution of CA certificates is handled automatically. The web browser comes pre-installed with a set of public CA root certificates. Organizations also push their private CA root certificate to clients through various software distribution methods.

The certificate enrollment process is used by a host system to enroll with a PKI. To do so, CA certificates are retrieved in-band over a network, and the authentication is done out-of-band (OOB) using the telephone. The system enrolling with the PKI contacts a CA to request and obtain a digital identity certificate for itself and to get the CA's self-signed certificate. The final stage verifies that the CA certificate was authentic and is performed using an OOB method such as the Plain Old Telephone System (POTS) to obtain the fingerprint of the valid CA identity certificate.

The first part of the certificate enrollment process consists of acquiring the CA's self-signed certificate.

Click the plus signs (+) in Figure 1 to understand how CA certificates are retrieved.

After retrieving the CA certificate, Alice and Bob submit certificate requests to the CA. Click the plus signs in Figure 2 for more information.

Having installed certificates signed by the same CA, Bob and Alice are now ready to authenticate each other. Click the plus signs in Figure 3 for more information.

Authentication no longer requires the presence of the CA server, and each user exchanges their certificates containing public keys.

Certificate must sometimes be revoked. For example, a digital certificate can be revoked if key is compromised or if it is no longer needed.

Here are two of the most common methods of revocation:

- **Certificate Revocation List (CRL)** - A list of revoked certificate serial numbers that have been invalidated because they expired. PKI entities regularly poll the CRL repository to receive the current CRL.

- **Online Certificate Status Protocol (OCSP)** - An Internet protocol used to query an OCSP server for the revocation status of an X.509 digital certificate. Revocation information is immediately pushed to an online database.

Refer to
Lab Activity
for this chapter

9.2.2.7   Lab - Certificate Authority Stores

In this lab, you will complete the following objectives:

- Certificates Trusted by Your Browser

- Checking for Man-In-Middle

9.2.3 Applications and Impacts of Cryptography

Refer to
Online Course
for Illustration

9.2.3.1 PKI Applications

Where can PKI be used by an enterprise? The following provides a short list of common use of PKIs:

- SSL/TLS certificate-based peer authentication
- Secure network traffic using IPsec VPNs
- HTTPS Web traffic
- Control access to the network using 802.1x authentication
- Secure email using the S/MIME protocol
- Secure instant messaging
- Approve and authorize applications with Code Signing
- Protect user data with the Encryption File System (EFS)
- Implement two-factor authentication with smart cards
- Securing USB storage devices

Refer to
Online Course
for Illustration

9.2.3.2 Encrypting Network Transactions

A security analysis must be able to recognize and solve potential problems related to permitting PKI-related solutions on the enterprise network.

Consider how the increase of SSL/TLS traffic poses a major security risk to enterprises because the traffic is encrypted and cannot be intercepted and monitored by normal means. Users can introduce malware or leak confidential information over an SSL/TLS connection.

Threat actors can use SSL/TLS to introduce regulatory compliance violations, viruses, malware, data loss, and intrusion attempts in a network.

Other SSL/TLS-related issues may be associated with validating the certificate of a web server. When this occurs, web browsers will display a security warning. PKI-related issues that are associated with security warnings include:

- **Validity date range -** The X.509v3 certificates specify "not before" and "not after" dates. If the current date is outside the range, the web browser displays a message. Expired certificates may simply be the result of administrator oversight, but they may also reflect more serious conditions.

- **Signature validation error -** If a browser cannot validate the signature on the certificate, there is no assurance that the public key in the certificate is authentic. Signature validation will fail if the root certificate of the CA hierarchy is not available in the browser's certificate store.

The figure is displaying an example of a signature validation error with the Cisco AnyConnect Mobility Client.

Some of these issues can be avoided due to the fact that the SSL/TLS protocols are extensible and modular. This is known as a cipher suite. The key components of the cipher suite are the Message Authentication Code Algorithm (MAC), the encryption algorithm, the key exchange algorithm, and the authentication algorithm. These can be changed without replacing the entire protocol. This is very helpful because the different algorithms continue to evolve. As cryptanalysis continues to reveal flaws in these algorithms, the cipher suite can be updated to patch these flaws. When the protocol versions within the cipher suite change, the version number of SSL/TLS changes as well.

Refer to
Online Course
for Illustration

9.2.3.3 Encryption and Security Monitoring

Network monitoring becomes more challenging when packets are encrypted. However, security analysts must be aware of those challenges and address them as best as possible. For instance, when site-to-site VPNs are used, the IPS should be positioned so it can monitor unencrypted traffic.

However, the increase of HTTPS in the enterprise network introduces new challenges. Since HTTPS introduces end-to-end encrypted HTTP traffic (via TLS/SSL), it is not as easy to peek into user traffic.

Security analysts must know how to circumvent and solve these issues. Here is a list of some of the things that a security analyst could do:

- Configure rules to distinguish between SSL and non-SSL traffic, HTTPS and non-HTTPS SSL traffic.

- Enhance security through server certificate validation using CRLs and OCSP.

- Implement antimalware protection and URL filtering of HTTPS content.

- Deploy a Cisco SSL Appliance to decrypt SSL traffic and send it to intrusion prevention system (IPS) appliances to identify risks normally hidden by SSL.

Cryptography is dynamic and always changing. A security analyst must maintain a good understanding of cryptographic algorithms and operations to be able to investigate cryptography-related security incidents.

There are two main ways in which cryptography impacts security investigations. First, attacks can be directed to specifically target the encryption algorithms themselves. After the algorithm has been cracked and the attacker has obtained the keys, any encrypted data that has been captured can be decrypted by the attacker and read, thus exposing private data. The security investigation is also affected because data can be hidden in plain sight by encrypting it. For example, command and control traffic that is encrypted with TLS/SSL most likely cannot be seen by a firewall. The command and control traffic between a command and control server and an infected computer in a secure network cannot be stopped if it cannot be seen and understood. The attacker would be able to continue using encrypted commands to infect more computers and possibly create a botnet. This type of traffic can be detected by decrypting the traffic and comparing it with known attack signatures, or by detecting anomalous TLS/SSL traffic. This is either very difficult and time consuming, or a hit-or-miss process.

9.3   Summary

9.3.1   Conclusion

Refer to
Online Course
for Illustration

9.3.1.1   Chapter 9: Cryptography and the Public Key Infrastructure

In this chapter, you learned about the various cryptographic techniques and how their use affects network security monitoring. Securing communications with cryptography consists of four elements:

■ Data confidentiality to guarantee that only authorized users can read the message.

■ Data integrity to guarantee that the message was not altered.

■ Origin authentication guarantees that the message is not a forgery and does actually come from whom it states.

■ Data non-repudiation to guarantee that the sender cannot repudiate, or refute, the validity of a message sent.

One of the main ways to verify and ensure data integrity is through the use of hash functions. Hash functions make it computationally infeasible for two different sets of data to come up with the same hash output. Three well-known hash functions include:

■ MD5 with a 128-bit digest

■ SHA-1

■ SHA-2

To include authentication along with message integrity, an HMAC is added to as an input to a hash function. If two parties share a secret key and use HMAC functions for authentication, a properly constructed HMAC digest of a message that a party has received indicates that the other party was the originator of the message.

Confidentiality of the data is ensured through one of two types of encryption: symmetric and asymmetric.

Symmetric encryption uses the same key to encrypt and decrypt data. Well-known symmetric encryption algorithms include:

■ Data Encryption Standard (DES)

■ 3DES (Triple DES)

■ Advanced Encryption Standard (AES)

■ Software-Optimized Encryption Algorithm (SEAL)

■ Rivest Ciphers (RC)

Asymmetric encryption uses different keys to encrypt and decrypt data. Examples of protocols that use asymmetric key algorithms include:

- Internet Key Exchange (IKE)

- Secure Socket Layer (SSL)

- Secure Shell (SSH)

- Pretty Good Privacy (PGP)

Diffie-Hellman (DH) is an asymmetric mathematical algorithm that allows two computers to generate an identical shared secret key without having communicated before. The new shared secret key is never actually exchanged between the sender and receiver.

The Public Key Infrastructure (PKI) relies on digital certificates. Digital certificates provide a digital signature that authenticates the source, guarantees the integrity of the data, and provides nonrepudiation for the transaction. The three Digital Signature Standards (DSS) are:

- Digital Signature Algorithm (DSA)

- Rivest-Shamir Adelman Algorithm (RSA)

- Elliptic Curve Digital Signature Algorithm (ECDSA)

Trusted third party organizations such as VeriSign validate the authenticity of digital certificates. Digital certificates are used in a variety of PKI applications including:

- IPsec VPNs

- HTTPS traffic

- 802.1x authentication

- Email and instant message security

- Code signing

- Encryption File System (EFS)

- Two-factor authentication

- USB device security

Go to the online course to take the quiz and exam.

Chapter 9 Quiz

This quiz is designed to provide an additional opportunity to practice the skills and knowledge presented in the chapter and to prepare for the chapter exam. You will be allowed multiple attempts and the grade does not appear in the gradebook.

Chapter 9 Exam

The chapter exam assesses your knowledge of the chapter content.

Your Chapter Notes

Endpoint Security and Analysis

10.0 Introduction

10.0.1 Welcome

Refer to
Online Course
for Illustration

10.0.1.1 Chapter 10: Endpoint Security and Analysis

Endpoints are the most numerous devices on a network; therefore, they are the targets of the majority of network attacks. A cybersecurity analyst must be familiar with the threats to endpoints, the methods for protecting endpoints from attacks, and the methods for detecting compromised endpoints.

This chapter discusses how to investigate endpoint vulnerabilities and attacks.

10.1 Endpoint Protection

10.1.1 Antimalware Protection

Refer to
Interactive Graphic
in online course

10.1.1.1 Endpoint Threats

The term "endpoint" is defined in various ways. For the purpose of this course, we can define endpoints as hosts on the network that can access or be accessed by other hosts on the network. This obviously includes computers and servers, however many other devices can also access the network. With the rapid growth of the Internet of Things (IoT), other types of devices are now endpoints on the network. This includes networked security cameras, controllers, and even light bulbs and appliances. Each endpoint is potentially a way for malicious software to gain access to a network. In addition, new technologies, such as cloud, expand the boundaries of enterprise networks to include locations on the Internet for which the enterprises are not responsible.

Devices that remotely access networks through VPNs are also endpoints that need to be considered. These endpoints could inject malware into the VPN network from the public network.

The following points summarize some of the reasons why malware remains a major challenge:

- Over 75% of organizations experienced adware infections from 2015-2016.

- From 2016 to early 2017, global spam volume increased dramatically (Figure 1). 8 to 10 percent of this spam can be considered to be malicious (Figure 2).

- Malware that targets the Android mobile operating system was in the top ten most common types of malware found in 2016.

- Several common types of malware have been found to significantly change features in less than 24 hours in order to evade detection.

Refer to
Online Course
for Illustration

10.1.1.2   Endpoint Security

News media commonly cover external network attacks on enterprise networks. These are some examples of such attacks:

- DoS attacks on an organization's network to degrade or even halt public access to it

- Breach of an organization's Web server to deface their web presence

- Breach of an organization's data servers and hosts to steal confidential information

Various network security devices are required to protect the network perimeter from outside access. As shown in the figure, these devices could include a hardened router that is providing VPN services, a next generation firewall (ASA, in the figure), an IPS appliance, and an authentication, authentication, and accounting services (AAA server, in the figure).

However, many attacks originate from inside the network. Therefore, securing an internal LAN is nearly as important as securing the outside network perimeter. Without a secure LAN, users within an organization are still susceptible to network threats and outages that can directly affect an organization's productivity and profit margin. After an internal host is infiltrated, it can become a starting point for an attacker to gain access to critical system devices, such as servers and sensitive information.

Specifically, there are two internal LAN elements to secure:

- **Endpoints -** Hosts commonly consist of laptops, desktops, printers, servers, and IP phones, all of which are susceptible to malware-related attacks.

- **Network infrastructure -** LAN infrastructure devices interconnect endpoints and typically include switches, wireless devices, and IP telephony devices. Most of these devices are susceptible to LAN-related attacks including MAC address table overflow attacks, spoofing attacks, DHCP related attacks, LAN storm attacks, STP manipulation attacks, and VLAN attacks.

This chapter focuses on securing endpoints.

Refer to
Interactive Graphic
in online course

10.1.1.3   Host-Based Malware Protection

The network perimeter is always expanding. People access corporate network resources with mobile devices that use remote access technologies such as VPN. These same devices are also used on unsecured, or minimally secured, public and home networks. Host-based antimalware/antivirus software and host-based firewalls are used to protect these devices.

Antivirus/Antimalware Software

This is software that is installed on a host to detect and mitigate viruses and malware. Examples are Windows Defender (Figure 1), Norton Security, McAfee, Trend Micro, and others. Antimalware programs may detect viruses using three different approaches:

- **Signature-based -** This approach recognizes various characteristics of known malware files.

- **Heuristics-based -** This approach recognizes general features shared by various types of malware.

- **Behavior-based -** This approach employs analysis of suspicious behavior.

Many antivirus programs are able to provide real-time protection by analyzing data as it is used by the endpoint. These programs also scan for existing malware that may have entered the system prior to it being recognizable in real time.

Host-based antivirus protection is also known as agent-based. Agent-based antivirus runs on every protected machine. Agentless antivirus protection performs scans on hosts from a centralized system. Agentless systems have become popular for virtualized environments in which multiple OS instances are running on a host simultaneously. Agent-based antivirus running in each virtualized system can be a serious drain on system resources. Agentless antivirus for virtual hosts involves the use of a special security virtual appliance that performs optimized scanning tasks on the virtual hosts. An example of this is VMware's vShield.

Host-based Firewall

This software is installed on a host. It restricts incoming and outgoing connections to connections initiated by that host only. Some firewall software can also prevent a host from becoming infected and stop infected hosts from spreading malware to other hosts. This function is included in some operating systems. For example, Windows includes Windows Defender and Windows Firewall (Figure 2). Other solutions are produced by other companies or organizations. The Linux IPtables and TCP Wrapper tools are examples. Host-based firewalls are discussed in more detail later in the chapter.

Host-based Security Suites

It is recommended to install a host-based suite of security products on home networks as well as business networks. These host-based security suites include antivirus, anti-phishing, safe browsing, Host-based intrusion prevention system, and firewall capabilities. These various security measures provide a layered defense that will protect against most common threats.

In addition to the protection functionality provided by host-based security products, is the telemetry function. Most host-based security software includes robust logging functionality that is essential to cybersecurity operations. Some host-based security programs will submit logs to a central location for analysis.

There are many host-based security programs and suites available to users and enterprises. The independent testing laboratory AV-TEST, shown in Figure 3, provides high-quality reviews of host-based protections, as well as information about many other security products.

Click here to learn more about AV-TEST.

Refer to **Interactive Graphic** in online course

10.1.1.4 Network-Based Malware Protection

New security architectures for the borderless network address security challenges by having endpoints use network scanning elements. These devices provide many more layers of scanning than a single endpoint possibly could. Network-based malware prevention devices are also capable of sharing information among themselves to make better informed decisions.

Protecting endpoints in a borderless network can be accomplished using network-based, as well as host-based techniques, as shown in Figure 1. The following are examples of devices and techniques that implement host protections and the network level.

- **Advanced Malware Protection (AMP)** - This provides endpoint protection from viruses and malware.

- **Email Security Appliance (ESA)** - This provides filtering of SPAM and potentially malicious emails before they reach the endpoint. An example is the Cisco ESA.

- **Web Security Appliance (WSA)** - This provides filtering of websites and blacklisting to prevent hosts from reaching dangerous locations on the web. The Cisco WSA provides control over how users access the Internet and can enforce acceptable use policies, control access to specific sites and services, and scan for malware.

- **Network Admission Control (NAC)** - This permits only authorized and compliant systems to connect to the network.

These technologies work in concert with each other to give more protection than host-based suites can provide, as shown in Figure 2.

Refer to
Online Course
for Illustration

10.1.1.5   Cisco Advanced Malware Protection (AMP)

Cisco Advanced Malware Protection (AMP) addresses all phases of a malware attack, from breach prevention to detection, response, and remediation. AMP is an integrated, enterprise-class malware analysis and protection solution. It provides comprehensive protection for organizations across the attack continuum:

- **Before an attack** - AMP uses global threat intelligence from Cisco's Talos Security Intelligence and Research Group, and Threat Grid's threat intelligence feeds to strengthen defenses and protect against known and emerging threats.

- **During an attack** - AMP uses that intelligence coupled with known file signatures and Cisco Threat Grid's dynamic malware analysis technology. It identifies and blocks policy-violating file types and exploit attempts, as well as malicious files trying to infiltrate the network.

- **After an attack** - The solution goes beyond point-in-time detection capabilities and continuously monitors and analyzes all file activity and traffic, regardless of disposition, searching for any indications of malicious behavior. This happens not only after an attack, but also after a file is initially inspected. If a file with an unknown or previously deemed "good" disposition starts behaving badly, AMP will detect it and instantly alert security teams with an indication of compromise. It then provides visibility into where the malware originated, what systems were affected, and what the malware is doing. It also provides the controls to rapidly respond to the intrusion and remediate it with a few clicks. This gives security teams the level of deep visibility and control they need to quickly detect attacks, determine the impact, and contain malware before it causes damage.

Cisco AMP is very flexible and can be deployed on endpoints, on ASA and FirePOWER firewalls, and on various other appliances, such as ESA, WSA, and Meraki MX.

Click here for a video overview of the core Cisco AMP functionalities.

Refer to
Interactive Graphic
in online course

10.1.1.6   Activity - Identify Antimalware Terms and Concepts

10.1.2   Host-Based Intrusion Protection

Refer to
Interactive Graphic
in online course

10.1.2.1   Host-Based Firewalls

Host-based personal firewalls are standalone software programs that control traffic entering or leaving a computer. Firewall apps are also available for Android phones and tablets.

Host-based firewalls may use a set of predefined policies, or profiles, to control packets entering and leaving a computer. They also may have rules that can be directly modified or created to control access based on addresses, protocols, and ports. Host-based firewall applications can also be configured to issue alerts to users if suspicious behavior is detected. They can then offer the user the ability to allow an offending application to run or to be prevented from running in the future.

Logging varies depending on the firewall application. It typically includes date and time of the event, whether the connection was allowed or denied, information about the source or destination IP addresses of packets, and the source and destination ports of the encapsulated segments. In addition, common activities such as DNS lookups and other routine events can show up in host-based firewall logs, so filtering and other parsing techniques are useful for inspecting large amounts of log data.

One approach to intrusion prevention is the use of distributed firewalls. Distributed firewalls combine features of host-based firewalls with centralized management. The management function pushes rules to the hosts and may also accept log files from the hosts.

Whether installed completely on the host or distributed, host-based firewalls are an important layer of network security along with network-based firewalls. Here are some examples of host-based firewalls:

- **Windows Firewall** - First included with Windows XP, Windows Firewall uses a profile-based approach to configuring firewall functionality. Access to public networks is assigned the restrictive Public firewall profile. The Private profile is for computers that are isolated from the Internet by other security devices, such as a home router with firewall functionality. The Domain profile is the third available profile. It is chosen for connections to a trusted network, such as a business network that is assumed to have an adequate security infrastructure. Windows Firewall has logging functionality and can be centrally managed with customized group security policies from a management server such as System Center 2012 Configuration Manager.

- **iptables** - This is an application that allows Linux system administrators to configure network access rules that are part of the Linux kernel Netfilter modules.

- **nftables** - The successor to iptables, nftables is a Linux firewall application that uses a simple virtual machine in the Linux kernel. Code is executed within the virtual machine that inspects network packets and implements decision rules regarding packet acceptance and forwarding.

- **TCP Wrapper** - This is a rule-based access control and logging system for Linux. Packet filtering is based on IP addresses and network services.

Refer to
Online Course
for Illustration

10.1.2.2   Host-Based Intrusion Detection

The distinction between host-based intrusion detection and intrusion prevention is blurred. In fact, some sources refer to host-based intrusion detection and prevention systems (HIPDS). Because the industry seems to favor the use of the acronym HIDS, we will use it in our discussion here.

A host-based intrusion detection system (HIDS) is designed to protect hosts against known and unknown malware. A HIDS can perform detailed monitoring and reporting on the system configuration and application activity. It can provide log analysis, event correlation, integrity checking, policy enforcement, rootkit detection, and alerting. A HIDS will frequently include a management server endpoint, as shown in the figure.

A HIDS is a comprehensive security application that combines the functionalities of anti-malware applications with firewall functionality. A HIDS not only detects malware but also can prevent it from executing if it should reach a host. Because the HIDS software must run directly on the host, it is considered an agent-based system.

Refer to **Online Course** for Illustration

10.1.2.3 HIDS Operation

It can be said that host-based security systems function as both detection and prevention systems because they prevent known attacks and detect unknown potential attacks. A HIDS uses both proactive and reactive strategies. A HIDS can prevent intrusion because it uses signatures to detect known malware and prevent it from infecting a system. However, this strategy is only good against known threats. Signatures are not effective against new, or zero day, threats. In addition, some malware families exhibit polymorphism. This means that variations of a type, or family, of malware may be created by attackers that will evade signature-based detections by changing aspects of the malware signature just enough so that it will not be detected. An additional set of strategies are used to detect the possibility of successful intrusions by malware that evades signature detection:

- **Anomaly-based** - Host system behavior is compared to a learned baseline model. Significant deviations from the baseline are interpreted as the result of some sort of intrusion. If an intrusion is detected, the HIDS can log details of the intrusion, send alerts to security management systems, and take action to prevent the attack. The measured baseline is derived from both user and system behavior. Because many things other than malware can cause system behavior to change, anomaly detection can create many erroneous results which can increase the workload for security personnel and also lower the credibility of the system.

- **Policy-based** - Normal system behavior is described by rules, or the violation of rules, that are predefined. Violation of these policies will result in action by the HIDS. The HIDS may attempt to shut down software processes that have violated the rules and can log these events and alert personnel to violations. Most HIDS software comes with a set of predefined rules. With some systems, administrators can create custom policies that can be distributed to hosts from a central policy management system.

Refer to **Online Course** for Illustration

10.1.2.4 HIDS Products

There are a number of HIDS products on the market today. Most of them utilize software on the host and some sort of centralized security management functionality that allows integration with network security monitoring services and threat intelligence. Examples are Cisco AMP, AlienVault USM, Tripwire, and Open Source HIDS SECurity (OSSEC).

OSSEC uses a central manager server and agents that are installed on individual hosts. Currently, agents only exist for Microsoft Windows platforms. For other platforms, OSSEC can also operate as an agentless system, and can be deployed in virtual environments. The OSSEC server can also receive and analyze alerts from a variety of network devices and firewalls over syslog. OSSEC monitors system logs on hosts and also conducts file integrity checking. OSSEC can detect rootkits, and can also be configured to run scripts or applications on hosts in response to event triggers.

Click here to learn more about OSSEC.

Refer to **Interactive Graphic** in online course

10.1.2.5 Activity - Identify the Host-Based Intrusion Protection Terminology

10.1.3   Application Security

Refer to
Online Course
for Illustration

10.1.3.1   Attack Surface

Recall that a vulnerability is a weakness in a system or its design that could be exploited by a threat. An attack surface is the total sum of the vulnerabilities in a given system that is accessible to an attacker. The attack surface can consist of open ports on servers or hosts, software that runs on Internet-facing servers, wireless network protocols, and even users.

The attack surface is continuing to expand, as shown in the figure. More devices are connecting to networks through the Internet of Things (IoT) and Bring Your Own Device (BYOD). Much of network traffic now flows between devices and some location in the cloud. Mobile device use continues to increase. All of these trends contribute to a prediction that global IP traffic will increase threefold in the next five years.

The SANS Institute describes three components of the attack surface:

- **Network Attack Surface -** The attack exploits vulnerabilities in networks. This can include conventional wired and wireless network protocols, as well as other wireless protocols used by smartphones or IoT devices. Network attacks also exploit vulnerabilities at the network and transport layers.

- **Software Attack Surface -** The attack is delivered through exploitation of vulnerabilities in web, cloud, or host-based software applications.

- **Human Attack Surface -** The attack exploits weaknesses in user behavior. Such attacks include social engineering, malicious behavior by trusted insiders, and user error.

Refer to
Interactive Graphic
in online course

10.1.3.2   Application Blacklisting and Whitelisting

One way of decreasing the attack surface is to limit access to potential threats by creating lists of prohibited applications. This is known as blacklisting.

Application blacklists can dictate which user applications are not permitted to run on a computer. Similarly, whitelists can specify which programs are allowed to run, as shown in Figure 1. In this way, known vulnerable applications can be prevented from creating vulnerabilities on network hosts.

Whitelists are created in accordance with a security baseline that has been established by an organization. The baseline establishes an accepted amount of risk, and the environmental components that contribute to that level of risk. Non-whitelisted software can violate the established security baseline by increasing risk.

Figure 2 shows the Windows Local Group Policy Editor blacklisting and whitelisting settings. Figure 3 shows how entries can be added, in this case to the list of blacklisted applications.

Click here for an interesting discussion by Kevin Townsend on the issues around whitelisting and blacklisting.

Websites can also be whitelisted and blacklisted. These blacklists can be manually created, or they can be obtained from various security services. Blacklists can be continuously updated by security services and distributed to firewalls and other security systems that use them. Cisco's FireSIGHT security management system is an example of a device that can access the Cisco Talos security intelligence service to obtain blacklists. These blacklists can then be distributed to security devices within an enterprise network.

Click here for information on SpamHaus, an example of a free blacklist service.

Refer to
Online Course
for Illustration

10.1.3.3   System-Based Sandboxing

Sandboxing is a technique that allows suspicious files to be executed and analyzed in a safe environment. Automated malware analysis sandboxes offer tools that analyze malware behavior. These tools observe the effects of running unknown malware so that features of malware behavior can be determined and then used to create defenses against it.

As mentioned previously, polymorphic malware changes frequently and new malware appears regularly. Malware will enter the network despite the most robust perimeter and host-based security systems. HIDS and other detection systems can create alerts on suspected malware that may have entered the network and executed on a host. Systems such as Cisco AMP can track the trajectory of a file through the network, and can "roll back" network events to obtain a copy of the downloaded file. This file can then be executed in a sandbox, such as Cisco Threat Grid Glovebox, and the activities of the file documented by the system. This information can then be used to create signatures to prevent the file from entering the network again. The information can also be used to create detection rules and automated plays that will identify other systems that have been infected.

Cuckoo Sandbox is a free malware analysis system sandbox. It can be run locally and have malware samples submitted to it for analysis. Click here for more information on Cuckoo Sandbox.

A number of online public sandboxes also exist. These services allow malware samples to be uploaded for analysis. Some of these services are VirusTotal, Payload Security VxStream Sandbox (shown in the figure), and Malwr.

Refer to **Video**
in online course

10.1.3.4   Video Demonstration - Using a Sandbox to Launch Malware

Click Play to view a demonstration of using sandbox environment to launch and analyze a malware attack.

Click here to read a transcript of the video.

10.2   Endpoint Vulnerability Assessment

10.2.1   Network and Server Profiling

Refer to
Online Course
for Illustration

10.2.1.1   Network Profiling

In order to detect serious security incidents, it is important to understand, characterize, and analyze information about normal network functioning. Networks, servers, and hosts all exhibit typical behavior for a given point in time. Network and device profiling can provide a baseline that serves as a reference point. Unexplained deviations from the baseline may indicate a compromise.

Increased utilization of WAN links at unusual times can indicate a network breach and exfiltration of data. Hosts that begin to access obscure Internet servers, resolve domains that are obtained through dynamic DNS, or use protocols or services that are not needed by the system user can also indicate compromise. Deviations in network behavior are difficult to detect if normal behavior is not known.

Tools like NetFlow and Wireshark can be used to characterize normal network traffic characteristics. Because organizations can make different demands on their networks depending on the time of day or day of the year, network baselining should be carried out over an extended period of time. Some questions to ask when establishing a network baseline, as shown in the figure, address important elements of the network profile:

- **Session duration** - This is the time between the establishment of a data flow and its termination.

- **Total throughput** - This is the amount of data passing from a given source to a given destination in a given period of time.

- **Ports used** - This is a list of TCP or UDP processes that are available to accept data.

- **Critical asset address space** - These are the IP addresses or the logical location of essential systems or data.

In addition, a profile of the types of traffic that typically enter and leave the network is an important tool in understanding network behavior. Malware can use unusual ports that may not be typically seen during normal network operation. Host-to-host traffic is another important metric. Most network clients communicate directly with servers, so an increase of traffic between clients can indicate that malware is spreading laterally through the network. Finally, changes in user behavior, as revealed by AAA, server logs, or a user profiling system like Cisco Identity Services Engine (ISE) is another valuable indicator. Knowing how individual users typically use the network leads to detection of potential compromise of user accounts. A user who suddenly begins logging in to the network at strange times from a remote location should raise alarms if this behavior is a deviation from a known norm.

Refer to
Online Course
for Illustration

10.2.1.2   Server Profiling

Server profiling is used to establish the accepted operating state of servers. A server profile is a security baseline for a given server. It establishes the network, user, and application parameters that are accepted for a specific server.

In order to establish a server profile, as shown in the figure, it is important to understand the function that a server is intended to perform in a network. From there, various operating and usage parameters can be defined and documented. A server profile may establish the following:

- **Listening ports** - These are the TCP and UDP daemons and ports that are allowed to be open on the server.

- **User accounts** - These are the parameters defining user access and behavior.

- **Service accounts** - These are the definitions of the type of service that an application is allowed to run on a given host.

- **Software environment** - These are the tasks, processes, and applications that are permitted to run on the server.

Refer to
Online Course
for Illustration

10.2.1.3   Network Anomaly Detection

Network behavior is described by a large amount of diverse data such as the features of packet flow, features of the packets themselves, and telemetry from multiple sources. One approach to detection of network attacks is the analysis of this diverse, unstructured data using Big Data analytics techniques.

This entails the use of sophisticated statistical and machine learning techniques to compare normal performance baselines with network performance at a given time. Significant deviations can be indicators of compromise.

Anomaly detection can recognize network congestion caused by worm traffic that exhibits scanning behavior. Anomaly detection also can identify infected hosts on the network that are scanning for other vulnerable hosts.

The figure illustrates a simplified version of an algorithm designed to detect an unusual condition at the border routers of an enterprise. For example, the cybersecurity analyst could provide the following values:

- $X = 5$
- $Y = 100$
- $Z = 30$
- $N = 500$

Now, the algorithm can be interpreted as: Every 5th minute, get a sampling of 1/100th of the flows during second 30. If the number of flows is greater than 500, generate an alarm. If the number of flows is less than 500, do nothing. This is a simple example of using a traffic profile to identify the potential for data loss.

Refer to **Online Course** for Illustration

10.2.1.4   Network Vulnerability Testing

Most organizations connect to public networks in some way due to the need to access the Internet. These organizations must also provide Internet facing services of various types to the public. Because of the vast number of potential vulnerabilities, and the fact that new vulnerabilities can be created within an organization network and its Internet facing services, periodic security testing is essential. Network security can be tested using a variety of tools and services. Various types of tests can be performed:

- **Risk Analysis** - This is a discipline in which analysts evaluate the risk posed by vulnerabilities to a specific organization. A risk analysis includes assessment of the likelihood of attacks, identifies types of likely threat actors, and evaluates the impact of successful exploits on the organization.

- **Vulnerability Assessment** - This test employs software to scan Internet facing servers and internal networks for various types of vulnerabilities. These vulnerabilities include unknown infections, weaknesses in web-facing database services, missing software patches, unnecessary listening ports, etc. Tools for vulnerability assessment include the open source OpenVAS platform, Microsoft Baseline Security Analyzer, Nessus, Qualys, and FireEye Mandiant services. Vulnerability assessment includes, but goes beyond, port scanning.

- **Penetration Testing** - This type of test uses authorized simulated attacks to test the strength of network security. Internal personnel with hacker experience, or professional ethical hackers, identify assets that could be targeted by threat actors. A series of exploits is used to test security of those assets. Simulated exploit software tools are frequently used. Penetration testing does not only verify that vulnerabilities exist, it actually exploits those vulnerabilities to determine the potential impact of a successful exploit. An individual penetration test is often known as a pen test. Metasploit is a tool used in penetration testing. CORE Impact offers penetration testing software and services.

Refer to
Interactive Graphic
in online course

10.2.1.5 Activity - Identify the Elements of Network Profiling

10.2.2 Common Vulnerability Scoring System (CVSS)

Refer to
Online Course
for Illustration

10.2.2.1 CVSS Overview

The Common Vulnerability Scoring System (CVSS) is a risk assessment designed to convey the common attributes and severity of vulnerabilities in computer hardware and software systems. The third revision, CVSS 3.0, is a vendor-neutral, industry standard, open framework for weighting the risks of a vulnerability using a variety of metrics. These weights combine to provide a score of the risk inherent in a vulnerability. The numeric score can be used to determine the urgency of the vulnerability, and the priority of addressing it. The benefits of the CVSS can be summarized as follows:

- It provides standardized vulnerability scores that should be meaningful across organizations.

- It provides an open framework with the meaning of each metric openly available to all users.

- It helps prioritize risk in a way that is meaningful to individual organizations.

The Forum of Incident Response and Security Teams (FIRST) has been designated as the custodian of the CVSS to promote its adoption globally. Version 3.0 was under development for 3 years, and Cisco and other industry partners contributed to the standard. The figure displays the specification page for the CVSS at the FIRST website.

Refer to
Online Course
for Illustration

10.2.2.2 CVSS Metric Groups

Before performing a CVSS assessment, it is important to know key terms that are used in the assessment instrument.

Many of the metrics address the role of what the CVSS calls an authority. An authority is a computer entity, such as a database, operating system, or virtual sandbox, which grants and manages access and privileges to users.

As shown in the figure, the CVSS uses three groups of metrics to assess vulnerability:

Base Metric Group

This represents the characteristics of a vulnerability that are constant over time and across contexts. It has two classes of metrics:

- **Exploitability** - These are features of the exploit such as the vector, complexity, and user interaction required by the exploit.

- **Impact metrics** - The impacts of the exploit are rooted in the CIA triad of confidentiality, integrity, and availability.

Temporal Metric Group

This measures the characteristics of a vulnerability that may change over time, but not across user environments. Over time, the severity of a vulnerability will change as it is detected and measures to counter it are developed. The severity of a new vulnerability may be high, but will decrease as patches, signatures, and other countermeasures are developed.

Environmental Metric Group

This measures the aspects of a vulnerability that are rooted in a specific organization's environment. These metrics help to guide consequences within an organization and also allow adjustment of metrics that are less relevant to what an organization does.

Refer to **Online Course** for Illustration

10.2.2.3 CVSS Base Metric Group

The Base Metric Group Exploitability metrics include the following criteria:

- **Attack vector** - This is a metric that reflects the proximity of the threat actor to the vulnerable component. The more remote the threat actor is to the component, the higher the severity. Threat actors close to your network or inside your network are easier to detect and mitigate.

- **Attack complexity** - This is a metric that expresses the number of components, software, hardware, or networks, that are beyond the attacker's control and that must be present in order for a vulnerability to be successfully exploited.

- **Privileges required** - This is a metric that captures the level of access that is required for a successful exploit of the vulnerability.

- **User interaction** - This metric expresses the presence or absence of the requirement for user interaction in order for an exploit to be successful.

- **Scope** - This metric expresses whether multiple authorities must be involved in an exploit. This is expressed as whether the initial authority changes to a second authority during the exploit.

The Base Metric Group Impact metrics increase with the degree or consequence of loss due to the impacted component. Impact metric components include:

- **Confidentiality Impact** - This is a metric that measures the impact to confidentiality due to a successfully exploited vulnerability. Confidentiality refers to the limiting of access to only authorized users.

- **Integrity Impact** - This is a metric that measures the impact to integrity due to a successfully exploited vulnerability. Integrity refers to the trustworthiness and authenticity of information.

- **Availability Impact** - This is a metric that measures the impact to availability due to a successfully exploited vulnerability. Availability refers to the accessibility of information and network resources. Attacks that consume network bandwidth, processor cycles, or disk space all impact the availability.

Refer to **Interactive Graphic** in online course

10.2.2.4 The CVSS Process

The CVSS Base Metrics Group is designed as a way to assess security vulnerabilities found in software and hardware systems. It describes the severity of a vulnerability based on the characteristics of a successful exploit of the vulnerability. The other metric groups modify the base severity score by accounting for how the base severity rating is affected by time and environmental factors.

The CVSS process uses a tool called the CVSS v3.0 Calculator, shown in Figure 1. The calculator is similar to a questionnaire in which choices are made that describe the vulnerability for each metric group. After all choices are made, a score is generated. Pop-up text that offers an explanation for each metric and metric value are displayed by hovering a mouse over each. Choices are made by choosing one of the values for the metric. Only one choice can be made per metric.

Click here to explore the CVSS calculator.

A detailed user guide that defines metric criteria, examples of assessments of common vulnerabilities, and the relationship of metric values to the final score is available to support the process.

After the Base Metric group is completed, the numeric severity rating is displayed, as shown in Figure 2. A vector string is also created that summarizes the choices made. If other metric groups are completed, those values are appended to the vector string. The string consists of the initial(s) for the metric, and an abbreviated value for the selected metric value separated by a colon. The metric-value pairs are separated by slashes. An example vector for the Base Metric group is shown in the Figure 3. The vector strings allow the results of the assessment to be easily shared and compared.

In order for a score to be calculated for the Temporal or Environmental metric groups, the Base Metric group must first be completed. The Temporal and Environmental metric values then modify the Base Metric results to provide an overall score. The interaction of the scores for the metric groups is shown in Figure 4.

Refer to
Online Course
for Illustration

10.2.2.5   CVSS Reports

The ranges of scores and the corresponding qualitative meaning is shown in the figure. Frequently, the Base and Temporal metric group scores will be supplied to customers by the application or security vendor in whose product the vulnerability has been discovered. The affected organization completes the environmental metric group to tailor the vendor-supplied scoring to the local context.

The resulting score serves to guide the affected organization in the allocation of resources to address the vulnerability. The higher the severity rating, the greater the potential impact of an exploit and the greater the urgency in addressing the vulnerability. While not as precise as the numeric CVSS scores, the qualitative labels are very useful for communicating with stakeholders who are unable to relate to the numeric scores.

In general, any vulnerability that exceeds 3.9 should be addressed. The higher the rating level, the greater the urgency for remediation.

Refer to
Interactive Graphic
in online course

10.2.2.6   Other Vulnerability Information Sources

There are other important vulnerability information sources. These work together with the CVSS to provide a comprehensive assessment of vulnerability severity. There are two systems that operate in the United States:

Common Vulnerabilities and Exposures (CVE)

This is a dictionary of common names, in the form of CVE identifiers, for known cybersecurity vulnerabilities. The CVE identifier provides a standard way to research a reference to vulnerabilities. When a vulnerability has been identified, CVE identifiers can be used to access fixes. In addition, threat intelligence services use CVE identifiers, and they appear in various security system logs. The CVE Details website provides a linkage between CVSS scores and CVE information. It allows browsing of CVE vulnerability records by CVSS severity rating.

Click here for more information on CVE (Figure 1). Click here to explore the linkages between CVE and CVSS.

National Vulnerability Database (NVD)

This utilizes CVE identifiers and supplies additional information on vulnerabilities such as CVSS threat scores, technical details, affected entities, and resources for further investigation. The database was created and is maintained by the U.S. government National Institute of Standards and Technology (NIST) agency.

Click here for more information on NVD (Figure 2).

Figure 3 illustrates an example of the NVD CVSS page for CVE-2016-0051, the WebDAV Elevation of Privilege Vulnerability.

Refer to
Interactive Graphic
in online course

10.2.2.7 Activity - Identify CVSS Metrics

10.2.3 Compliance Frameworks

Refer to
Online Course
for Illustration

10.2.3.1 Compliance Regulations

Recent history is full of instances in which sensitive information has been lost to threat actors. Recent security breaches at large retailers have resulted in the loss of personally identifiable information for millions of people. Corporations have lost valuable intellectual property which has resulted in the loss of millions of dollars in revenue. In addition, security breaches have resulted in the loss of sensitive information related to national security.

To prevent similar losses, a number of security compliance regulations have emerged. The regulations offer a framework for practices that enhance information security while also stipulating incidence response actions and penalties for failure to comply. Organizations can verify compliance through the process of compliance assessment and audit. Assessments verify compliance or non-compliance for informational purposes. Audits also verify compliance but can result in consequences, such as financial penalties or loss of business opportunity.

This topic will discuss and differentiate the important and far reaching compliance regulations shown in the figure.

Refer to
Online Course
for Illustration

10.2.3.2 Overview of Regulatory Standards

There are five major regulatory compliance regulations.

Payment Card Industry Data Security Standard (PCI-DSS)

PCI-DSS is a proprietary, non-governmental standard maintained by the Payment Card Industry Security Standards Council which was formed by the five major credit card companies. The standard specifies requirements for the secure handling of customer credit card data by merchants and service providers. It dictates standards for how credit card information is to be stored and transmitted, and when customer information must be removed from storage systems.

The PCI-DSS applies to any entity that stores, processes, and/or transmits data about credit cardholders. As shown in the figure, cardholder data includes:

- Cardholder name
- Primary account number (PAN)
- Expiration date

- Service Code (part of the magnetic strip)

- Card Verification Code (CVC), Card Verification Value (CVV), Card Security Code (CSC)

- Card Identification Code (CID)

- Sensitive Data stored on magnetic strip or chip

Many network management platforms include compliance reporting in their security-management related functionalities.

Click here for more information on PCI-DSS.

Federal Information Security Management Act of 2002 (FISMA)

FISMA was established by NIST by an act of the US Congress. FISMA regulations specify security standards for U.S. government systems and contractors to the U.S. government. FISMA also provides standards for the categorization of information and information systems according to a range of risk levels, and requirements for the security of information in each risk category.

Click here for more information on FISMA.

Sarbanes-Oxley Act of 2002 (SOX)

SOX set new or expanded requirements for all U.S. public company boards, management, and public accounting firms regarding the way in which corporations control and disclose financial information. The act is designed to ensure the integrity of financial practices and reporting. It also dictates controls for access to financial information and information systems.

Click here for more information on SOX.

Gramm-Leach-Bliley Act (GLBA)

GLBA established that financial institutions must ensure the security and confidentiality of customer information; protect against any anticipated threats or hazards to the security or integrity of such information; and protect against unauthorized access to or use of customer information that could result in substantial harm or inconvenience to any customer. Financial institutions are considered to be banks, brokerages, insurance companies, etc.

Click here for more information on GLBA.

Health Insurance Portability and Accountability Act (HIPAA)

HIPAA requires that all patient personally identifiable healthcare information be stored, maintained, and transmitted in ways that ensure patient privacy and confidentiality. HIPAA stipulates controlled access policies and data encryption of patient information. HIPAA specifies detailed administrative safeguards and implementation specifications in the areas of security management, workforce security, and information access management, among others.

Click here for more information on HIPAA.

Note Although the scope of this course and the CCNA Cybersecurity Operations certification are limited to United States regulations, click here to learn more about European Union cybersecurity regulations.

Refer to
Interactive Graphic
in online course

10.2.3.3 Activity - Identify Regulatory Standards

10.2.4   Secure Device Management

Refer to **Online Course** for Illustration

10.2.4.1   Risk Management

Risk management involves the selection and specification of security controls for an organization. It is part of an ongoing organization-wide information security program that involves the management of the risk to the organization or to individuals associated with the operation of a system.

Risk management is an ongoing, multi-step, cyclical process, as shown in the figure.

Risk is determined as the relationship between threat, vulnerability, and the nature of the organization. It first involves answering the following questions as part of a risk assessment:

- Who are the threat actors who want to attack us?

- What vulnerabilities can threat actors exploit?

- How would we be affected by attacks?

- What is the likelihood that different attacks will occur?

NIST Special Publication 800-30 describes risk assessment as:

> *...the process of identifying, estimating, and prioritizing information security risks. Assessing risk requires the careful analysis of threat and vulnerability information to determine the extent to which circumstances or events could adversely impact an organization and the likelihood that such circumstances or events will occur.*

Click here to download the full NIST Special Publication 800-30.

A mandatory activity in risk assessment is the identification of threats and vulnerabilities and the matching of threats with vulnerabilities in what is often called threat-vulnerability (T-V) pairing. The T-V pairs can then be used as a baseline to indicate risk before security controls are implemented. This baseline can then be compared to ongoing risk assessments as a means of evaluating risk management effectiveness. This part of risk assessment is referred to as determining the inherent risk profile of an organization.

After the risks are identified, they may be scored or weighted as a way of prioritizing risk reduction strategies. For example, vulnerabilities that are found to have corresponded with multiple threats can receive higher ratings. In addition, T-V pairs that map to the greatest institutional impact will also receive higher weightings.

There are four potential ways to respond to risks that have been identified, based on their weightings or scores:

- **Risk avoidance** - Stop performing the activities that create risk. It is possible that as a result of a risk assessment, it is determined that the risk involved in an activity outweighs the benefit of the activity to the organization. If this is found to be true, then it may be determined that the activity should be discontinued.

- **Risk reduction** - Decrease the risk by taking measures to reduce vulnerability. This involves implementing management approaches discussed earlier in this chapter. For example, if an organization uses server operating systems that are frequently targeted by threat actors, risk can be reduced through ensuring that the servers are patched as soon as vulnerabilities have been addressed.

- **Risk sharing** - Shift some of the risk to other parties. For example, a risk-sharing technique might be to outsource some aspects of security operations to third-parties. Hiring a security as a service (SECaaS) CSIRT to perform security monitoring is an example. Another example is to buy insurance that will help to mitigate some of the financial losses due to a security incident.

- **Risk retention** - Accept the risk and its consequences. This strategy is acceptable for risks that have low potential impact and relatively high cost of mitigation or reduction. Other risks that may be retained are those that are so dramatic that they cannot realistically be avoided, reduced, or shared.

Refer to **Interactive Graphic** in online course

10.2.4.2   Activity - Identify the Risk Response

Refer to **Interactive Graphic** in online course

10.2.4.3   Vulnerability Management

According to NIST, vulnerability management is a security practice designed to proactively prevent the exploitation of IT vulnerabilities that exist within an organization. The expected result is to reduce the time and money spent dealing with vulnerabilities and the exploitation of those vulnerabilities. Proactively managing vulnerabilities of systems will reduce or eliminate the potential for exploitation, and involve considerably less time and effort than responding after an exploitation has occurred.

Vulnerability management requires a robust means of identifying vulnerabilities based on vendor security bulletins and other information systems such as CVE. Security personnel must be competent in assessing the impact, if any, of vulnerability information they have received. Solutions should be identified with effective means of implementing and assessing the unanticipated consequences of implemented solutions. Finally, the solution should be tested to verify that the vulnerability has been eliminated.

The steps in the Vulnerability Management Life Cycle, shown in the figure, are described below.

- **Discover** - Inventory all assets across the network and identify host details, including operating systems and open services, to identify vulnerabilities. Develop a network baseline. Identify security vulnerabilities on a regular automated schedule.

- **Prioritize Assets** - Categorize assets into groups or business units, and assign a business value to asset groups based on their criticality to business operations.

- **Assess** - Determine a baseline risk profile to eliminate risks based on asset criticality, vulnerability, threats, and asset classification.

- **Report** - Measure the level of business risk associated with your assets according to your security policies. Document a security plan, monitor suspicious activity, and describe known vulnerabilities.

- **Remediate** - Prioritize according to business risk and address vulnerabilities in order of risk.

- **Verify** - Verify that threats have been eliminated through follow-up audits.

Refer to **Online Course** for Illustration

10.2.4.4   Asset Management

Asset management involves the implementation of systems that track the location and configuration of networked devices and software across an enterprise. As part of any security management plan, organizations must know what equipment accesses the network, where that equipment is within the enterprise and logically on the network, and what software and data those systems store or can access. Asset management not only tracks corporate assets and other authorized devices, but also can be used to identify devices that are not authorized on the network.

NIST specifies in publication NISTIR 8011 Volume 2, the detailed records that should be kept for each relevant device. NIST describes potential techniques and tools for operationalizing an asset management process:

- Automated discovery and inventory of the actual state of devices

- Articulation of the desired state for those devices using policies, plans, and procedures in the organization's information security plan

- Identification of non-compliant authorized assets

- Remediation or acceptance of device state, possible iteration of desired state definition

- Repeat the process at regular intervals, or ongoing

The figure provides an overview of this process.

Click here to download the NISTIR 8011 Volume 2 document.

Refer to
Online Course
for Illustration

10.2.4.5 Mobile Device Management

Mobile device management (MDM), especially in the age of BYOD, presents special challenges to asset management. Mobile devices cannot be physically controlled on the premises of an organization. They can be lost, stolen, or tampered with, putting data and network access at risk. Part of an MDM plan is taking action when devices leave the custody of the responsible party. Measures that can be taken include disabling the lost device, encrypting the data on the device, and enhancing device access with more robust authentication measures.

Due to the diversity of mobile devices it is possible that some devices that will be used on the network are inherently less secure than others. Network administrators should assume that all mobile devices are untrusted until they have been properly secured by the organization.

MDM systems, such as Cisco Meraki Systems Manager, shown in the figure, allow security personnel to configure, monitor and update a very diverse set of mobile clients from the cloud.

Click here to learn more about Cisco Meraki, watch some video demonstrations, and access a self-enroll course.

Refer to
Online Course
for Illustration

10.2.4.6 Configuration Management

Configuration management addresses the inventory and control of hardware and software configurations of systems. Secure device configurations reduce security risk. For example, an organization provides many computers and laptops to its workers. This enlarges the attack surface for the organization, because each system may be vulnerable to exploits. To manage this, the organization may create baseline software images and hardware configurations for each type of machine. These images may include a basic package of required software, endpoint security software, and customized security policies that control user access to aspects of the system configuration that could be made vulnerable. Hardware configurations may specify the permitted types of network interfaces and the permitted types of external storage.

Configuration management extends to the software and hardware configuration of networking devices and servers as well. As defined by NIST, configuration management:

comprises a collection of activities focused on establishing and maintaining the integrity of products and systems, through control of the processes for initializing, changing, and monitoring the configurations of those products and systems.

Click here to download the complete NIST Special Publication 800-128 on configuration management for network security.

For internetworking devices, software tools are available that will backup configurations, detect changes in configuration files, and enable bulk change of configurations across a number of devices.

With the advent of cloud data centers and virtualization, management of numerous servers presents special challenges. Configuration management tools like Puppet, Chef, Ansible, and SaltStack were developed to allow efficient management of servers that enable cloud-based computing.

10.2.4.7   Enterprise Patch Management

Refer to **Online Course** for Illustration

Patch management is related to vulnerability management. Vulnerabilities frequently appear in critical client, server, and networking device operating systems and firmware. Application software, especially Internet applications and frameworks like Acrobat, Flash, and Java, also are frequently discovered to have vulnerabilities. Patch management involves all aspects of software patching, including identifying required patches, acquiring, distributing, installing, and verifying that the patch is installed on all required systems. Installing patches is frequently the most effective way to mitigate software vulnerabilities. Sometimes, they are the only way to do so.

Patch management is required by some security compliance regulations, such as SOX and HIPAA. Failure to implement patches in a systematic and timely manner could result in audit failure and penalties for non-compliance. Patch management depends on asset management data to identify systems that are running software that requires patching. The figure shows a screen shot of the SolarWinds Patch Manager tool.

10.2.4.8   Patch Management Techniques

Refer to **Interactive Graphic** in online course

At the enterprise level, patch management is most efficiently run from a patch management system. Most patch management systems incorporate a client-centralized server architecture, as do other end point-related security systems. There are three patch management technologies.

■ **Agent-based** - This requires a software agent to be running on each host to be patched. The agent reports whether vulnerable software is installed on the host. The agent communicates with the patch management server, determines if patches exist that require installation, and installs the patches. The agent runs with sufficient privileges to allow it to install the patches. Agent-based approaches are the preferred means of patching mobile devices (Figure 1).

- **Agentless scanning** - Patch management servers scan the network for devices that require patching. The server determines which patches are required and installs those patches on the clients. Only devices that are on scanned network segments can be patched in this way. This can be a problem for mobile devices (Figure 2).

- **Passive network monitoring** - Devices requiring patching are identified through the monitoring of traffic on the network. This approach is only effective for software that includes version information in its network traffic (Figure 3).

Refer to
Interactive Graphic
in online course

10.2.4.9   Activity - Identify Device Management Activities

10.2.5   Information Security Management Systems

Refer to
Online Course
for Illustration

10.2.5.1   Security Management Systems

An Information Security Management System (ISMS) consists of a management framework through which an organization identifies, analyzes, and addresses information security risks. ISMSs are not based in servers or security devices. Instead, an ISMS consists of a set of practices that are systematically applied by an organization to ensure continuous improvement in information security. ISMSs provide conceptual models that guide organizations in planning, implementing, governing, and evaluating information security programs.

ISMSs are a natural extension of the use of popular business models, such as Total Quality Management (TQM) and Control Objectives for Information and Related Technologies (COBIT), into the realm of cybersecurity.

An ISMS is a systematic, multi-layered approach to cybersecurity. The approach includes people, processes, technologies, and the cultures in which they interact in a process of risk management.

An ISMS often incorporates the "plan-do-check-act" framework, known as the Deming cycle, from TQM. It is seen as an elaboration on the process component of the People-Process-Technology-Culture model of organizational capability, as shown in the figure.

Refer to
Interactive Graphic
in online course

10.2.5.2   ISO-27001

ISO is the International Organization for Standardization. ISO's voluntary standards are internationally accepted and facilitate business conducted between nations.

ISO partnered with the International Electrotechnical Commission (IEC) to develop the ISO/IEC 27000 family of specifications for ISMSs, as shown in Figure 1.

The ISO 27001 Certification is a global, industry-wide specification for an ISMS. Figure 2 illustrates the relationship of actions stipulated by the standard with the plan-do-check-act cycle. Certification means an organization's security policies and procedures have been independently verified to provide a systematic and proactive approach for effectively managing security risks to confidential customer information.

Refer to
Interactive Graphic
in online course

10.2.5.3   NIST Cybersecurity Framework

NIST is very effective in the area of cybersecurity, as we have seen in this chapter. More NIST standards will be discussed later in the course.

NIST has developed the Cybersecurity Framework, which, like ISO/IEC 27000, is a set of standards designed to integrate existing standards, guidelines, and practices to help better manage and reduce cybersecurity risk. The framework was first issued in February, 2014 and continues to undergo development.

The framework consists of a set of activities suggested to achieve specific cybersecurity outcomes, and references examples of guidance to achieve those outcomes. The core functions, defined in Figure 1, are split into major categories and subcategories. The major categories provide an understanding of the types of activities related to each function, as shown in Figure 2.

Organizations of many types are using the Framework in a number of ways. Many have found it helpful in raising awareness and communicating with stakeholders within their organization, including executive leadership. The Framework is also improving communications across organizations, allowing cybersecurity expectations to be shared with business partners, suppliers, and among sectors. By mapping the Framework to current cybersecurity management approaches, organizations are learning and showing how they match up with the Framework's standards, guidelines, and best practices. Some parties are using the Framework to reconcile internal policy with legislation, regulation, and industry best practice. The Framework also is being used as a strategic planning tool to assess risks and current practices.

Click here to learn more about the NIST Cybersecurity Framework.

Refer to
Interactive Graphic
in online course

10.2.5.4   Activity - Identify the ISO 27001 Activity Cycle

Refer to
Interactive Graphic
in online course

10.2.5.5   Activity - Identify the Stages in the NIST Cybersecurity Framework

10.3   Summary

10.3.1   Conclusion

Refer to
Online Course
for Illustration

10.3.1.1   Chapter 10: Endpoint Security and Analysis

In this chapter, you learned how to investigate endpoint vulnerabilities and attacks. Antimalware for network devices and hosts provides a method for mitigating the impact of attacks. Host-based personal firewalls are standalone software programs that control traffic entering or leaving a computer. A host-based intrusion detection system (HIDS) is designed to protect hosts against known and unknown malware. A HIDS is a comprehensive security application that combines the functionalities of antimalware applications with firewall functionality. Host-based security solutions are essential to protecting the expanding attack surfaces.

Cybersecurity analysts and security experts use a variety of tools to perform endpoint vulnerability assessments. Network and device profiling provide a baseline that serves as a reference point for identifying deviations from normal operations. Similarly, server profiling is used to establish the accepted operating state of servers. Network security can be evaluated using a variety of tools and services including:

- Risk analysis to evaluate the risk posed by vulnerabilities to a specific organization.

- Vulnerability assessment, which uses software to scan Internet-facing servers and internal networks for various types of vulnerabilities.

- Penetration testing, which uses authorized simulated attacks to test the strength of network security.

The Common Vulnerability Scoring System (CVSS) is a risk assessment designed to convey the common attributes and severity of vulnerabilities in computer hardware and software systems. The benefits of CVSS include:

- Standardized vulnerability scores that should be meaningful across organizations

- Open framework with the meaning of each metric openly available to all users

- Prioritization of risk in a way that is meaningful to individual organizations

A number of security compliance regulations have emerged including:

- **Federal Information Security Management Act of 2002 (FISMA)** - This provides security standards for U.S. government systems and contractors to the U.S. government.

- **Sarbanes-Oxley Act of 2002 (SOX)** - This provides the requirements for the way in which U.S. corporations control and disclose financial information.

- **Gramm-Leach-Bliley Act (GLBA)** - This states that financial institutions must secure customer information, protect against threats to customer information, and protect against unauthorized access to customer information.

- **Health Insurance Portability and Accountability Act (HIPAA)** - This requires that all patient personally identifiable healthcare information be stored, maintained, and transmitted in ways that ensure patient privacy and confidentiality.

- **Payment Card Industry Data Security Standard (PCI-DSS)** - This is a proprietary, non-governmental standard for the secure handling of customer credit card data.

Risk management involves the selection and specification of security controls for an organization. There are four potential ways to respond to risks that have been identified, based on their weightings or scores:

- Risk avoidance if it is determined that the activity should be discontinued.

- Risk reduction by implementing management approaches to reduce vulnerability.

- Risk sharing to shift risk by outsourcing some aspects of security operations to third-parties.

- Risk retention and acceptance for risks that have low potential impact and/or relatively high cost of mitigation or reduction.

Risk management tools include:

- Vulnerability management
- Asset management
- Mobile device management
- Configuration management
- Enterprise patch management

Organizations can use an Information Security Management System (ISMS) to identify, analyze, and address information security risks. Standards for managing cybersecurity risk are available from ISO and NIST.

Go to the online course to take the quiz and exam.

Chapter 10 Quiz

This quiz is designed to provide an additional opportunity to practice the skills and knowledge presented in the chapter and to prepare for the chapter exam. You will be allowed multiple attempts and the grade does not appear in the gradebook.

Chapter 10 Exam

The chapter exam assesses your knowledge of the chapter content.

Your Chapter Notes

Security Monitoring

11.0 Introduction

11.0.1 Welcome

Refer to
Online Course
for Illustration

11.0.1.1 Chapter 11: Security Monitoring

Network security monitoring (NSM) uses various types of data to detect, verify, and contain exploits. The primary task of the cybersecurity analyst is to verify successful or attempted exploits using NSM data and tools.

In this chapter, you will learn about the security technologies and log files used in security monitoring.

11.1 Technologies and Protocols

11.1.1 Monitoring Common Protocols

Refer to
Online Course
for Illustration

11.1.1.1 Syslog and NTP

Various protocols that commonly appear on networks have features that make them of special interest in security monitoring. For example, syslog and Network Time Protocol (NTP) are essential to the work of the cybersecurity analyst.

The syslog standard is used for logging event messages from network devices and endpoints, as shown in the figure. The standard allows for a system-neutral means of transmitting, storing, and analyzing messages. Many types of devices from many different vendors can use syslog to send log entries to central servers that run a syslog daemon. This centralization of log collection helps to make security monitoring practical. Servers that run syslog typically listen on UDP port 514.

Because syslog is so important to security monitoring, syslog servers may be a target for threat actors. Some exploits, such as those involving data exfiltration, can take a long time to complete due to the very slow ways in which data is secretly stolen from the network. Some attackers may try to hide the fact that exfiltration is occurring. They attack syslog servers that contain the information that could lead to detection of the exploit. Hackers may attempt to block the transfer of data from syslog clients to servers, tamper with or destroy log data, or tamper with software that creates and transmits log messages. The next generation (ng) syslog implementation, known as syslog-ng, offers enhancements that can help prevent some of the exploits that target syslog.

Click here to learn more about syslog-ng.

Refer to
Online Course
for Illustration

11.1.1.2 NTP

Syslog messages are usually timestamped. This allows messages from different sources to be organized by time to provide a view of network communication processes. Because the messages can come from many devices, it is important that the devices share a consistent timeclock. One way that this can be achieved is for the devices to use Network Time Protocol (NTP). NTP uses a hierarchy of authoritative time sources to share time information between devices on the network, as shown in the figure. In this way, device messages that share consistent time information can be submitted to the syslog server. NTP operates on UDP port 123.

Because events that are connected to an exploit can leave traces across every network device on their path to the target system, timestamps are essential for detection. Threat actors may attempt to attack the NTP infrastructure in order to corrupt time information used to correlate logged network events. This can serve to obfuscate traces of ongoing exploits. In addition, threat actors have been known to use NTP systems to direct DDoS attacks through vulnerabilities in client or server software. While these attacks do not necessarily result in corrupted security monitoring data, they can disrupt network availability.

Refer to
Online Course
for Illustration

11.1.1.3 DNS

Domain Name Service (DNS) is used by millions of people daily. Because of this, many organizations have less stringent policies in place to protect against DNS-based threats than they have to protect against other types of exploits. Attackers have recognized this and commonly encapsulate different network protocols within DNS to evade security devices. DNS is now used by many types of malware. Some varieties of malware use DNS to communicate with command-and-control (CnC) servers and to exfiltrate data in traffic disguised as normal DNS queries. Various types of encoding, such as Base64, 8-bit binary, and Hex can be used to camouflage the data and evade basic data loss prevention (DLP) measures.

For example, malware could encode stolen data as the subdomain portion of a DNS lookup for a domain where the nameserver is under control of an attacker. A DNS lookup for 'long-string-of-exfiltrated-data.example.com' would be forwarded to the nameserver of example.com, which would record 'long-string-of-exfiltrated-data' and reply back to the malware with a coded response. This use of the DNS subdomain is shown in the figure. The exfiltrated data is the encoded text shown in the box. The threat actor collects this encoded data, decodes and combines it, and now has access to an entire data file, such as a username/password database.

It is likely that the subdomain part of such requests would be much longer than usual requests. Cyber analysts can use the distribution of the lengths of subdomains within DNS requests to construct a mathematical model that describes normality. They can then use this to compare their observations and identify an abuse of the DNS query process. For example, it would not be normal to see a host on your network sending a query to aW4gc-GxhY2UgdG8gcHJvdGVjdC.example.com.

DNS queries for randomly generated domain names, or extremely long random-appearing subdomains, should be considered suspicious, especially if their occurrence spikes dramatically on the network. DNS proxy logs can be analyzed to detect these conditions. Alternatively, services such as the Cisco Umbrella passive DNS service can be used to block requests to suspected CnC and exploit domains.

Refer to
Interactive Graphic
in online course

11.1.1.4 HTTP and HTTPS

Hypertext Transfer Protocol (HTTP) is the backbone protocol of the World Wide Web. However, all information carried in HTTP is transmitted in plaintext from the source computer to the destination on the Internet. HTTP does not protect data from alteration or interception by malicious parties, which is a serious threat to privacy, identity, and information security. All browsing activity should be considered to be at risk.

A common exploit of HTTP is called iFrame (inline frame) injection. Most web-based threats consist of malware scripts that have been planted on webservers. These webservers then direct browsers to infected servers by loading iframes. In iFrame injection, a threat actor compromises a webserver and plants malicious code which creates an invisible iFrame on a commonly visited webpage. When the iFrame loads, malware is downloaded, frequently from a different URL than the webpage that contains the iFrame code. Network security services, such as Cisco Web Reputation filtering, can detect when a website attempts to send content from an untrusted website to the host, even when sent from an iFrame, as shown in Figure 1.

To address the alteration or interception of confidential data, many commercial organizations have adopted HTTPS or implemented HTTPS-only policies to protect visitors to their websites and services.

HTTPS adds a layer of encryption to the HTTP protocol by using secure socket layer (SSL), as shown in Figure 2. This makes the HTTP data unreadable as it leaves the source computer until it reaches the server. Note that HTTPS is not a mechanism for web server security. It only secures HTTP protocol traffic while it is in transit.

Unfortunately, the encrypted HTTPS traffic complicates network security monitoring. Some security devices include SSL decryption and inspection; however, this can present processing and privacy issues. In addition, HTTPS adds complexity to packet captures due to the additional messaging involved in establishing the encrypted connection. This process is summarized in Figure 3 and represents additional overhead on top of HTTP.

Refer to
Online Course
for Illustration

11.1.1.5 Email Protocols

Email protocols such as SMTP, POP3, and IMAP can be used by threat actors to spread malware, exfiltrate data, or provide channels to malware CnC servers, as shown in the figure.

SMTP sends data from a host to a mail server and between mail servers. Like DNS and HTTP, it is a common protocol to see leaving the network. Because there is so much SMTP traffic, it is not always monitored. However, SMTP has been used in the past by malware to exfiltrate data from the network. In the 2014 hack of Sony Pictures, one of the exploits used SMTP to exfiltrate user details from compromised hosts to CnC servers. This information may have been used to help develop exploits of secured resources within the Sony Pictures network. Security monitoring could reveal this type of traffic based on features of the email message.

IMAP and POP3 are used to download email messages from a mail server to the host computer. For this reason, they are the application protocols that are responsible for bringing malware to the host. Security monitoring can identify when a malware attachment entered the network and which host it first infected. Retrospective analysis can then track the behavior of the malware from that point forward. In this way, the malware behavior can better be understood and the threat identified. Security monitoring tools may also allow recovery of infected file attachments for submission to malware sandboxes for analysis.

Refer to
Online Course
for Illustration

11.1.1.6   ICMP

ICMP has many legitimate uses, however the ICMP functionality has been used to craft a number of types of exploits. ICMP can be used to identify hosts on a network, the structure of a network, and determine the operating systems at use on the network. It can also be used as a vehicle for various types of DoS attacks.

ICMP can also be used for data exfiltration. Because of the concern that ICMP can be used to surveil or deny service from outside of the network, ICMP traffic from inside the network is sometimes overlooked. However, some varieties of malware use crafted ICMP packets to transfer files from infected hosts to threat actors using this method, which is known as ICMP tunneling.

Click here for a detailed explanation of the well-known LOKI exploit.

A number of tools exist for crafting tunnels, such as Hans and Ping Tunnel.

Refer to
Interactive Graphic
in online course

11.1.1.7   Activity - Identify the Monitored Protocol

11.1.2   Security Technologies

Refer to
Interactive Graphic
in online course

11.1.2.1   ACLs

Many technologies and protocols can have impacts on security monitoring. Access Control Lists (ACLs) are among these technologies. ACLs can give a false sense of security if they are overly relied upon. ACLs, and packet filtering in general, are technologies that contribute to an evolving set of network security protections.

The figure illustrates the use of ACLs to permit only specific types of Internet Control Message Protocol (ICMP) traffic. The server at 192.168.1.10 is part of the inside network and is allowed to send ping requests to the outside host at 209.165.201.3. The outside host's return ICMP traffic is allowed if it is an ICMP reply, source quench (tells the source to reduce the pace of traffic), or any ICMP unreachable message. All other ICMP traffic types are denied. For example, the outside host cannot initiate a ping request to the inside host. The outbound ACL is allowing ICMP messages that report various problems. This will allow ICMP tunneling and data exfiltration.

Attackers can determine which IP addresses, protocols, and ports are allowed by ACLs. This can be done either by port scanning or penetration testing, or through other forms of reconnaissance. Attackers can craft packets that use spoofed source IP addresses. Applications can establish connections on arbitrary ports. Other features of protocol traffic can also be manipulated, such as the established flag in TCP segments. Rules cannot be anticipated and configured for all emerging packet manipulation techniques.

In order to detect and react to packet manipulation, more sophisticated behavior and context-based measures need to be taken. Cisco Next Generation firewalls, Advanced Malware Protection (AMP), and email and web content appliances are able to address the shortcomings of rule-based security measures.

Refer to
Online Course
for Illustration

11.1.2.2   NAT and PAT

Network Address Translation (NAT) and Port Address Translation (PAT) can complicate security monitoring. Multiple IP addresses are mapped to one or more public addresses that are visible on the Internet, hiding the individual IP addresses that are inside the network (inside addresses).

The figure illustrates the relationship between internal and external addresses that are used as source addresses (SA) and destination addresses (DA). These internal and external addresses are in a network that is using NAT to communicate with a destination on the Internet. If PAT is in effect, and all IP addresses leaving the network use the 209.165.200.226 inside global address for traffic to the Internet, it could be difficult to log the specific inside device that is requesting and receiving the traffic when it enters the network.

This problem can be especially relevant with NetFlow data. NetFlow flows are unidirectional and are defined by the addresses and ports that they share. NAT will essentially break a flow that passes a NAT gateway, making flow information beyond that point unavailable. Cisco offers security products that will "stitch" flows together even if the IP addresses have been replaced by NAT.

NetFlow is discussed in more detail later in the chapter.

Refer to
Online Course
for Illustration

11.1.2.3   Encryption, Encapsulation, and Tunneling

As mentioned with HTTPS, encryption can present challenges to security monitoring by making packet details unreadable. Encryption is part of VPN technologies. In VPNs, a commonplace protocol like IP, is used to carry encrypted traffic. The encrypted traffic essentially establishes a virtual point-to-point connection between networks over public facilities. Encryption makes the traffic unreadable to any other devices but the VPN endpoints.

A similar technology can be used to create a virtual point-to-point connection between an internal host and threat actor devices. Malware can establish an encrypted tunnel that rides on a common and trusted protocol, and use it to exfiltrate data from the network. A similar method of data exfiltration was discussed previously for DNS.

Refer to
Interactive Graphic
in online course

11.1.2.4   Peer-to-Peer Networking and Tor

In peer-to-peer (P2P) networking, shown in Figure 1, hosts can operate in both client and server roles. Three types of P2P applications exist: file sharing, processor sharing, and instant messaging. In file sharing P2P, files on a participating machine are shared with members of the P2P network. Examples of this are the once popular Napster and Gnutella. Bitcoin is a P2P operation that involves the sharing of a distributed database, or ledger, that records Bitcoin balances and transactions. BitTorrent is a P2P file sharing network.

Any time that unknown users are provided access to network resources, security is a concern. File-sharing P2P applications should not be allowed on corporate networks. P2P network activity can circumvent firewall protections and is a common vector for the spread of malware. P2P is inherently dynamic. It can operate by connecting to numerous destination IP addresses, and it can also use dynamic port numbering. Shared files are often infected with malware, and threat actors can position their malware on P2P clients for distribution to other users.

Processor sharing P2P networks donate processor cycles to distributed computational tasks. Cancer research, searching for extraterrestrials, and scientific research use donated processor cycles to distribute computational tasks.

Instant messaging (IM) is also considered to be a P2P application. IM has legitimate value within organizations that have geographically distributed project teams. In this case, specialized IM applications are available, such as the Cisco Jabber platform, which are more secure than IM that uses public servers.

Tor, shown in Figure 2, is a software platform and network of P2P hosts that function as Internet routers on the Tor network. The Tor network allows users to browse the Internet anonymously. Users access the Tor network by using a special browser. When a browsing session is begun, the browser constructs a layered end-to-end path across the Tor server network that is encrypted, as shown in Figure 3. Each encrypted layer is "peeled away" like the layers of an onion (hence "onion routing") as the traffic traverses a Tor relay. The layers contain encrypted next-hop information that can only be read by the router that needs to read the information. In this way, no single device knows the entire path to the destination, and routing information is readable only by the device that requires it. Finally, at the end of the Tor path, the traffic reaches its Internet destination. When traffic is returned to the source, an encrypted layered path is again constructed.

Tor presents a number of challenges to cybersecurity analysts. First, Tor is widely used by criminal organizations on the "dark net." In addition, Tor has been used as a communications channel for malware CnC. Because the destination IP address of Tor traffic is obfuscated by encryption, with only the next-hop Tor node known, Tor traffic avoids blacklists that have been configured on security devices.

Refer to
Online Course
for Illustration

11.1.2.5   Load Balancing

Load balancing involves the distribution of traffic between devices or network paths to prevent overwhelming network resources with too much traffic. If redundant resources exist, a load balancing algorithm or device will work to distribute traffic between those resources, as shown in the figure.

One way this is done on the Internet is through various techniques that use DNS to send traffic to resources that have the same domain name but multiple IP addresses. In some cases, the distribution may be to servers that are distributed geographically. This can result in a single Internet transaction being represented by multiple IP addresses on the incoming packets. This may cause suspicious features to appear in packet captures. In addition, some load balancing manager (LBM) devices use probes to test for the performance of different paths and the of health different resources. For example, an LBM may send probes to the different servers that it is load balancing traffic to in order to detect that the servers are operating. This is done to avoid sending traffic to a resource that is not available. These probes can appear to be suspicious traffic if the cybersecurity analyst is not aware that this traffic is part of the operation of the LBM.

Refer to
Interactive Graphic
in online course

11.1.2.6   Activity - Identify the Impact of the Technology on Security and Monitoring

11.2   Log Files

11.2.1   Types of Security Data

Refer to
Online Course
for Illustration

11.2.1.1   Alert Data

Alert data consists of messages generated by intrusion prevention systems (IPSs) or intrusion detection systems (IDSs) in response to traffic that violates a rule or matches the signature of a known exploit. A network IDS (NIDS), such as Snort, comes configured with rules for known exploits. Alerts are generated by Snort and are made readable and searchable by applications such as Snorby and Sguil, which are part of the Security Onion suite of NSM tools.

A testing site that is used to determine if Snort is operating is www.testmyids.com. It consists of a webpage that displays only the text **uid=0(root) gid=0(root) groups=0(root)**. If Snort is operating correctly and a host visits this site, a signature will be matched and an alert will be triggered. This is an easy and harmless way to verify that the NIDS is running.

The Snort rule that is triggered is:

```
alert ip any any -> any any (msg:"GPL ATTACK_RESPONSE id check returned
root"; content:"uid=0|28|root|29|"; fast_pattern:only; classtype:bad-
unknown; sid:2100498; rev:8;)
```

This rule generates an alert if any IP address in the network receives data from an external source that contains the text matching the pattern of **uid=0(root)**. The alert contains the message **GPL ATTACK_RESPONSE id check returned root**. The ID of the Snort rule that was triggered is **2100498**.

The figure illustrates a series of alerts that have been accessed and displayed on the Security Onion console application Sguil.

> Refer to
> **Interactive Graphic**
> in online course

11.2.1.2 Session and Transaction Data

Session data is a record of a conversation between two network endpoints, often a client and a server. The server could be inside the enterprise network or at a location accessed over the Internet. Session data is data about the session, not the data retrieved and used by the client. Session data will include identifying information such as the five tuples of source and destination IP addresses, source and destination port numbers, and the IP code for the protocol in use. Data about the session typically includes a session ID, the amount of data transferred by source and destination, and information related to the duration of the session.

Bro is a network security monitoring tool you will use in labs later in the course. Figure 1 shows a partial output for three HTTP sessions from a Bro connection log. Click the plus signs (+) in the figure for an explanation of each field.

Transaction data consists of the messages that are exchanged during network sessions. These transactions can be viewed in packet capture transcripts. Device logs kept by servers also contain information about the transactions that occur between clients and servers. For example, a session might include the downloading of content from a webserver, as shown in Figure 2. The transactions representing the requests and replies would be logged in an access log on the server or by a NIDS like Bro. The session is all traffic involved in making up the request, the transaction is the request itself.

> Refer to
> **Online Course**
> for Illustration

11.2.1.3 Full Packet Captures

Full packet captures are the most detailed network data that is generally collected. Because of the amount of detail, they are also the most storage and retrieval intensive types of data used in NSM. Full packet captures contain not only data about network conversations, like session data. Full packet captures contain the actual contents of the conservations themselves. Full packet captures contain the text of email messages, the HTML in webpages, and the files that enter or leave the network. Extracted content can be recovered from full packet captures and analyzed for malware or user behavior that violates business and security policies. The familiar tool Wireshark is very popular for viewing full packet captures and accessing the data associated with network conversations.

The figure illustrates the interface for the Network Analysis Monitor component of Cisco Prime Infrastructure system, which, like Wireshark, can display full packet captures.

Refer to **Online Course** for Illustration

11.2.1.4 Statistical Data

Like session data, statistical data is about network traffic. Statistical data is created through the analysis of other forms of network data. From these analysis, conclusions can be made that describe or predict network behavior. Statistical characteristics of normal network behavior can be compared to current network traffic in an effort to detect anomalies. Statistics can be used to characterize normal amounts of variation in network traffic patterns in order to identify network conditions that are significantly outside of those ranges. Statistically significant differences should raise alarms and prompt investigation.

Network Behavior Analysis (NBA) and Network Behavior Anomaly Detection (NBAD) are approaches to network security monitoring that use advanced analytical techniques to analyze NetFlow or Internet Protocol Flow Information Export (IPFIX) network telemetry data. Techniques such as predictive analytics and artificial intelligence perform advanced analyses of detailed session data to detect potential security incidents.

Note IPFIX is the open standard version of Cisco's NetFlow.

An example of a NSM tool that utilizes statistical analysis is Cisco Cognitive Threat Analytics. It is able to find malicious activity that has bypassed security controls, or entered through unmonitored channels (including removable media), and is operating inside an organization's environment. Cognitive Threat Analytics is a cloud-based product that uses machine learning and statistical modeling of networks. It creates a baseline of the traffic in a network and identifies anomalies. It analyzes user and device behavior, and web traffic, to discover command-and-control communications, data exfiltration, and potentially unwanted applications operating in the infrastructure. The figure illustrates an architecture for Cisco Cognitive Threat Analytics.

Refer to **Interactive Graphic** in online course

11.2.1.5 Activity - Identify Types of Network Monitoring Data

11.2.2 End Device Logs

Refer to **Online Course** for Illustration

11.2.2.1 Host Logs

As previously discussed, host-based intrusion protection (HIDS) runs on individual hosts. HIDS not only detects intrusions, but in the form of host-based firewalls, can also prevent intrusion. This software creates logs and stores them on the host. This can make it difficult to get a view of what is happening on hosts in the enterprise, so many host-based protections have a way to submit logs to centralized log management servers. In this way, the logs can be searched from a central location using NSM tools..

HIDS systems can use agents to submit logs to management servers. OSSEC, a popular open-source HIDS, includes a robust log collection and analysis functionality. Microsoft Windows includes several methods for automated host log collection and analysis. Tripwire, a HIDS for Linux, includes similar functionality. All can scale to larger enterprises.

Microsoft Windows host logs are visible locally through Event Viewer. Event Viewer keeps four types of logs:

- **Application logs** - These contain events logged by various applications.

- **System logs** - These include events regarding the operation of drivers, processes, and hardware.

- **Setup logs** - These record information about the installation of software, including Windows updates.

- **Security logs** - These record events related to security, such as logon attempts and operations related to file or object management and access.

Various logs can have different event types. The figure lists the Windows host log event types. Security logs consist only of audit success or failure messages. On Windows computers, security logging is carried out by the Local Security Authority Subsystem Service (LSASS), which is also responsible for enforcing security policies on a Windows host. LSASS runs as lsass.exe. It is frequently faked by malware. It should be running from the Windows System32 directory. If a file with this name, or a camouflaged name, such as 1sass.exe, is running or running from another directory, it could be malware.

Windows Events are identified by ID numbers and brief descriptions. Click here for an encyclopedia of security event IDs, some with additional details.

Refer to **Interactive Graphic** in online course

11.2.2.2 Syslog

Syslog incudes specifications for message formats, a client-server application structure, and network protocol. Many different types of network devices can be configured to use the syslog standard to log events to centralized syslog servers.

Syslog is a client/server protocol. Syslog was defined within the Syslog working group of the IETF (RFC 5424) and is supported by a wide variety of devices and receivers across multiple platforms.

The Syslog sender sends a small (less than 1KB) text message to the Syslog receiver. The Syslog receiver is commonly called "syslogd," "Syslog daemon," or "Syslog server." Syslog messages can be sent via UDP (port 514) and/or TCP (typically, port 5000). While there are some exceptions, such as SSL wrappers, this data is typically sent in plaintext over the network.

The full format of a Syslog message seen on the wire has three distinct parts, as shown in Figure 1.

- PRI (priority)

- HEADER

- MSG (message text)

The PRI consists of two elements, the Facility and Severity of the message, which are both integer values, as shown in Figure 2. The Facility consists of broad categories of sources that generated the message, such as the system, process, or application. The Facility value can be used by logging servers to direct the message to the appropriate log file. The Severity is a value from 0-7 that defines the severity of the message. The Priority (PRI) value is calculated by multiplying the Facility value by 8, and then adding it to the Severity value, as shown below.

Priority = (Facility * 8) + Severity

The Priority value is the first value in a packet and occurs between angled brackets (<>).

The HEADER section of the message contains the timestamp in **MMM DD HH:MM:SS** format. If the timestamp is preceded by the period (.) or asterisk (*) symbols, a problem is indicated with NTP. The HEADER section also includes the hostname or IP address of the device that is the source of the message.

The MSG portion contains the meaning of the syslog message. This can vary between device manufacturers and can be customized. Therefore, this portion of the message is the most meaningful and useful to the cybersecurity analyst.

Refer to **Online Course** for Illustration

11.2.2.3   Server Logs

Server logs are an essential source of data for network security monitoring. Network application servers such as email and web servers keep access and error logs. Especially important are DNS proxy server logs which document all the DNS queries and responses that occur on the network. DNS proxy logs are useful for identifying hosts that may have visited dangerous websites and for identifying DNS data exfiltration and connections to malware command-and-control servers. Many UNIX and Linux servers use syslog. Others may use proprietary logging. The contents of log file events depend on the type of server.

Two important log files to be familiar with are the Apache webserver access logs and Microsoft Internet Information Server (IIS) access logs. Examples of each are shown in the figure.

Refer to **Online Course** for Illustration

11.2.2.4   Apache Webserver Access Logs

Apache webserver access logs record the requests for resources from clients to the server. The logs can be in two formats. The first is common log format (CLF), and second is combined log format, which is CLF with the addition of the referrer and user agent fields, as shown in the figure.

The fields in the Apache access log in CLF are as follows:

- **IP address of requesting host**

- **Identity of client** - This is unreliable, and is frequently replaced by the hyphen (-) placeholder which is used to represent missing or unavailable data.

- **User ID** - If the user is authenticated to the webserver, this is the username for the account. Much access to webservers is anonymous, so this value will frequently be replaced by a hyphen.

- **Timestamp** - The time the request was received in **DD/MMM/YYYY:HH:MM:SS (+I-)** zone format.

- **Request** - The request method, the requested resource, and the request protocol.

- **Status code** - Three-digit numeric code representing the status of request. Codes beginning with 2 represent success, such as the 200 in the figure. Codes that begin with a 3 represent redirection. Codes that begin with a 4 represent client errors. Codes that begin with a 5 represent server errors. Click here for a list of HTTP status codes, with detailed explanations.

- **Size of the response** - Size, in bytes, of data returned to the client.

The combined log format adds the following two fields:

- **Referrer** - The URL of the resource from which the request was made. If the request is made directly by the user typing the URL into the browser, from a bookmark, or from a URL in a document, the value will be normally be a hyphen.

- **User agent** - The identifier for the browser that made the request. Click here for an explanation of the user agent field, with examples for common browsers.

Note The terms Uniform Resource Identifier (URI) and Uniform Resource Locator (URL) are not the same. A URI is a compact method of referring to a source such as example.com. A URL specifies the method for accessing the resource, such as https://www.example.com or ftp://www.example.com. Click here for more information of the difference between URI and URL.

Refer to **Online Course** for Illustration

11.2.2.5 IIS Access Logs

Microsoft IIS creates access logs that can be viewed from the server with Event Viewer. Event viewer makes viewing the native IIS log format much easier. An ASCII text example of a raw log file entry, with explanation of the fields, is shown in the figure. The native IIS log format is not customizable. However, IIS can log in more standard formats such as W3C Extended format, which does allow customization.

Refer to **Online Course** for Illustration

11.2.2.6 SIEM and Log Collection

Security Information and Event Management (SIEM) technology is used in many organizations to provide real-time reporting and long-term analysis of security events, as shown in Figure 1.

SIEM combines the essential functions of security event management (SEM) and security information management (SIM) tools to provide a comprehensive view of the enterprise network using the following functions:

- **Log collection** - These event records from sources throughout the organization provide important forensic information and help to address compliance reporting requirements.

- **Normalization** - This maps log messages from different systems into a common data model, enabling the organization to connect and analyze related events, even if they are initially logged in different source formats.

- **Correlation** - This links logs and events from disparate systems or applications, speeding detection of and reaction to security threats.

- **Aggregation** - This reduces the volume of event data by consolidating duplicate event records.

- **Reporting** - This presents the correlated, aggregated event data in real-time monitoring and long-term summaries, including graphical interactive dashboards.

- **Compliance** - This is reporting to satisfy the requirements of various compliance regulations.

A popular SIEM is Splunk, which is made by a Cisco partner. Figure 2 shows the Splunk Botnet Dashboard. Splunk is widely used in SOCs. Another popular and open source SIEM solution is ELK, which consists of the integrated Elasticsearch, Logstash, and Kibana applications.

Refer to
Interactive Graphic
in online course

11.2.2.7 Activity - Identify Information in Logged Events

11.2.3 Network Logs

Refer to
Online Course
for Illustration

11.2.3.1 Tcpdump

The tcpdump command line tool is a very popular packet analyzer. It can display packet captures in real time or write packet captures to a file. It captures detailed packet protocol and content data. Wireshark is a GUI built on tcpdump functionality.

The structure of tcpdump captures varies depending on the protocol captured and the fields requested.

Refer to
Interactive Graphic
in online course

11.2.3.2 NetFlow

NetFlow is a protocol that was developed by Cisco as a tool for network troubleshooting and session-based accounting. NetFlow efficiently provides an important set of services for IP applications, including network traffic accounting, usage-based network billing, network planning, security, Denial of Service monitoring capabilities, and network monitoring. NetFlow provides valuable information about network users and applications, peak usage times, and traffic routing.

NetFlow does not capture the entire contents of a packet as does full packet capture. Instead, NetFlow records information about the packet flow. For example, a full packet capture is viewed in Wireshark or tcpdump. NetFlow collects metadata, or data about the flow, not the flow data itself.

Cisco invented NetFlow and then allowed it to be used as a basis for an IETF standard called IPFIX. IPFIX is based on Cisco NetFlow Version 9.

NetFlow information can be viewed with tools such as the nfdump tool. Similar to tcpdump, nfdump provides a command line utility for viewing NetFlow data from the nfcapd capture daemon, or collector. Tools exist that add GUI functionality to viewing flows. Figure 1 shows a screen from the open source FlowViewer tool. The Cisco/Lancope Stealthwatch technology enhances the use of NetFlow data for NSM.

Traditionally, an IP Flow is based on a set of 5 and up to 7 IP packet attributes flowing in a single direction. A flow consists of all packets transmitted until the TCP conversation terminates. IP Packet attributes used by NetFlow are:

- IP source address
- IP destination address
- Source port
- Destination port
- Layer 3 protocol type
- Class of Service
- Router or switch interface

All packets with the same source/destination IP address, source/destination ports, protocol interface and class of service are grouped into a flow, and then packets and bytes are tallied. This methodology of fingerprinting or determining a flow is scalable because a large amount of network information is condensed into a database of NetFlow information called the NetFlow cache.

All NetFlow flow records will contain the first five items in the list above, and flow start and end timestamps. The additional information that may appear is highly variable and can be configured on the NetFlow Exporter device. Exporters are devices that can be configured to create flow records and transmit those flow records for storage on a NetFlow collector device. An example of a basic NetFlow flow record, in two different presentations, is shown in Figure 2.

A large number of attributes for a flow are available. The IANA registry of IPFIX entities lists several hundred, with the first 128 being the most common.

Although NetFlow was not initially conceived as tool for network security monitoring, it is seen as a useful tool in the analysis of network security incidents. It can be used to construct a timeline of compromise, understand individual host behavior, or to track the movement of an attacker or exploit from host to host within a network.

Refer to **Interactive Graphic** in online course

11.2.3.3   Application Visibility and Control

The Cisco Application Visibility and Control (AVC) system, depicted in Figure 1, combines multiple technologies to recognize, analyze, and control over 1000 applications. These include voice and video, email, file sharing, gaming, peer-to-peer (P2P), and cloud-based applications. AVC uses Cisco Next-generation network-based application recognition (NBAR2) to discover and classify the applications in use on the network. The NBAR2 application recognition engine supports over 1000 network applications.

To truly understand the importance of this technology, consider Figure 2. Identification of network applications by port provides very little granularity and visibility into user behavior. However, application visibility through the identification of application signatures identifies what users are doing, whether it be teleconferencing or downloading movies to their phones.

A management and reporting system, such as Cisco Prime, analyzes and presents the application analysis data into dashboard reports for use by network monitoring personnel. Application usage can also be controlled through quality of service classification and policies based on the AVC information.

Click here for a video overview of Cisco Application Visibility and Control.

Refer to **Online Course** for Illustration

11.2.3.4   Content Filter Logs

Devices that provide content filtering, such as the Cisco Email Security Appliance (ESA) and the Cisco Web Security Appliance (WSA), provide a wide range of functionalities for security monitoring. Logging is available for many of these functionalities.

The ESA, for example, has more than 30 logs that can be used to monitor most aspects of email delivery, system functioning, antivirus, antispam operations, and blacklist and whitelist decisions. Most of the logs are stored in text files and can be collected on syslog servers, or can be pushed to FTP or SCP servers. In addition, alerts regarding the functioning of the appliance itself and its subsystems can be monitored by email to administrators who are responsible for monitoring and operating the device.

WSA devices offer a similar depth of functioning. WSA effectively acts as a web proxy, meaning that it logs all inbound and outbound transaction information for HTTP traffic. These logs can be quite detailed and are customizable. They can be configured in a W3C compatibility format. The WSA can be configured to submit the logs to a server in various ways, including syslog, FTP, and SCP.

Other logs that are available to the WSA include ACL decision logs, malware scan logs, and web reputation filtering logs.

The figure illustrates the "drill-down" dashboards available from Cisco content filtering devices.

Refer to
Online Course
for Illustration

11.2.3.5   Logging from Cisco Devices

Cisco security devices can be configured to submit events and alerts to security management platforms using SNMP or syslog. The figure illustrates a syslog message generated by a Cisco ASA device and a syslog message generated by a Cisco IOS device.

Note that there are two meanings used for the term facility in Cisco syslog messages. The first is the standard set of Facility values that were established by the syslog standards. These values are used in the PRI message part of the syslog packet to calculate the message priority. Cisco uses some of the values between 15 and 23 to identify Cisco log Facilities, depending on the platform. For example, Cisco ASA devices use syslog Facility 20 by default, which corresponds to local4. The other Facility value is assigned by Cisco, and occurs in the MSG part of the syslog message.

Cisco devices may use slightly different syslog message formats, and may use mnemonics instead of message IDs, as shown in the figure. A dictionary of Cisco ASA syslog messages can be found here.

Refer to
Interactive Graphic
in online course

11.2.3.6   Proxy Logs

Proxy servers, such as those used for web and DNS requests, contain valuable logs that are a primary source of data for network security monitoring.

Proxy servers are devices that act as intermediaries for network clients. For example, an enterprise may configure a web proxy to handle web requests on the behalf of clients. Instead of requests for web resources being sent directly to the server from the client, the request is sent to a proxy server first. The proxy server requests the resources and returns them to the client. The proxy server generates logs of all requests and responses. These logs can then be analyzed to determine which hosts are making the requests, whether the destinations are safe or potentially malicious, and to also gain insights into the kind of resources that have been downloaded.

Web Proxies

Web proxies provide data that helps determine whether responses from the web were generated in response to legitimate requests, or have been manipulated to appear to be responses but are in fact exploits. It is also possible to use web proxies to inspect outgoing traffic as means of data loss prevention (DLP). DLP involves scanning outgoing traffic to detect whether the data that is leaving the web contains sensitive, confidential, or secret information. Examples of popular web proxies are Squid, CCProxy, Apache Traffic Server, and WinGate.

Figure 1 illustrates an example of a Squid web proxy log in the Squid-native format. Explanations of the field values appear below the log entry.

Note   Open web proxies, which are proxies that are available to any Internet user, can be used to obfuscate threat actor IP addresses. Open proxy addresses may be used in blacklisting Internet traffic.

OpenDNS

OpenDNS, a Cisco company, offers a hosted DNS service that extends the capability of DNS to include security enhancements. Rather than organizations hosting and maintaining blacklisting, phishing protection, and other DNS-related security, OpenDNS provides these protections on their own DNS service. OpenDNS is able to apply many more resources to managing DNS than most organizations can afford. OpenDNS functions in part as a DNS super proxy in this regard. The OpenDNS suite of security products apply real-time threat intelligence to managing DNS access and the security of DNS records. DNS access logs are available from OpenDNS for the subscribed enterprise. Figure 2 shows an example of an OpenDNS proxy log. Instead of using local or ISP DNS servers, an organization can choose to subscribe to OpenDNS for DNS services.

> Refer to **Online Course** for Illustration

11.2.3.7   NextGen IPS

As we know, NextGen IPS devices extend network security beyond IP addresses and Layer 4 port numbers to the application layer and beyond. NexGen IPS are advanced devices that provided much more functionality than previous generations of network security devices. One of those functionalities is reporting dashboards with interactive features that allow quick point-and-click reports on very specific information without the need for SIEM or other event correlators.

Cisco's line of next generation IPS devices (NGIPS) use FirePOWER Services to consolidate multiple security layers into a single platform. This helps to contain costs and simplify management. FirePOWER services include application visibility and control, FirePOWER NGIPS, reputation and category-based URL filtering, and Advanced Malware Protection (AMP). FirePOWER devices allow monitoring network security through a web-enabled GUI called Event Viewer.

Common NGIPS events include:

- **Connection Event -** Connection logs contain data about sessions that are detected directly by the NGIPS. Connection events include basic connection properties such as timestamps, source and destination IP addresses, and metadata about why the connection was logged, such as which access control rule logged the event.

- **Intrusion Event -** The system examines the packets that traverse the network for malicious activity that could affect the availability, integrity, and confidentiality of a host and its data. When the system identifies a possible intrusion, it generates an intrusion event, which is a record of the date, time, type of exploit, and contextual information about the source of the attack and its target.

- **Host or Endpoint Event -** When a host appears on the network it can be detected by the system and details of the device hardware, IP addressing, and the last known presence on the network can be logged.

- **Network Discovery Event -** Network discovery events represent changes that have been detected in the monitored network. These changes are logged in response to network discovery policies that specify the kinds of data to be collected, the network segments to be monitored, and the hardware interfaces of the device that should be used for event collection.

- **Netflow Event -**Network discovery can use a number of mechanisms, one of which is to use exported NetFlow flow records to generate new events for hosts and servers.

Refer to
Interactive Graphic
in online course

11.2.3.8   Activity - Identify the Security Technology from the Data Description

Refer to
Interactive Graphic
in online course

11.2.3.9   Activity - Identify the NextGen IPS Event Type

Refer to **Packet
Tracer Activity**
for this chapter

11.2.3.10   Packet Tracer - Explore a NetFlow Implementation

In this Packet Tracer activity, you will explore an implementation of NetFlow.

Refer to **Packet
Tracer Activity**
for this chapter

11.2.3.11   Packet Tracer - Logging from Multiple Sources

In this activity, you will use Packet Tracer to compare network data generated by multiple sources including syslog, AAA, and NetFlow.

11.3   Summary

11.3.1   Conclusion

Refer to
Lab Activity
for this chapter

11.3.1.1   Lab - Setup a Multi-VM Environment

In this lab, you will set up a virtual network environment by connecting multiple virtual machines in Virtualbox. This environment will be used for the rest of the labs in this course.

Click Play to view a demonstration of how to setup the multi-VM lab environment.

Click here to read the transcript for this video.

Refer to
Online Course
for Illustration

11.3.1.2   Chapter 11: Security Monitoring

In this chapter, you learned how cybersecurity analysts use various tools and techniques to identify network security alerts. Syslog is a common monitoring protocol that can log a variety of events. NTP is used to timestamp these events. Protocols that are particularly vulnerable, such as DNS, HTTP, email protocols, and ICMP, should be actively monitored by the cybersecurity analyst.

Security technologies used to protect the privacy of our data also make it more difficult for security monitoring. ACLs can give a false sense of security if they are overly relied upon. NAT and PAT can complicate security monitoring, hiding the individual IP addresses that are inside the network. Encrypted traffic is difficult to monitor because the data is unreadable to any other devices but the VPN endpoints. P2P network activity can circumvent firewall protections, is difficult to monitor, and is a common vector for the spread of malware.

Log files are the data used by cybersecurity analysts to monitor the security of the network. Security data includes:

- Alert data
- Session and transaction data
- Full packet captures
- Statistical data

The sources for these security data include a variety of logs:

- Host logs
- Syslog
- Server logs
- Web logs
- Network logs

security impact. These messages can be filtered from NSM data. Similarly, syslog may store messages of very low severity that should be disregarded to diminish the quantity of NSM data to be handled.

Refer to
Interactive Graphic
in online course

12.2.1.3   Data Normalization

Data normalization is the process of combining data from a number of data sources into a common format. ELSA provides a series of plugins that process security data and transform it before it is added to ELSA databases. Additional plugins can be created to suit the needs of the organization.

A common schema will specify the names and formats for the required data fields. Formatting of the data fields can vary widely between sources. However, if searching is to be effective, the data fields must be consistent. For example, as shown in Figure 1, IPv6 addresses, MAC addresses, and date and time information can be represented in varying formats. Similarly, subnet masks, DNS records, and so on can vary in format between data sources.

Data normalization is required to simplify searching for correlated events. If differently formatted values exist in the NSM data for IPv6 addresses, for example, a separate query term would need to be created for every variation in order for correlated events to be returned by the query.

When ELSA displays a log file entry, the original entry is shown in bold, and the normalized entry appears below it with the ELSA field identifiers and their values, as shown in Figure 2.

Refer to
Online Course
for Illustration

12.2.1.4   Data Archiving

Everyone would love the security of collecting and saving everything, just in case. However, retaining NSM data indefinitely is not feasible due to storage and access issues. It should be noted that the retention period for certain types of network security information may be specified by compliance frameworks. For example, the Payment Card Industry Security Standards Council (PCI DSS) requires and that an audit trail of user activities related to protected information be retained for one year.

Security Onion has different data retention periods for different types of NSM data. For pcaps and raw Bro logs, a value assigned in the **securityonion.conf** file controls the percentage of disk space that can be used by log files. By default, this value is set to 90%. For ELSA, retention of archived logs is dependent on values set in the **elsa_node.conf** file. These values are related to the amount of storage space that is available. By default, Security Onion is configured with a log size limit of 3GB. The guideline is that this value should be 90-95% of the total disk space that ELSA is using. By default, ELSA will use 33% of the configured log size limit for archived logs. ELSA can optionally be configured to retain data for a period of time. The provided value for this in the configuration file is 90 days.

Squil alert data is retained for 30 days by default. This value is set in the **securityonion.conf** file.

Security Onion is known to require a lot of storage and RAM to run properly. Depending on the size of the network, multiple terabytes of storage may be required. Of course, Security Onion data can always be archived to external storage by a data archive system, depending on the needs and capabilities of the organization.

Note   The storage locations for the different types of Security Onion data will vary based on the Security Onion implementation.

Refer to
Lab Activity
for this chapter

12.2.1.5   Lab - Convert Data into a Universal Format

Log entries are generated by network devices, operating systems, applications, and various types of programmable devices. A file containing a time-sequenced stream of log entries is called a log file.

By nature, log files record events that are relevant to the source. The syntax and format of data within log messages are often defined by the application developer.

Therefore, the terminology used in the log entries often varies from source to source. For example, depending on the source, the terms login, logon, authentication event, and user connection, may all appear in log entries to describe a successful user authentication to a server.

It is often desirable to have a consistent and uniform terminology in logs generated by different sources. This is especially true when all log files are being collected by a centralized point.

The term normalization refers to the process of converting parts of a message, in this case a log entry, to a common format.

In this lab, you will use command line tools to manually normalize log entries. In Part 2, the timestamp field must be normalized. In Part 3, the IPv6 field is the one that requires normalization.

Refer to
Online Course
for Illustration

12.2.1.6   Investigating Process or API Calls

Application programs interact with an operating system (OS) through system calls to the OS application programming interface (API), as shown in the figure. These system calls allow access to many aspects of system operation such as:

- software process control
- file management
- device management
- information management
- communication

Malware can also make system calls. If malware can fool an OS kernel into allowing it to make system calls, many exploits are possible.

HIDS software tracks the operation of a host OS. OSSEC rules detect changes in host-based parameters like the execution of software processes, changes in user privileges, registry modifications, among many others. OSSEC rules will trigger an alert in Sguil. Pivoting to ELSA on the host IP address allows you to choose the type of alert based on the program that created it. Choosing OSSEC as the source program in ELSA results in a view of the OSSEC events that occurred on the host, including indicators that malware may have interacted with the OS kernel.

12.2.2   Investigating Network Data

Refer to
Online Course
for Illustration

12.2.2.1   Working in Sguil

The primary duty of a cybersecurity analyst is the verification of security alerts. Depending on the organization, the tools used to do this will vary. For example, a ticketing system may be used to manage task assignment and documentation. In Security Onion, the first place that a cybersecurity analyst will go to verify alerts is Sguil.

Sguil automatically correlates similar alerts into a single line and provides a way to view correlated events represented by that line. In order to get a sense of what has been happening in the network, it may be useful to sort on the **CNT** column to display the alerts with the highest frequency.

Note In the figure, the title of the **CNT** column is hidden. The **CNT** column is column two between the **ST** and **Sensor** columns.

Right-clicking the **CNT** value and selecting **View Correlated Events** opens a tab displaying all the correlated events. This can help the cybersecurity analyst understand the time frame during which the correlated events were received by Sguil. Note that each event receives a unique event ID. Only the first event ID in the series of correlated events is displayed in the RealTime tab. The figure shows Sguil alerts sorted on **CNT** with the **View Correlated Events** menu open.

Refer to **Interactive Graphic** in online course

12.2.2.2   Sguil Queries

Queries can be constructed in Sguil using the Query Builder. It simplifies constructing queries to a certain degree, but the cybersecurity analyst must know the field names and some issues with field values. For example, Sguil stores IP addresses in an integer representation. In order to query on an IP address in dotted decimal notation, the IP address value must be placed within the **INET_ATON()** function. Query Builder is opened from the Sguil **Query** menu. Select **Query Event Table** to search active events.

Figure 1 shows the names of the event table fields that can be queried directly. Selecting **Show DataBase Tables** from the **Query** menu displays a reference to the field names and types for each of the tables that can be queried. Figure 2 shows a simple timestamp and IP address query made in the Query Builder window. Note the use of the **INET_ATON()** function to simplify entering an IP address.

In Figure 3, the cybersecurity analyst is investigating a source port 40754 that is associated with an Emerging Threats alert. Towards the end of the query, the **WHERE event. src_port = '40754'** portion was created by the user in Query Builder. The remainder of the Query is supplied automatically by Sguil and concerns how the data that is associated with the events is to be retrieved, displayed, and presented.

Refer to **Online Course** for Illustration

12.2.2.3   Pivoting from Sguil

Sguil provides the ability for the cybersecurity analyst to pivot to other information sources and tools. Log files are available in ELSA, relevant packet captures can be displayed in Wireshark, and transcripts of TCP sessions and Bro information are also available. The menu shown in the figure was opened by right-clicking on an Alert ID. Selecting from this menu will open information about the alert in other tools, which provides rich, contextualized information to the cybersecurity analyst.

Additionally, Sguil can provide pivots to Passive Real-time Asset Detection System (PRADS) and Security Analyst Network Connection Profiler (SANCP) information.

PRADS gathers network profiling data, including information about the behavior of assets on the network. PRADS is an event source, like Snort and OSSEC. It can also be queried through Sguil when an alert indicates that an internal host may have been compromised. Executing a PRADS query out of Sguil can provide information about the services, applications, and payloads that may be relevant to the alert. In addition, PRADS detects when new assets appear on the network.

Note   The Sguil interface refers to PADS instead of PRADS. PADS was the predecessor to PRADS. PRADS is the tool that is actually used in Security Onion. PRADS is also used to populate SANCP tables. In Security Onion, the functionalities of SANCP have been replaced by PRADS, however the term SANCP is still used in the Sguil interface. PRADS collects the data, and a SANCP agent records the data in a SANCP data table.

The SANCP functionalities concern collecting and recording statistical information about network traffic and behavior. SANCP provides a means of verifying that network connections are valid. This is done through the application of rules that indicate which traffic should be recorded and the information with which the traffic should be tagged.

Refer to
Online Course
for Illustration

12.2.2.4   Event Handling in Sguil

Finally, Sguil is not only a console that facilitates investigation of alerts. It is also a tool for addressing alerts. Three tasks can be completed in Sguil to manage alerts. First, alerts that have been found to be false positives can be expired. This can be done by using the right-click menu or by pressing the F8 key. An expired event disappears from the queue. Second, if the cybersecurity analyst is uncertain how to handle an event, it can be escalated by pressing the F9 key. The alert will be moved to the Sguil Escalated Events tab. Finally, an event can be categorized. Categorization is for events that have been identified as true positives.

Sguil includes seven pre-built categories that can be assigned by using the menu, which is shown in the figure, or by pressing the corresponding function key. For example, an event would be categorized as Cat I by pressing the F1 key. In addition, criteria can be created that will automatically categorize an event. Categorized events are assumed to have been handled by the cybersecurity analyst. When an event is categorized, it is removed from the list of **RealTime Events**. The event remains in the database however, and it can be accessed by queries that are issued by category.

This course covers Sguil at a basic level. Click here for additional information about using Sguil.

Refer to
Online Course
for Illustration

12.2.2.5   Working in ELSA

ELSA provides access to a large number of log file entries. Because the number of logs that could be displayed in ELSA is so large, several default values have been set to minimize the number of records that ELSA displays when it is launched. It is important to know that ELSA will only retrieve the first 100 records for the previous 48 hours. If no records have been generated for that period (unlikely in a production network) the ELSA window will be empty. To increase the number of records displayed, the directive **limit:1000** can be added to the query. This specifies the limit for the number of records to be returned by the query, in this case 1000.

In order to see log file records for a different period of time, the **From** and **To** dates in the ELSA query can be changed by clicking on **From** or **To** and using the calendar pop-up menus, or by entering dates and times manually. The figure shows the calendar pop-up menu. In addition, ELSA must have a query submitted in order to display records. Changing the dates is not enough to refresh the list of log file entries.

The easiest way to see information in ELSA is to issue the built-in queries that appear to the left of the ELSA window and then adjust the dates and resubmit the query using the Submit Query button. There are many useful searches available. When clicked, the queries appear in the query field and can be edited there if necessary.

Refer to
Interactive Graphic
in online course

12.2.2.6   Queries in ELSA

Constructing queries is very simple in ELSA. There are many shortcuts available for refining queries without doing any typing. ELSA uses a very natural syntax roughly based on Google search syntax. A query consisting of just an IP address will work. However, because of the large numbers of records that are potentially returned, a number of operators and directives exist for narrowing searches and stipulating which records should be displayed.

Note   Advanced ELSA queries are beyond the scope of this course. In the labs, you will be provided with the complex query statements, if necessary.

Figure 1 shows a query executed on an IP address. This will result in all records that contain the IP address for the given time and date range being returned. This is not very useful. However, it is easy to narrow the query by clicking on an entry in the **Field Summary** list that summarizes the search results.

Clicking an entry will display a summary screen with bar graphs that depict all of the unique values and their frequencies that appear for the results of the query, as shown in Figure 2. Clicking an entry in the Value column will display the query with the value added to the previous query. This process can be repeated to narrow down search results easily. In this way, queries can be constructed for the five tuples and a wide range of other values.

ELSA provides field summary and value information for every field that is indexed in the query results. This permits refining queries based on a wide range of values. In addition, queries can be created by simply clicking on a value or attribute in the ELSA-normalized portion of a log file entry.

ELSA queries can also use regular expressions to create advanced patterns for matching specific packet contents. Regular expressions are executed in ELSA using the grep function. Grep serves as a transform in ELSA queries. This means it is used to process the results from a query. The grep transform serves as a text-based filter that tells ELSA which records should be displayed. The grep function is passed the field name to match, and a regular expression pattern to apply, as in *grep(field,pattern)*. Unix-like pipes, using the | symbol, can be used to direct the output of ELSA queries through ELSA plugins and transforms.

ELSA queries may be saved as named macros. These queries can then be called in the query box by entering the name of the query preceded by the dollar sign symbol ($). Query macros can also be combined with other query elements.

Refer to
Online Course
for Illustration

12.2.2.7   Investigating Process or API Calls

Application programs interact with an operating system (OS) through system calls to the OS application programming interface (API), as shown in the figure. These system calls allow access to many aspects of system operation such as:

- Software process control

- File management

- Device management

- Information management

- Communication

Malware can also make system calls. If malware can fool an OS kernel into allowing it to make system calls, many exploits are possible.

HIDS software tracks the operation of a host OS. OSSEC rules detect changes in host-based parameters like the execution of software processes, changes in user privileges, and registry modifications, among many others. OSSEC rules will trigger an alert in Sguil. Pivoting to ELSA on the host IP address allows you to choose the type of alert based on the program that created it. Choosing OSSEC as the source program in ELSA results in a view of the OSSEC events that occurred on the host, including indicators that malware may have interacted with the OS kernel.

Refer to
Interactive Graphic
in online course

12.2.2.8   Investigating File Details

When ELSA is opened directly, a query short cut exists for **Files**. By opening the **Files** queries and selecting **Mime Types** in the menu, a list of the types of files that have been downloaded, and their frequencies, is displayed, as shown in Figure 1. If the cybersecurity analyst is interested in the executable files, clicking **application/XML** will display records for all logged instances in which executable files were downloaded during the time scope of the query.

Figure 2 shows details of a record returned by this query. File details, such as the file size, sending and receiving hosts, and protocol used to download the file are displayed. In addition, the MD5 and SHA-1 hashes for the file have been calculated. If the cybersecurity analyst is suspicious of the file, the hash value can be submitted to an online site, such as VirusTotal, to determine if the file is known malware. The hash value can be submitted from the Search tab on the VirusTotal page.

Refer to
Lab Activity
for this chapter

12.2.2.9   Lab - Regular Expression Tutorial

A regular expression (regex) is a pattern of symbols that describes data to be matched in a query or other operation. Regular expressions are constructed similarly to arithmetic expressions, by using various operators to combine smaller expressions. There are two major standards of regular expression, POSIX and Perl.

In this lab, you will use an online tutorial to explore regular expressions. You will also describe the information that matches given regular expressions.

Refer to
Lab Activity
for this chapter

12.2.2.10   Lab - Extract an Executable from a PCAP

Looking at logs is very important but it is also important to understand how network transactions happen at the packet level.

In this lab, you will analyze the traffic in a previously captured pcap file and extract an executable from the file.

12.2.3   Enhancing the Work of the Cybersecurity Analyst

Refer to
Online Course
for Illustration

12.2.3.1   Dashboards and Visualizations

Dashboards provide a combination of data and visualizations designed to improve the access of individuals to large amounts of information. Dashboards are usually interactive. They allow cybersecurity analysts to focus on specific details and information by clicking on elements of the dashboard. For example, clicking on a bar in a bar chart could provide a breakdown of the information for the data represented by that bar. ELSA includes the capability of designing custom dashboards. In addition, other tools that are included in Security Onion, such as Squert, provide a visual interface to NSM data.

Cisco Talos provides an interactive dashboard that allows investigation of the threat landscape, as shown in the figure.

Refer to
Online Course
for Illustration

12.2.3.2   Workflow Management

Because of the critical nature of network security monitoring, it is essential that workflows are managed. This enhances efficiency of the cyberoperations team, increases the account-ability of staff, and ensures that all potential alerts are treated properly. In large security organizations, it is conceivable that thousands of alerts will be received daily. Each alert should be systematically assigned, processed, and documented by cyberoperations staff.

Runbook automation, or workflow management systems, provide the tools necessary to streamline and control processes in a cybersecurity operations center. Squil provides basic workflow management. However, it is not a good choice for large operations with many employees. Instead, third party workflow management systems are available that can be customized to suit the needs of cybersecurity operations.

In addition, automated queries are useful for adding efficiency to the cyberoperations work-flow. These queries, sometimes known as plays, or playbooks, automatically search for complex security incidents that may evade other tools. For example, an ELSA query can be configured as an alert rule that can be run regularly. ELSA can notify cybersecurity analysts by email, or other means, that a suspected exploit has been detected by the query. Playbooks can also be created in a scripting language such as Python and integrated into workflow management systems to ensure that the alerts are processed, documented, and reported along with other alerts.

12.3   Digital Forensics

12.3.1   Evidence Handling and Attack Attribution

Refer to
Interactive Graphic
in online course

12.3.1.1   Digital Forensics

Now that you have investigated and identified valid alerts, what do you do with the evidence? The cybersecurity analyst will inevitably uncover evidence of criminal activity. In order to protect the organization and to prevent cybercrime, it is necessary to identify threat actors, report them to the appropriate authorities, and provide evidence to support prosecution. Tier 1 cybersecurity analysts are usually the first to uncover wrong doing. Cybersecurity analysts must know how to properly handle evidence and attribute it to threat actors.

Digital forensics is the recovery and investigation of information found on digital devices as it relates to criminal activity. This information could be data on storage devices, in volatile computer memory, or the traces of cybercrime that are preserved in network data, such as pcaps and logs.

Cybercriminal activity can be broadly characterized as originating from inside of or outside of the organization. Private investigations are concerned with individuals inside the organization. These individuals could simply be behaving in ways that violate user agreements or other non-criminal conduct. When individuals are suspected of involvement in criminal activity involving the theft or destruction of intellectual property, an organization may choose to involve law enforcement authorities, in which case the investigation becomes public. Internal users could also have used the organization's network to conduct other criminal activities that are unrelated to the organizational mission but are in violation of various legal statutes. In this case, public officials will carry out the investigation.

When an external attacker has exploited a network and stolen or altered data, evidence needs to be gathered to document the scope of the exploit. Various regulatory bodies specify a range of actions that an organization must take when various types of data have been compromised. The results of forensic investigation can help to identify the actions that need to be taken.

For example, under HIPAA, if a data breach has occurred that involves patient information, notification of the breach must be made to the affected individuals. If the breach involves more than 500 individuals in a state or jurisdiction, the media, as well as the affected individuals, must be notified. Digital forensic investigation must be used to determine which individuals were affected, and to certify the number of affected individuals so that appropriate notification can be made in compliance with HIPAA regulations.

It is possible that the organization itself could be the subject of an investigation. Cybersecurity analysts may find themselves in direct contact with digital forensic evidence that details the conduct of members of the organization. Analysts must know the requirements regarding the preservation and handling of such evidence. Failure to do so could result in criminal penalties for the organization and even the cybersecurity analyst if the intention to destroy evidence is established.

Refer to **Online Course** for Illustration

12.3.1.2 The Digital Forensics Process

It is important than an organization develop well-documented processes and procedures for digital forensic analysis. Regulatory compliance may require this documentation, and this documentation may be inspected by authorities in the event of a public investigation.

NIST Special Publication 800-86 *Guide to Integrating Forensic Techniques into Incident Response* is a valuable resource for organizations that require guidance in developing digital forensics plans.

NIST describes the digital forensics process as involving four steps, as shown in the figure.

Step 1.   Collection - This is the identification of potential sources of forensic data and acquisition, handling, and storage of that data. This stage is critical because special care must be taken not to damage, lose, or omit important data.

Step 2.   Examination - This entails assessing and extracting relevant information from the collected data. This may involve decompression or decryption of the data. Information that is irrelevant to the investigation may need to be removed. Identifying actual evidence in large collections of data can be very difficult and time-consuming.

Step 3.   Analysis - This entails drawing conclusions from the data. Salient features, such as people, places, times, events, and so on should be documented. This step may also involve the correlation of data from multiple sources.

Step 4.   Reporting - This entails preparing and presenting information that resulted from the analysis. Reporting should be impartial and alternative explanations should be offered if appropriate. Limitations of the analysis and problems encountered should be included. Suggestions for further investigation and next steps should also be made.

In the figure, note the transition from media, to data, to information, to evidence that occurs during the forensics process.

Refer to **Online Course** for Illustration

12.3.1.3 Types of Evidence

In legal proceedings, evidence is broadly classified as either direct or indirect. Direct evidence is evidence that was indisputably in the possession of the accused, or is eyewitness evidence from someone who observed criminal behavior.

Evidence is further classified as:

- **Best evidence** - This is evidence that is in its original state. This evidence could be storage devices used by an accused, or archives of files that can be proven to be unaltered.

- **Corroborating evidence** - This is evidence that supports an assertion that is developed from best evidence.

- **Indirect evidence** - This is evidence that, in combination with other facts, establishes a hypothesis. This is also known as circumstantial evidence. For example, evidence that an individual has committed similar crimes can support the assertion that the person committed the crime of which they are accused.

Refer to **Online Course** for Illustration

12.3.1.4   Evidence Collection Order

IETF RFC 3227 provides guidelines for the collection of digital evidence. It describes an order for the collection of digital evidence based on the volatility of the data. Data stored in RAM is the most volatile, and it will be lost when the device is turned off. In addition, important data in volatile memory could be overwritten by routine machine processes. Therefore, the collection of digital evidence should begin with the most volatile evidence and proceed to the least volatile. An example of most volatile to least volatile evidence collection order is as follows:

1. Memory registers, caches

2. Routing table, ARP cache, process table, kernel statistics, RAM

3. Temporary file systems

4. Non-volatile media, fixed and removable

5. Remote logging and monitoring data

6. Physical interconnections and topologies

7. Archival media, tape or other backups

Details of the systems from which the evidence was collected, including who has access to those systems and at what level of permissions should be recorded. Such details should include hardware and software configurations for the systems from which the data was obtained.

Refer to **Interactive Graphic** in online course

12.3.1.5   Chain of Custody

Although evidence may have been gathered from sources that support attribution to an accused individual, it can be argued that the evidence could have been altered or fabricated after it was collected. In order to counter this argument, a rigorous chain of custody must be defined and followed.

Chain of custody involves the collection, handling, and secure storage of evidence. Detailed records should be kept of the following:

- Who discovered and collected the evidence.

- All details about the handling of evidence including times, places, and personnel involved.

- Who has primary responsibility for the evidence, when responsibility was assigned, and when custody changed.

- Who has physical access to the evidence while it was stored? Access should be restricted to only the most essential personnel.

Refer to
Online Course
for Illustration

12.3.1.6   Data Integrity and Preservation

When collecting data, it is important that it is preserved in its original condition. Time-stamping of files should be preserved. For this reason, the original evidence should be copied, and analysis should only be conducted on copies of the original. This is to avoid accidental loss or alteration of the evidence. Because timestamps may be part of the evidence, opening files from the original media should be avoided.

The process used to create copies of the evidence that is used in the investigation should be recorded. Whenever possible, the copies should be direct bit-level copies of the original storage volumes. Volatile memory could contain forensic evidence, so special tools should be used to preserve that evidence before the device is shut down and evidence is lost. Users should not disconnect, unplug, or turn off infected machines unless explicitly told to do so by security personnel.

Refer to
Online Course
for Illustration

12.3.1.7   Attack Attribution

After the extent of the cyberattack has been assessed and evidence collected and preserved, incident response can move to identifying the source of the attack. As we know, a wide range of threat actors exist, ranging from disgruntled individuals, hackers, cybercriminals and criminal gangs, or nation states. Some criminals act from inside the network, while others can be on the other side of world. Sophistication of cybercrime varies as well. Nation states may employ large groups of highly-trained individuals to carry out an attack and hide their tracks, while other threat actors may openly brag about their criminal activities.

Threat attribution refers to the act of determining the individual, organization, or nation responsible for a successful intrusion or attack incident.

Identifying responsible threat actors should occur through the principled and systematic investigation of the evidence. While it may be useful to also speculate as to the identity of threat actors by identifying potential motivations for an incident, it is important not to let this bias the investigation. For example, attributing an attack to a commercial competitor may lead the investigation away from the possibility that a criminal gang or nation state was responsible.

In an evidence-based investigation, the incident response team correlates Tactics, Techniques, and Procedures (TPP) that were used in the incident with other known exploits. Cybercriminals, much like other criminals, have specific traits that are common to most of their crimes. Threat intelligence sources can help to map the TTP identified by an investigation to known sources of similar attacks. However, this highlights a problem with threat attribution. Evidence of cybercrime is seldom direct evidence. Identifying commonalities between TTPs for known and unknown threat actors is circumstantial evidence.

Some aspects of a threat that can aid in attribution are the location of originating hosts or domains, features of the code used in malware, the tools used, and other techniques. Sometimes, at the national security level, threats cannot be openly attributed because doing so would expose methods and capabilities that need to be protected.

For internal threats, asset management plays a major role. Uncovering the devices from which an attack was launched can lead directly to the threat actor. IP addresses, MAC addresses, and DHCP logs can help track the addresses used in the attack back to a specific device. AAA logs are very useful in this regard, as they track who accessed what network resources at what time.

Refer to
Interactive Graphic
in online course

12.3.1.8   Activity - Identify the Type of Evidence

Refer to
Interactive Graphic
in online course

12.3.1.9   Activity - Identify the Forensic Technique Terminology

12.4   Summary

12.4.1   Conclusion

Refer to
Lab Activity
for this chapter

12.4.1.1   Lab - Interpret HTTP and DNS Data to Isolate Threat Actor

MySQL is a popular database used by numerous web applications. Unfortunately, SQL injection is a common web hacking technique. It is a code injection technique where an attacker executes malicious SQL statements to control a web application's database server.

Domain name service (DNS) traffic can be used to exfiltrate data.

In this lab, you will perform an SQL injection to access the SQL database on the server. You will also use the DNS service to facilitate data exfiltration.

Refer to
Lab Activity
for this chapter

12.4.1.2   Lab - Isolate Compromised Host using 5-Tuple

In this lab, you will exploit a vulnerable server using known exploits. You will also review the logs to determine the compromised hosts and file using the 5-tuples.

Refer to
Online Course
for Illustration

12.4.1.3   Chapter 12: Intrusion Data Analysis

In this chapter, you learned how to work with the Security Onion suite of applications and analyze intrusion data. You also learned about the proper handling of evidence in a digital forensics investigation.

Security Onion contains a variety of detection and analysis tools including:

- CapME
- Snort
- Bro
- OSSEC
- Suricata
- Wireshark
- Elsa
- Squil

After completing all the labs in this chapter and working with your multi-VM environment, you should now be familiar with these tools, their uses, and importance to the cybersecurity analyst. Some organizations use a variety of other tools and supplement Security Onion with additional tools. However, basic understanding of Security Onion should transfer easily during your training period in your new job.

Go to the online course to take the quiz and exam.

Chapter 12 Quiz

This quiz is designed to provide an additional opportunity to practice the skills and knowledge presented in the chapter and to prepare for the chapter exam. You will be allowed multiple attempts and the grade does not appear in the gradebook.

Chapter 12 Exam

The chapter exam assesses your knowledge of the chapter content.

Your Chapter Notes

Incident Response and Handling

13.0 Introduction

13.0.1 Welcome

Refer to
Online Course
for Illustration

13.0.1.1 Chapter 13: Incident Response and Handling

In cybersecurity, threat actors are always developing new techniques. New threats constantly emerge that must be detected and contained so that assets and communication are restored as quickly as possible. Many attackers use extortion, fraud, and identity theft for financial gain. The need to consistently defend against these attacks led to the creation of several incident response models.

This chapter covers incident response and handling models and procedures. These include the Cyber Kill Chain, the Diamond Model, the VERIS schema, and NIST guidelines for the structure of Computer Security Incident Response Teams (CSIRTs) and processes for handling an incident.

13.1 Incident Response Models

13.1.1 The Cyber Kill Chain

Refer to
Online Course
for Illustration

13.1.1.1 Steps of the Cyber Kill Chain

The Cyber Kill Chain was developed by Lockheed Martin to identify and prevent cyber intrusions. As the figure shows, there are seven steps to the Cyber Kill Chain, which help analysts understand the techniques, tools, and procedures of threat actors. When responding to an incident, the objective is to detect and stop the attack as early as possible in the kill chain progression. The earlier the attack is stopped; the less damage is done and the less the attacker learns about the target network.

The Cyber Kill Chain specifies what an attacker must complete to accomplish their goal. The steps in the Cyber Kill Chain are as follows:

1. Reconnaissance
2. Weaponization
3. Delivery
4. Exploitation
5. Installation
6. Command & Control (CnC)
7. Action on Objectives

If the attacker is stopped at any stage, the chain of attack is broken. Breaking the chain means the defender successfully thwarted the threat actor's intrusion. Threat actors are successful only if they reach Step 7.

Note   Threat actor is the term used throughout this course to refer to the party instigating the attack. However, Lockheed Martin uses the term "adversary" in its description of the Cyber Kill Chain. The two terms, adversary and threat actor, are used interchangeably in this topic.

Refer to **Online Course** for Illustration

13.1.1.2   Reconnaissance

Reconnaissance is when the threat actor performs research, gathers intelligence, and selects targets. This will inform the threat actor if the attack is worth performing. Any public information may help to determine the what, where, and how the attack could be performed. There is a lot of publicly available information, especially for larger organizations including news articles, websites, conference proceedings, and public-facing network devices. Increasing amounts of information surrounding employees is available through social media outlets.

The threat actor will choose targets that have been neglected or unprotected because they will have a higher likelihood of becoming penetrated and compromised. All information obtained by the threat actor is reviewed to determine its importance and if it reveals possible additional avenues of attack.

The figure summarizes some of the tactics and defenses used during this step.

Refer to **Online Course** for Illustration

13.1.1.3   Weaponization

The goal of this step is to use the information from the earlier reconnaissance to develop a weapon against specific targeted systems in the organization. To develop this weapon, the designer will use the vulnerabilities of the assets that were discovered and build them into a tool that can be deployed. After the tool has been used, it is expected that the threat actor has achieved their goal of gaining access into the target system or network, degrading the health of a target, or the entire network. The threat actor will further examine network and asset security to expose additional weaknesses, gain control over other assets, or deploy additional attacks.

It is not difficult to choose a weapon for the attack. The threat actor needs to look at what attacks are available for the vulnerabilities they have discovered. There are many attacks that have already been created and tested at large. One problem is that because these attacks are so well known, they are most likely also known by the defenders. It is often more effective to use a zero-day attack to avoid detection methods. The threat actor may wish to develop their own weapon that is specifically designed to avoid detection, using the information about the network and systems that they have learned.

The figure summarizes some of the tactics and defenses used during this step.

Refer to **Online Course** for Illustration

13.1.1.4   Delivery

During this step, the weapon is transmitted to the target using a delivery vector. This may be through the use of a website, removable USB media, or an email attachment. If the weapon is not delivered, the attack will be unsuccessful. The threat actor will use many different methods to increase the odds of delivering the payload such as encrypting communications, making the code look legitimate, or obfuscating the code. Security sensors are so advanced that they will detect the code as malicious unless it is altered to avoid detection. The code may be altered to seem innocent, yet still perform the necessary actions, even though it may take longer to execute.

The figure summarizes some of the tactics and defenses used during this step.

Refer to
Online Course
for Illustration

13.1.1.5   Exploitation

After the weapon has been delivered, the threat actor uses it to break the vulnerability and gain control of the target. The most common exploit targets are applications, operating system vulnerabilities, and users. The attacker must use an exploit that gains the effect they desire. This is very important because if the wrong exploit is conducted, obviously the attack will not work, but unintended side effects such as a DoS or multiple system reboots will cause undue attention that could easily inform cybersecurity analysts of the attack and the threat actor's intentions.

The figure summarizes some of the tactics and defenses used during this step.

Refer to
Online Course
for Illustration

13.1.1.6   Installation

This step is where the threat actor establishes a back door into the system to allow for continued access to the target. To preserve this backdoor, it is important that remote access does not alert cybersecurity analysts or users. The access method must survive through antimalware scans and rebooting of the computer to be effective. This persistent access can also allow for automated communications, especially effective when multiple channels of communication are necessary when commanding a botnet.

The figure summarizes some of the tactics and defenses used during this step.

Refer to
Online Course
for Illustration

13.1.1.7   Command and Control

In this step, the goal is to establish command and control (CnC or C2) with the target system. Compromised hosts usually beacon out of the network to a controller on the Internet. This is because most malware requires manual interaction in order to exfiltrate data from the network. CnC channels are used by the threat actor to issue commands to the software that they installed on the target. The cybersecurity analyst must be able to detect CnC communications in order to discover the compromised host. This may be in the form of unauthorized Internet Relay Chat (IRC) traffic or excessive traffic to suspect domains.

The figure summarizes some of the tactics and defenses used during this step.

Refer to
Online Course
for Illustration

13.1.1.8   Actions on Objectives

The final step of the Cyber Kill Chain describes the threat actor achieving their original objective. This may be data theft, performing a DDoS attack, or using the compromised network to create and send spam. At this point the threat actor is deeply rooted in the systems of the organization, hiding their moves and covering their tracks. It is extremely difficult to remove the threat actor from the network.

The figure summarizes some of the tactics and defenses used during this step.

Refer to
Interactive Graphic
in online course

13.1.1.9   Activity - Identify the Kill Chain Step

13.1.2   The Diamond Model of Intrusion

Refer to
Online Course
for Illustration

13.1.2.1   Diamond Model Overview

The Diamond Model of intrusion is made up of four parts and represents a security incident or event, as shown in the figure. In the Diamond Model, an event is a time-bound activity restricted to a specific step where an adversary uses a capability over some infrastructure against a victim to achieve a specific result.

The four core features of an intrusion event are adversary, capability, infrastructure, and victim:

- **Adversary** - These are the parties responsible for the intrusion.

- **Capability** - This is a tool or technique that the adversary uses to attack the victim.

- **Infrastructure** - This is the network path or paths that the adversaries use to establish and maintain command and control over their capabilities.

- **Victim** - This is the target of the attack. However, a victim might be the target initially and then used as part of the infrastructure to launch other attacks.

The adversary uses capabilities over infrastructure to attack the victim. Each line in the model shows how each part reached the other. For example, a capability like malware might be used over email by an adversary to attack a victim.

Meta-features expand the model slightly to include the following important elements:

- **Timestamp** - This indicates the start and stop time of an event and is an integral part of grouping malicious activity.

- **Step** - This is analogous to steps in the Cyber Kill Chain; malicious activity includes two or more steps executed in succession to achieve the desired result.

- **Results** - This delineates what the adversary gained from the event. Results can be documented as one or more of the following: confidentiality compromised, integrity compromised, and availability compromised.

- **Direction** - This indicates the direction of the event across the Diamond Model. These include Adversary-to-Infrastructure, Infrastructure-to-Victim, Victim-to-Infrastructure, and Infrastructure-to-Adversary.

- **Methodology** - This is used to classify the general type of event, such as port scan, phishing, content delivery attack, syn flood, etc.

- **Resources** - These are one or more external resources used by the adversary for the intrusion event, such as software, adversary's knowledge, information (e.g., username/passwords), and assets to carry out the attack (hardware, funds, facilities, network access).

Refer to
Online Course
for Illustration

13.1.2.2   Pivoting Across the Diamond Model

As a cybersecurity analyst, you may be called on to use the Diamond Model to diagram a series of intrusion events. The Diamond Model is ideal for illustrating how the adversary pivots from one event to the next.

For example, in the figure an employee reports that his computer is acting abnormally. A host scan by the security technician indicates that the computer is infected with malware.

An analysis of the malware reveals that the malware contains a list of CnC domain names. These domain names resolve to a list of IP addresses. These IP addresses are then used to identify the adversary, as well as investigate logs to determine if other victims in the organization are using the CnC channel.

13.1.2.3   The Diamond Model and the Cyber Kill Chain

Refer to **Online Course** for Illustration

Adversaries do not operate in just a single event. Instead, events are threaded together in a chain in which each event must be successfully completed before the next event. This thread of events can be mapped to the Cyber Kill Chain previously discussed in the chapter.

The following example, shown in the figure, illustrates the end-to-end process of an adversary as they vertically traverse the Cyber Kill Chain, use a compromised host to horizontally pivot to another victim, and then begin another activity thread:

1. Adversary conducts a web search for victim company Gadgets, Inc. receiving as part of the results their domain gadgets.com.

2. Adversary uses the newly discovered domain gadets.com for a new search "network administrator gadget.com" and discovers forum postings from users claiming to be network administrators of gadget.com. The user profiles reveal their email addresses.

3. Adversary sends phishing emails with a Trojan horse attached to the network administrators of gadget.com.

4. One network administrator (NA1) of gadget.com opens the malicious attachment. This executes the enclosed exploit allowing for further code execution.

5. NA1's compromised host sends an HTTP Post message to an IP address, registering it with a CnC controller. NA1's compromised host receives an HTTP Response in return.

6. It is revealed from reverse engineering that the malware has additional IP addresses configured which act as a back-up if the first controller does not respond.

7. Through a CnC HTTP response message sent to NA1's host, the malware begins to act as a proxy for new TCP connections.

8. Through the proxy established on NA1's host, Adversary does a web search for "most important research ever" and finds Victim 2, Interesting Research Inc.

9. Adversary checks NA1's email contact list for any contacts from Interesting Research Inc. and discovers the contact for the Interesting Research Inc. Chief Research Officer.

10. Chief Research Officer of Interesting Research Inc. receives a spear-phish email from Gadget Inc.'s NA1's email address sent from NA1's host with the same payload as observed in Event 3.

The adversary now has two compromised victims from which additional attacks can be launched. For example, the adversary could mine the Chief Research Officer's email contacts for the additional potential victims. The adversary might also setup another proxy to exfiltrate all of the Chief Research Officer's files.

Note   This example is a modification of the U.S. Department of Defense's example in the publication "The Diamond Model of Intrusion Analysis". Click here to download the publication.

Refer to **Interactive Graphic** in online course

13.1.2.4 Activity - Identify the Diamond Model Features

13.1.3 The VERIS Schema

Refer to **Online Course** for Illustration

13.1.3.1 What is the VERIS Schema?

The Vocabulary for Event Recording and Incident Sharing (VERIS) is a set of metrics designed to create a way to describe security incidents in a structured and repeatable way. VERIS was created to share quality information about security events to the community, anonymously. The VERIS Community Database (VCDB) is an open and free collection of publicly-reported security incidents in VERIS format. You can use unformatted, raw data or the dashboard to find VERIS entries. The VCDB is a central location for the security community to learn from experience and help with decision making, before, during, and after a security incident.

Click here to access the VCDB interactive dashboard.

Click here to access VCDB raw data.

In the VERIS schema, risk is defined as the intersection of four landscapes of Threat, Asset, Impact, and Control, as shown in the figure. Information from each landscape helps to understand the level of risk to the organization. VERIS helps to determine these landscapes using real security incidents to help risk management assessment.

Refer to **Interactive Graphic** in online course

13.1.3.2 Create a VERIS Record

When creating records to add to the database, start with the basic facts about the incident. It is helpful to use the VERIS elements outlined by the community. Figure 1 shows the most basic record that can exist. The framework does not need to be complicated. The only required fields in the record are those where the attribute is present. As more is known about the incident, data can be added.

When an incident is recorded, it is most likely that you will have more specific information than just the year when the incident occurred. For example, the month and day can be documented by adding VERIS labels to the existing record, as shown in Figure 2. The way the incident was discovered, a summary of what happened, and any other notes about the type of incident should also be recorded using VERIS labels. Any variable, data, or text can be recorded as part of the VERIS record using VERIS labels. For example, in Figure 2 variables were added to document that Debbie in Sales reported that her computer was infected with malware. It was determined, through an interview with Debbie and a scan of her computer, that a rootkit was installed via an infected USB drive.

After the initial records are created, additional details should be added to aid in data analysis. The only two required in the VERIS schema are whether the incident was a real security incident, and how the incident was discovered. Most ticketing systems will allow new fields to be added to forms. To add more details to the record, just add a new field and designate a VERIS enumeration for it. A Word document, Excel spreadsheet, or other software can be used to create these records as well. You could also create a dedicated reporting tool for incident recording.

Click here for an example of a VERIS incident recording tool.

After the major details have been recorded, even more detail can be added as you continue to document the incident. Every bit of information that can be entered into the record may be helpful to your organization and others who respond to the incident and prevent and detect future incidents of this type. The more data available to the community, the better chance there is of preventing future incidents.

VERIS can record the details of the organization that was affected such as industry, number of employees, or the country of the organization. This information can be useful in the overall picture when multiple organizations have a record of a similar incident. This demographic information can be shared without revealing specific, private information about the affected organization.

Refer to **Interactive Graphic** in online course

13.1.3.3 Top-Level and Second-Level Elements

There are five top-level elements of the VERIS schema, each of which provides a different aspect of the incident. Each top-level element contains several second-level elements, as shown in Figure 1. These elements are useful for classifying data that has been collected about an incident.

Impact Assessment

For any incident, there is impact, whether it is minor or widespread. It is often very difficult to determine the scope of the impact until well after an incident has occurred, or even after it has been remediated. The second-level elements used for impact assessment are as follows:

- **Loss Categorization** - Identifies the types of losses that occurred due to the incident.

- **Loss Estimation** - This is an estimate of the total losses that were incurred because of the incident.

- **Estimation Currency** - Uses the same currency when multiple types are involved.

- **Impact Rating** - This is a rating that indicates the overall impact of the incident. It could be a number between 1 and 100, or another scale such as a grading scale.

- **Notes** - Additional details that may be of use are recorded here.

Discovery and Response

This section is for recording the timeline of events, the method of incident discovery, and what the response was to the incident, including how it was remediated. The second-level elements used for discovery and response are as follows:

- **Incident Timeline** - The timeline of all events from the discovery of the incident to the time the incident has been contained or restored to a fully functional state. This section is very important for gathering metrics such as readiness, the actions of the threat actors, and the response of the affected organization, along with many others.

- **Discovery Method** - Identifies the way in which the incident was discovered. This may be accidental, or by design.

- **Root Causes** - Identifies any weakness or failure in security allowing the incident to take place.

- **Corrective Actions** - This variable is for recording what will be done to detect or prevent this type of incident in the future.

- **Targeted vs. Opportunistic** - Identifies if the incident was a deliberate, targeted attack, or if it was a random incident, based on a found opportunity by an attacker.

Incident Description

To describe an incident completely, VERIS uses the A4 threat model that was developed by the RISK team at Verizon. The second-level elements used for incident description, also known as the 4 As, are as follows:

- **Actors** - Whose actions affected the asset?

- **Actions** - What actions affected the asset?

- **Assets** - Which assets were affected?

- **Attributes** - How the asset was affected?

Each of these elements should be further refined through the use of their associated sub-elements by answering the questions in Figure 2 and Figure 3.

Victim Demographics

This section is for describing the organization that has experienced the incident. The characteristics of the organization can be compared to other organizations to determine if there are aspects of an incident that are common. The second-level elements used for victim demographics are as follows:

- **Victim ID** - Identifies incidents with the organization that experienced them.

- **Primary Industry** - Identifies the industry in which the affected organization conducts business. The six-digit North American Industry Classification System (NAICS) code is entered here. Click here for the NAICS codes.

- **Country of Operation** - Used to record the country where the primary location of the organization operates.

- **State** - Only used when the organization operates in the United States.

- **Number of Employees** - This is for recording the size of the entire organization, not a department or branch.

- **Annual Revenue** - This variable can be rounded for privacy.

- **Locations Affected** - Identifies any additional regions or branches that were affected by the incident.

- **Notes** - Additional details that may be of use are recorded here.

Incident Tracking

This is for recording general information about the incident so organizations can identify, store, and retrieve incidents over time. The second-level elements used for incident tracking are as follows:

- **Incident ID** - This is a unique identifier for storage and tracking.

- **Source ID** - Identifies the incident in the context of who reported it.

- **Incident Confirmation** - Differentiates the incident from those that are known or suspected as being non-incidents.

- **Incident Summary** - Provides a short description of the incident.

- **Related Incidents** - Allows the incident to be associated with similar incidents.

- **Confidence Rating** - Provides a rating as to how accurate the reported incident information is.

- **Incident Notes** - Allows recording of any information not captured in other VERIS fields.

Refer to
Online Course
for Illustration

13.1.3.4   The VERIS Community Database

There are some organizations that collect data for security incidents, but either the data is not available to the public for free, or it is not in a format that allows for manipulation or transformation that may be required to make it useful. This makes it difficult for researchers who study security incident trends and organizations to make reliable risk management calculations.

This is where the VERIS Community Database (VCDB) is useful. Through the proper use of the VERIS schema and a willingness to participate, organizations can submit security incident details to the VCDB for the community to use. The larger and more robust the VCDB becomes, the more useful it will be in prevention, detection, and remediation of security incidents. It will also become a very useful tool for risk management, saving organizations data, time, effort, and money.

Click here for the VCDB.

Like any database, it can be used to determine answers to questions. It can also be used to find out how one organization compares to another when it is of the same approximate size and operating in the same kind of industry.

Refer to
Interactive Graphic
in online course

13.1.3.5   Activity - Apply the VERIS Schema to an Incident

13.2   Incident Handling

13.2.1   CSIRTs

Refer to
Online Course
for Illustration

13.2.1.1   CSIRT Overview

A computer security incident can be defined differently across organizations. Generally, a computer security incident is any malicious or suspicious act which violates a security policy or any event that threatens the security, confidentiality, integrity, or availability of an organization's assets, information systems, or data network. Although this definition may be considered vague, these are some common computer security incidents:

- Malicious code

- Denial of service

- Unauthorized entry

- Device theft

- Malicious scans or probes

- Security breach

- Violation of any security policy item

When a security incident takes place, an organization needs a way to respond. A Computer Security Incident Response Team (CSIRT) is an internal group commonly found within an organization that provides services and functions to secure the assets of that organization. A CSIRT does not necessarily only respond to incidents that have already happened. A CSIRT may also provide proactive services and functions such as penetration testing, intrusion detection, or even security awareness training. These types of services can help to prevent incidents, but also increase response time, and mitigate damage. In the case where a security incident needs to be contained and mitigated, the CSIRT coordinates and oversees these efforts.

Refer to **Online Course** for Illustration

13.2.1.2   Types of CSIRTs

In larger organizations, the CSIRT will focus on investigating computer security incidents. Information security teams (InfoSec) will focus on implementing security policies and monitoring for security incidents. Many times in smaller organizations, the CSIRT will handle the tasks of the InfoSec team. Every organization is different. The goals of the CSIRT must be in alignment with the goals of the organization. There are many different types of CSIRTs and related organizations:

- **Internal CSIRT** - Provides incident handling for the organization in which they reside. Any organization such as a hospital, bank, university, or a construction company, can have an internal CSIRT.

- **National CSIRT** - Provides incident handling for a country.

- **Coordination Centers** - Coordinates incident handling across multiple CSIRTs. One example is US-CERT. US-CERT responds to major incidents, analyzes threats and exchanges information with other cybersecurity experts and partners around the world.

- **Analysis Centers** - Use data from many sources to determine incident activity trends. Trends help to predict future incidents and provide early warning to prevent and mitigate damages as quickly as possible. The VERIS community is an example of an analysis center.

- **Vendor Teams** - Provide remediation for vulnerabilities in an organization's software or hardware. These teams often handle customer reports concerning security vulnerabilities. This team may also act as the internal CSIRT for an organization. For example, click here to learn more about Cisco's Product Security Incident Response Team (PSIRT).

- **Managed Security Service Providers (MSSP)** - Provide incident handling to other organizations as a fee-based service. Cisco, Symantec, Verizon, and IBM are all examples of managed security service providers.

Refer to **Online Course** for Illustration

13.2.1.3   CERT

Computer Emergency Response Teams (CERTs) are similar to CSIRTs, but are not the same. CERT is a trademarked acronym owned by Carnegie Mellon University. A CSIRT is an organization responsible for receiving, reviewing, and responding to security incidents.

A CERT provides security awareness, best practices, and security vulnerability information to their populations. CERTs do not directly respond to security incidents.

Many countries have asked for permission to use the CERT acronym. These are some of the more prominent CERTs:

- US-CERT: https://www.us-cert.gov

- Japan CERT Coordination Center: http://www.jpcert.or.jp/english/index.html

- Indian Computer Emergency Response Team: http://www.cert-in.org.in

- Singapore Computer Emergency Response Team: https://www.csa.gov.sg/singcert

- CERT Australia: https://cert.gov.au

Refer to
Interactive Graphic
in online course

13.2.1.4   Activity - Match the CSIRT with the CSIRT Goal

13.2.2   NIST 800-61r2

Refer to
Online Course
for Illustration

13.2.2.1   Establishing an Incident Response Capability

The NIST recommendations for incident response are detailed in their Special Publication 800-61, revision 2 entitled "Computer Security Incident Handling Guide" (Figure 1).

Click here to download the publication.

Note   Although this chapter summarizes much of the content in the NIST 800-61r2 standard, you should also read the entire publication as it covers six major exam topics for the Cybersecurity CCNA SECOPS exam.

The NIST 800-61r2 standard provides guidelines for incident handling, particularly for analyzing incident-related data and determining the appropriate response to each incident. The guidelines can be followed independently of particular hardware platforms, operating systems, protocols, or applications.

The first step for an organization is to establish a computer security incident response capability (CSIRC). NIST recommends creating policies, plans, and procedures for establishing and maintaining a CSIRC.

Policy

An incident response policy details how incidents should be handled based on the organization's mission, size, and function. The policy should be reviewed regularly to adjust it to meet the goals of the roadmap that has been laid out. Policy elements are listed in Figure 2.

Plan Elements

A good incident response plan helps to minimize damage caused by an incident. It also helps to make the overall incident response program better by adjusting it according to lessons learned. It will ensure that each party involved in the incident response has a clear understanding of not only what they will be doing, but what others will be doing as well. Plan elements are listed in Figure 3.

Procedure Elements

The procedures that are followed during an incident response should follow the incident response plan. Procedures such as following technical processes, using techniques, filling out forms and following checklists are standard operating procedures (SOPs). These SOPs should be detailed so that the mission and goals of the organization are in mind when these procedures are followed. SOPs minimize errors that may be caused by personnel that are under stress while participating in incident handling. It is important to share and practice these procedures, making sure that they are useful, accurate, and appropriate.

Refer to **Online Course** for Illustration

13.2.2.2   Incident Response Stakeholders

Other groups and individuals within the organization may also be involved with incident handling. It is important to ensure that they will cooperate before an incident is underway. Their expertise and abilities can help the CSIRT to handle the incident quickly and correctly. These are some of the stakeholders that may be involved in handing a security incident:

Management - Managers create the policies that everyone must follow. They also design the budget and are in charge of staffing all of the departments. Management must coordinate the incident response with other stakeholders and minimize the damage of an incident.

Information Assurance - This group may need to be called in to change things such as firewall rules during some stages of incident management such as containment or recovery.

IT Support - This is the group that works with the technology in the organization and understands it the most. Because IT support has a deeper understanding, it is more likely that they will perform the correct action to minimize the effectiveness of the attack or preserve evidence properly.

Legal Department - It is a best practice to have the legal department review the incident policies, plans, and procedures to make sure that they do not violate any local or federal guidelines. Also, if any incident has legal implications, a legal expert will need to become involved. This might include prosecution, evidence collection, or lawsuits.

Public Affairs and Media Relations - There are times when the media and the public might need to be informed of an incident, such as when their personal information has been compromised during an incident.

Human Resources - The human resources department might need to perform disciplinary measures if an incident caused by an employee occurs.

Business Continuity Planning - Security incidents may alter an organization's business continuity. It is important that those in charge of business continuity planning are aware of security incidents and the impact they have had on the organization as a whole. This will allow them to make any changes in plans and risk assessments.

Physical Security and Facilities Management - When a security incident happens because of a physical attack, such as tailgating or shoulder surfing, these teams might need to be informed and involved. It is also their responsibility to secure facilities that contain evidence from an investigation.

Refer to **Online Course** for Illustration

13.2.2.3   NIST Incident Response Life Cycle

NIST defines four steps in the incident response process life cycle, as shown in the figure.

- **Preparation** - The members of the CSIRT are trained in how to respond to an incident.

- **Detection and Analysis** - Through continuous monitoring, the CSIRT quickly identifies, analyzes, and validates an incident.

- **Containment, Eradication, and Recovery** - The CSIRT implements procedures to contain the threat, eradicate the impact on organizational assets, and use backups to restore data and software. This phase may cycle back to detection and analysis to gather more information, or to expand the scope of the investigation.

- **Post-Incident Activities** - The CSIRT then documents how the incident was handled, recommends changes for future response, and specifies how to avoid a reoccurrence.

The incident response life cycle is meant to be a self-reinforcing learning process whereby each incident informs the process for handling future incidents. Each of these phases are discussed in more detail in this topic.

Refer to
Online Course
for Illustration

13.2.2.4   Preparation

The preparation phase is when the CSIRT is created and trained. This phase is also when the tools and assets that will be needed by the team to investigate incidents are acquired and deployed. The following list has examples of actions that also take place during the preparation phase:

- Organizational processes are created to address communication between people on the response team. This includes such things as contact information for stakeholders, other CSIRTs, and law enforcement, an issue tracking system, smartphones, encryption software, etc.

- Facilities to host the response team and the SOC are created.

- Necessary hardware and software for incident analysis and mitigation is acquired. This may include forensic software, spare computers, servers and network devices, backup devices, packet sniffers, and protocol analyzers.

- Risk assessments are used to implement controls that will limit the number of incidents.

- Validation of security hardware and software deployment is performed on end-user devices, servers, and network devices.

- User security awareness training materials are developed.

Additional incident analysis resources might be required. Examples of these resources are a list of critical assets, network diagrams, port lists, hashes of critical files, and baseline readings of system and network activity. Mitigation software is also an important item when preparing to handle a security incident. An image of a clean OS and application installation files may be needed to recover a computer from an incident.

Often, the CSIRT may have a jump kit prepared. This is a portable box with many of the items listed above to help in establishing a swift response. Some of these items may be a laptop with appropriate software installed, backup media, and any other hardware, software, or information to help in the investigation. It is important to inspect the jump kit on a regular basis to install updates and make sure that all the necessary elements are available and ready for use. It is helpful to practice deploying the jump kit with the CSIRT to ensure that the team members know how to use its contents properly.

Refer to
Online Course
for Illustration

13.2.2.5   Detection and Analysis

Because there are so many different ways in which a security incident can occur, it is impossible to create instructions that completely cover each step to follow to handle them. Different types of incidents will require different responses.

Attack Vectors

An organization should be prepared to handle any incident, but should focus on the most common types of incidents so that they can be dealt with swiftly. These are some of the more common types of attack vectors:

- **Web** - Any attack that is initiated from a website or application hosted by a website.

- **Email** - Any attack that is initiated from an email or email attachment.

- **Loss or Theft** - Any equipment that is used by the organization such as a laptop, desktop, or smartphone can provide the required information for someone to initiate an attack.

- **Impersonation** - When something or someone is replaced for the purpose of malicious intent.

- **Attrition** - Any attack that uses brute force to attack devices, networks, or services.

- **Media** - Any attack that is initiated from external storage or removable media.

Detection

Some incidents are easy to detect while others may go undetected for months. The detection of security incidents might be the most difficult phase in the incident response process. Incidents are detected in many different ways and not all of these ways are very detailed or provide detailed clarity. There are automated ways of detection such as antivirus software or an IDS. There are also manual detections through user reports.

It is important to accurately determine the type of incident and the extent of the effects. There are two categories for the signs of an incident:

- **Precursor** - This is a sign that an incident might occur in the future. When precursors are detected, an attack might be avoided by altering security measures to specifically address the type of attack detected. Examples of precursors are log entries that show a response to a port scan, or a newly-discovered vulnerability to an organization's web server.

- **Indicator** - This is a sign that an incident might already have occurred or is currently occurring. Some examples of indicators are a host that has been infected with malware, multiple failed logins from an unknown source, or an IDS alert.

Analysis

Incident analysis is difficult because not all of the indicators are accurate. In a perfect world, each indicator should be analyzed to find out if it is accurate. This is nearly impossible due to the number and variety of logged and reported incidents. The use of complex algorithms and machine learning often help to determine the validity of security incidents. This is more prevalent in large organizations that have thousands or even millions of incidents daily. One method that can be used is network and system profiling. Profiling is measuring the characteristics of expected activity in networking devices and systems so that changes to it can be more easily identified.

When an indicator is found to be accurate, it does not necessarily mean that a security incident has occurred. Some indicators happen for other reasons besides security. A server that continually crashes, for example, may have bad RAM instead of a buffer overflow attack occurring. To be safe, even ambiguous or contradictory symptoms must be analyzed to determine if a legitimate security incident has taken place. The CSIRT must react quickly to validate and analyze incidents. This is performed by following a predefined process and documenting each step.

Scoping

When the CSIRT believes that an incident has occurred, it should immediately perform an initial analysis to determine the incident's scope, such as which networks, systems, or applications are affected, who or what originated the incident, and how the incident is occurring. This scoping activity should provide enough information for the team to prioritize subsequent activities, such as containment of the incident and deeper analysis of the effects of the incident.

Incident Notification

When an incident is analyzed and prioritized, the incident response team needs to notify the appropriate individuals so that all who need to be involved will play their roles. Examples of parties that are typically notified include:

- Chief Information Officer (CIO)
- Head of information security
- Local information security officer
- Other incident response teams within the organization
- External incident response teams (if appropriate)
- System owner
- Human resources (for cases involving employees, such as harassment through email)
- Public affairs (for incidents that may generate publicity)
- Legal department (for incidents with potential legal ramifications)
- US-CERT (required for Federal agencies and systems operated on behalf of the Federal government)
- Law enforcement (if appropriate)

Refer to
Online Course
for Illustration

13.2.2.6   Containment, Eradication, and Recovery

After a security incident has been detected and sufficient analysis has been performed to determine that the incident is valid, it must be contained in order to determine what to do about it. Strategies and procedures for incident containment need to be in place before an incident occurs and implemented before there is widespread damage.

Containment Strategy

For every type of incident, a containment strategy should be created and enforced. These are some conditions to determine the type of strategy to create for each incident type:

- How long it will take to implement and complete a solution?

- How much time and how many resources will be needed to implement the strategy?

- What is the process to preserve evidence?

- Can an attacker be redirected to a sandbox so that the CSIRT can safely document the attacker's methodology?

- What will be the impact to the availability of services?

- What is the extent of damage to resources or assets?

- How effective is the strategy?

During containment, additional damage may be incurred. For example, it is not always advisable to unplug the compromised host from the network. The malicious process could notice this disconnection to the CnC controller and trigger a data wipe or encryption on the target. This is where experience and expertise can help to contain an incident beyond the scope of the containment strategy.

Evidence

During an incident, evidence must be gathered to resolve it. Evidence is also important for subsequent investigation by authorities. Clear and concise documentation surrounding the preservation of evidence is critical. For evidence to be admissible in court, evidence collection must conform to specific regulations. After evidence collection, it must be accounted for properly. This is known as the chain of custody. These are some of the most important items to log when documenting evidence used in the chain of custody:

- Location of the recovery and storage of all evidence

- Any identifying criteria for all evidence such as serial number, MAC address, hostname, or IP address

- Identification information for all of the people that participated in collecting or handling the evidence

- Time and date that the evidence was collected and each instance it was handled

It is vital to educate anyone involved in evidence handling on how to preserve evidence properly.

Attacker Identification

Identifying attackers is secondary to containing, eradicating, and recovering hosts and services. However, identifying attackers will minimize the impact to critical business assets and services. These are some of the most important actions to perform to attempt to identify an attacking host during a security incident:

- Use incident databases to research related activity. This database may be in-house or located at organizations that collect data from other organizations and consolidate it into incident databases such as the VERIS community database.

- Validate the attacker's IP address to determine if it is a viable one. The host may or may not respond to a request for connectivity. This may be because it has been configured to ignore the requests, or the address has already been reassigned to another host.

- Use an Internet search engine to gain additional information about the attack. There may have been another organization or individual that has released information about an attack from the identified source IP address.

- Monitor the communication channels that some attackers use, such as IRC. Because users can be disguised or anonymized in IRC channels, they may talk about their exploits in these channels. Often, the information gathered from this type of monitoring is misleading, and should be treated as leads and not facts.

Eradication, Recovery, and Remediation

After containment, the first step to eradication is identifying all of the hosts that need remediation. All of the effects of the security incident must be eliminated. This includes malware infections and user accounts that have been compromised. All of the vulnerabilities that were exploited by the attacker must also be corrected or patched so that the incident does not occur again.

To recover hosts, use clean and recent backups, or rebuild them with installation media if no backups are available or they have been compromised. Also, fully update and patch the operating systems and installed software of all hosts. Change all host passwords and passwords for critical systems in accordance with the password security policy. This may be a good time to validate and upgrade network security, backup strategies, and security policies. Attackers often attack the systems again, or use a similar attack to target additional resources, so be sure to prevent this as best as possible. Focus on what can be fixed quickly while prioritizing critical systems and operations.

Refer to **Online Course** for Illustration

13.2.2.7   Post-Incident Activities

After incident response activities have eradicated the threats and the organization has begun to recover from the effects of the attack, it is important to take a step back and periodically meet with all of the parties involved to discuss the events that took place and the actions of all of the individuals while handling the incident. This will provide a platform to learn what was done right, what was done wrong, what could be changed, and what should be improved upon.

Lessons-based hardening

After a major incident has been handled, the organization should hold a "lessons learned" meeting to review the effectiveness of the incident handling process and identify necessary hardening needed for existing security controls and practices. Examples of good questions to answer during the meeting include the following:

- Exactly what happened, and at what times?

- How well did the staff and management perform while dealing with the incident?

- Were the documented procedures followed? Were they adequate?

- What information was needed sooner?

- Were any steps or actions taken that might have inhibited the recovery?

■ What would the staff and management do differently the next time a similar incident occurs?

■ How could information sharing with other organizations be improved?

■ What corrective actions can prevent similar incidents in the future?

■ What precursors or indicators should be watched for in the future to detect similar incidents?

■ What additional tools or resources are needed to detect, analyze, and mitigate future incidents?

Refer to
Online Course
for Illustration

13.2.2.8   Incident Data Collection and Retention

By having 'lessons learned' meetings, the collected data can be used to determine the cost of an incident for budgeting reasons, as well as to determine the effectiveness of the CSIRT, and identify possible security weaknesses throughout the system. The collected data needs to be actionable. Only collect data that can be used to define and refine the incident handling process.

A higher number of incidents handled can show that something in the incidence response methodology is not working properly and needs to be refined. It could also show incompetence in the CSIRT. A lower number of incidents might show that network and host security has been improved. It could also show a lack of incident detection. Separate incident counts for each type of incident may be more effective at showing strengths and weakness of the CSIRT and implemented security measures. These subcategories can help to target where a weakness resides, rather than whether there is a weakness at all.

The time of each incident provides insight into the total amount of labor used and the total time of each phase of the incident response process. The time until the first response is also important, as well as how long it took to report the incident and escalate it beyond the organization, if necessary.

It is important to perform an objective assessment of each Incident. The response to an incident that has been resolved can be analyzed to determine how effective it was. NIST Special Publication 800-61 provides the following examples of performing an objective assessment of an incident:

■ Reviewing logs, forms, reports, and other incident documentation for adherence to established incident response policies and procedures.

■ Identifying which precursors and indicators of the incident were recorded to determine how effectively the incident was logged and identified.

■ Determining if the incident caused damage before it was detected.

■ Determining if the actual cause of the incident was identified, and identifying the vector of attack, the vulnerabilities exploited, and the characteristics of the targeted or victimized systems, networks, and applications.

■ Determining if the incident is a recurrence of a previous incident.

■ Calculating the estimated monetary damage from the incident (e.g., information and critical business processes negatively affected by the incident).

■ Measuring the difference between the initial impact assessment and the final impact assessment.

- Identifying which measures, if any, could have prevented the incident.

- Subjective assessment of each incident requires that incident response team members assess their own performance, as well as that of other team members and of the entire team. Another valuable source of input is the owner of a resource that was attacked, in order to determine if the owner thinks the incident was handled efficiently and if the outcome was satisfactory.

There should be a policy in place in each organization that outlines how long evidence of an incident should be retained. Evidence is often retained for many months or many years after an incident has taken place. These are some of the determining factors for evidence retention:

- **Prosecution -** When an attacker will be prosecuted because of a security incident, the evidence should be retained until after all legal actions have been completed. This may be several months or many years. In legal actions, no evidence is should be overlooked or considered insignificant. An organization's policy may state that any evidence surrounding an incident that has been involved with legal actions must never be deleted or destroyed.

- **Data Type -** An organization may specify that specific types of data should be kept for a specific period of time. Items such as email or text may only need to be kept for 90 days. More important data such as that used in an incident response (that has not had legal action), may need to be kept for three years or more.

- **Cost -** If there is a lot of hardware and storage media that needs to be stored for a long time, it can become costly. Remember also that as technology changes, functional devices that can use outdated hardware and storage media must be stored as well.

13.2.2.9   Reporting Requirements and Information Sharing

Refer to **Online Course** for Illustration

Governmental regulations should be consulted by the legal team to determine precisely the organization's responsibility for reporting the incident. In addition, management will need to determine what additional communication is necessary with other stakeholders, such as customers, vendors, partners, etc.

Beyond the legal requirements and stakeholder considerations, NIST recommends that an organization coordinate with organizations to share details for the incident. For example, the organization could log the incident in the VERIS community database.

The critical recommendations from NIST for sharing information are as follows:

- Plan incident coordination with external parties before incidents occur.

- Consult with the legal department before initiating any coordination efforts.

- Perform incident information sharing throughout the incident response life cycle.

- Attempt to automate as much of the information sharing process as possible.

- Balance the benefits of information sharing with the drawbacks of sharing sensitive information.

- Share as much of the appropriate incident information as possible with other organizations.

Refer to
Interactive Graphic
in online course

Refer to
Interactive Graphic
in online course

Refer to
Interactive Graphic
in online course

Refer to
Lab Activity
for this chapter

13.2.2.10   Activity - Identify the Incident Response Plan Elements

13.2.2.11   Activity - Identify the Incident Handling Term

13.2.2.12   Activity - Identify the Incident Handling Step

13.2.2.13   Lab - Incident Handling

In this lab, you will apply your knowledge of security incident handling procedures to formulate questions about given incident scenarios.

13.3   Summary

13.3.1   Conclusion

Refer to
Online Course
for Illustration

13.3.1.1   Chapter 13: Incident Response and Handling

In this chapter, you learned about incident response models commonly used by cybersecurity analysts to manage network security incidents.

The Cyber Kill Chain specifies the steps that an attacker must complete to accomplish their goal. The steps in the Cyber Kill Chain are as follows:

1. Reconnaissance

2. Weaponization

3. Delivery

4. Exploitation

5. Installation

6. Command & Control

7. Action on Objectives

If the attacker is stopped at any stage, the chain of attack is broken.

The Diamond Model of intrusion is made up of four parts and represents a security incident or event: adversary, capability, infrastructure, and victim. As a cybersecurity analyst, you may be called on to use the Diamond Model to diagram a series of intrusion events. The Diamond Model is ideal for illustrating how the adversary pivots from one event to the next.

In the VERIS schema, risk is defined as the intersection of four landscapes of Threat, Asset, Impact, and Control. Through the proper use of the VERIS schema and a willingness to participate, organizations can submit security incident details to the VCDB for the community to use.

Generally, a computer security incident is any malicious or suspicious act which violates a security policy, or any event that threatens the security, confidentiality, integrity, or availability of an organization's assets, information systems, or data network.

A CSIRT is an internal group commonly found within an organization that provides services and functions to respond to security incidents.

The types of CSIRTs are:

- Internal CSIRT
- National CSIRT
- Coordination Centers
- Analysis Centers
- Vendor Teams
- Managed Security Service Providers

Unlike CSIRTs, CERTs provide security awareness, best practices, and security vulnerability information to their populations. CERTs do not directly respond to security incidents.

NIST 800-61r2 defines four phases in the incident response process life cycle:

- Preparation
- Detection and Analysis
- Containment, Eradication, and Recovery
- Post-Incident Activities

Go to the online
course to take the
quiz and exam.

Chapter 13 Quiz

This quiz is designed to provide an additional opportunity to practice the skills and knowledge presented in the chapter and to prepare for the chapter exam. You will be allowed multiple attempts and the grade does not appear in the gradebook.

Chapter 13 Exam

The chapter exam assesses your knowledge of the chapter content.

Your Chapter Notes